Ben Troke is a solicitor and a mediator with 25 years' experience working in health and social care, acting for the NHS and private sector providers and commissioners all over the country. His particular interest is in decisions about medical treatment and he regularly deals with urgent applications to court in emergency situations. Ben is independently rated as one of the leading practitioners in the country in the Court of Protection.

He currently sits on the Law and Ethics Policy Unit of the Faculty of Intensive Care Medicine, the clinical ethics committee of Alder Hey children's hospital, and the Mental Health and Disability Committee of the Law Society.

Demystifying the law is Ben's passion and he regularly speaks at conferences and provides training, in person and online.

A Practical Guide to the Law of Medical Treatment Decisions

Second edition

A Practical Guide to the Law of Medical Treatment Decisions

Second edition

Ben Troke, LLB, LLM

Solicitor and mediator

Law Brief Publishing

Published 2025 by Law Brief Publishing, an imprint of Law Brief Publishing Ltd
30 The Parks
Minehead
Somerset
TA24 8BT

www.lawbriefpublishing.com

Paperback: 978-1-916698-91-8

For my family, friends and colleagues;
and for all those who work in health
and social care, and those they care for.

ACKNOWLEDGEMENTS

I am writing in a personal capacity and so all the opinions, mistakes and misjudgements are entirely my own, of course. But I would like to record my gratitude to those who made the time to help me: Sam Cox at the Alzheimer's Society for her unstinting support; Nadine Montgomery for her insight and generosity in sharing her story; Dr Ian Thomas, Daniel Sokol, Vikram Sachdeva KC, Sophia Roper KC and Alex Ruck Keene KC, all of whom made wise comments and suggestions on parts of the book, and Damian Whitlam, Dr Sonya Daniel and Dr Dale Gardiner for their input on this second edition.

Finally, of course, to my own "next of kin": my supportive friends and family (especially my dad, whose first comment on the idea of the book – "Oh, I don't think anyone will be interested in that…" – has been so motivational); and above all to Cathy and our daughters Emma and Genevieve, without whom… this would have been finished so much sooner.

ALZHEIMER'S SOCIETY

Alzheimer's Society is the UK 's leading support and research charity for people with dementia, their families and carers.

There are currently estimated to be 982,000 people living with dementia in the UK and this is projected to rise to 1.4 million in 2040. The scale and the need to prevent, diagnose, support, live and die well with dementia will only become greater.

The Society provides information and support to people with any form of dementia and their carers through our publications, National Dementia Helpline, website and around 3,000 local services throughout England, Wales and Northern Ireland.

We support health and social care professionals by delivering high quality education, resources and training. We influence politicians and policy-makers, and campaign for better quality of life for people living with dementia and their carers and greater understanding of dementia.

We also fund innovative research in the areas of cause, cure, care and prevention. We work with scientists and people affected by dementia to ensure that the medical and social research programmes we fund have a positive impact on people's lives.

If you have any concerns about Alzheimer's disease or any other form of dementia, visit alzheimers.org.uk or call the Alzheimer's Society Dementia Support Line on 0300 222 11 22. (Interpreters are available in any language. Calls may be recorded or monitored for training and evaluation purposes.)

PREFACE

The murky area where medicine, law and ethics rub together has always fascinated me. The more we *can* do, as medicine and science take great strides, the more questions arise about what we *should* do, and the greater the need to tread carefully.

If I'm honest, though, I would never have had the stomach for medicine. I feel a lot of sympathy for the in-house NHS trust lawyer I heard of who fainted during the post-mortem they had to attend as part of their induction, and I can still feel queasy with the pictures I sometimes see in medical records.

So it was always going be the lawyers' side of this for me. Early in my career I lived near one of the largest teaching hospitals in the UK, thinking of the thrill it would be to be *their* lawyer! A few years later I was lucky enough to be working for them and, later still, privileged to sit on their ethics committee and to be their first port of call for advice on difficult medical treatment decisions and disputes.

That thrill can wane a little when those calls occasionally come at 3am, to be sure, but the pride of working alongside the clinicians has never faded.

It is a massive challenge for something the size of the NHS to nimbly share good ideas and best practice, and to learn collectively from mistakes or missed opportunities. And the independent sector providers of health and care have their own challenges, of course.

Without exception, though, the clinicians I have been fortunate to work with have been dedicated and driven to do their very best for the patients in their care. Their commitment has been inspiring, and when there are bad outcomes, I have seen these felt personally, painfully and for a long time.

But I appreciate that good intentions offer no comfort to the patients or their families when things go wrong, as they sometimes do, or when communication and relationships break down just when the most fraught and agonising decisions need to be made.

Some of those problems are not helped, I think, by commonplace misunderstandings of the legal framework for making decisions about medical treatment: can a patient insist on treatment, as well as refuse it? Should a patient get everything that is in his "best interests"? Can parents demand any treatment they want for their children? Who decides for a patient who cannot make a decision for themselves, and what role is there for "next of kin"[1]?

To manage expectations (something I learnt the importance of very early in my career): This is not a book about clinical negligence (though I will share the best evidence there is on how a doctor can avoid being sued), professional regulation of clinicians or care providers (eg GMC[2] / NMC[3] / CQC[4]) or inquests, or coercive treatment of mental disorders (under the Mental Health Act 1983).

Instead, this book is intended to offer a practical guide to the legal framework in England and Wales around making physical medical treatment decisions, covering decisions about offering treatment options and resource allocation, consent, mental capacity and best interests decisions, children and parental responsibility, and how disputes can be resolved including going to court.

One of the attractions of this area of work has always been that there are cases with no easy answers, even where the legal framework is relatively clear, so I am well aware of the dangers of trying to tackle some of these questions in black and white. Cases I refer to in this book are either entirely fictional, or are in the public domain as reported judgments.

---

1 Spoiler: None at all. There is no such thing (I'll get to this later).

2 General Medical Council, which regulates doctors.

3 Nursing and Midwifery Council which, of course, regulates nurses and midwives.

4 The Care Quality Commission, which regulates the organisations which provide health and social care.

The law is correct as at 25 July 2025, but can move quickly in this area and, of course, this cannot be legal advice on any of the issues covered.

If you want something more like an A-Z than a guidebook, there are some very much more thorough and heavyweight (in every sense) textbooks available. As a more *practical* guide, though, I will include some practicalities you won't typically get in a textbook, for example how to prepare a good witness statement or give evidence well in court.

My hope is to set out a practical overview that might be helpful not only to lawyers in the field, but also to clinicians and to anyone who has an interest in how crucial medical treatment decisions will be made for ourselves and our families.

So with apologies to the lawyers, I'll try to explain things in a way that is not exclusive to legally qualified readers, and there might be a few bits which the lawyers choose to skip. In the hope it might help those to whom it is an unfamiliar landscape, there is a glossary of some of the legal language at the back, including an introduction to the legal system and profession. There are also some resources in the Appendix for those who want to take steps now to exercise some control over those decisions for the future.

At the beginning, though, I think it is useful to set out a bit of context for some of the key themes that run throughout the book:

- An ethical framework – and autonomy v paternalism
- Doctor / patient relationships and trust; and
- Communication (and how to not get sued).

It has been my privilege to build a career in this field, supporting professionals dedicated to providing treatment and care. I have always been immensely proud to work alongside those who provide health and care, often in challenging situations, and when desperately difficult decisions have to be made.

The least we can try to do is be clear and open about the legal and ethical framework in which those decisions about medical treatment are made.

In updating this from the first edition, I have, broadly, tried to correct my own mistakes and make things clearer, and to add the highlights of the new case law since 2020. But it does not pretend to be capture every new case about medical treatment in the last five years any more than the first edition could include every case before then.

The most changes are where recent case law has been liveliest, or there have been significant developments, or I have taken the opportunity to plug what I now realise was a gap. In summary, I have added significant material on:

- The duty of candour and making good apologies
- Covert recording of consultations
- The sequence of the test for mental capacity (ie functional before diagnostic tests) according to the Supreme Court
- The role of "insight" and "executive function" in mental capacity
- The need for "belief" in the information about treatment to have capacity, and the role of hope
- The role of family in best interests decisions
- Another high-profile case about withdrawal of treatment from a child, the changes in the law around access for legal aid for these cases, and some proposals for reform
- The case law on gender dysphoria services and the ability of children & young people to make their own decisions about this
- Decision making and 16–17 year olds generally, and the "mature minor"

- The role of ethics committees, and some judicial criticism of this
- When to go to court, who should make the application, and the impact of delay
- The anonymity or naming of clinicians in litigation about medical treatment

I have also added a short Coda on the diagnosis of death, and disputes about this, since we have a brand-new Code of Practice on this from the Academy of Medical Royal Colleges, in effect since 1 January 2025 (see Chapter 6½).

I have taken a decision not to add anything about the proposed legislation on assisted dying, which (at the time of writing) is not clear whether it will come into law, or – if so – in what form, as it is still going through parliament. But while such a change in the law could radically alter the relationship between clinicians and patients, the latest estimate I have seen is that it would not come into force until October 2029 anyway, so there may yet be time to pick it up in another edition before then!

And (in the hope that this is not unduly optimistic), I have cut the sections of the first edition, having been published in the early days of the Covid 19 pandemic, which dealt specifically with the medico-legal issues that caused, including the imposition of treatment without consent, and the allocation (or rationing) of scarce resources in that context. I hope that those might prove only of historic interest, and – who knows – might prompt a roaring trade in the first editions.

I hope that this is helpful.

As with the first edition, all author's proceeds are donated to the Alzheimer's Society – www.alzheimers.org.uk

Ben Troke
July 2025

CONTENTS

CHAPTER 1

CONTEXT

This book is about making medical treatment decisions, for yourself and for others. We will need to think about who decides what options are even available; how we inform and support patients to make decisions, and how we establish when an adult cannot make a decision for themselves and what we do about it; how we deal with cases about children; and how we should resolve disputes. Finally, we will set out a few things you can think about now if you want to exercise some control over how this will work for you in future.

Before all that, though, there are three themes run through this book like a stick of rock, and it may be helpful to pick them out and put them into a little context before we start.

- An ethical framework – especially autonomy v paternalism
- Doctor / patient relationships and trust; and
- Communication (and how to not get sued), candour and contrition.

Ethics – autonomy v paternalism

We cherish the idea of consent out of respect for the fundamental ethical principle of autonomy – i.e. that our own lives should be determined by our own decisions as much as possible. (I have a picture by my front door based on the Dr Seuss version of this, that you can choose your own path, thanks to the brains in your head and the feet in your shoes.)

But **autonomy** is only one ethical principle. A competing principle is of **beneficence**: doing good. We will often want to intervene in someone else's life and decisions because it will be better for them if we do (or so we think), and those driven towards the caring professions might well be at higher risk of finding it very difficult to let someone do something we think will harm them.

Equally, we might consider the ethical principle of **non-maleficence** (more accessibly put as "do no harm")[1].

Finally, for these purposes, there is the principle of **justice** – of treating people fairly, for example in allocation of resources.[2]

Of course, the challenge lies in the inevitable situations where these four ethical principles, each in themselves undoubtedly good, pull in different directions.

For example:

- In what circumstances should we force treatment on someone who does not want it, because it will be good for them, or even save their life? At a larger scale, should we put flouride in drinking water for the common good, despite the fact that some would not agree to this, given a free choice? ("Mass medication without consent" sounds less appealing doesn't it?).

- What about vaccination? For each individual, it is no doubt better not to be vaccinated, given the risks, however small, as long as enough other people are to secure the "herd immunity" required for us all to feel the great benefit.

---

1 Primum non nocere – first do no harm, adapted from the Hippocratic Oath.

2 These are the four fundamental ethical principles set out in Beauchamp and Childress, Principles of Biomedical Ethics, 8th edition, 2019.

- How do we decide when to refuse funding of treatment – such as the latest expensive cancer drug – as a matter of fair resource allocation, when we know it would be good for someone, and they certainly want to have it?

- Topically, at the time of writing, should we respect people's choices even to the point where they want help to end their own lives, and make it a legal right to have assisted suicide?

- Should a surgeon operate to separate conjoined twins when we know it is the only way to save one life, though we know it will certainly kill the other? [3]

Many of these examples are beyond the scope of this book, but the first question, of treatment in someone's best interests, whether they want it or not, lies at its heart.

Of these four ethical principles, there is no doubt which is now the first among equals. Throughout society as a whole, at least in our western European culture, there is ever greater premium put on personal choice and individual rights. In health and social care we have seen this play out in some obvious and some more subtle ways.

One milestone was the Patient's Charter in 1991, which set out an NHS commitment to meet very much a rights-based set of expectations. Over time, this was reborn as the NHS Constitution, from 2013, which again emphasised the patient's right to be involved in decision-making, encapsulated in the phrase "no decision about me without me".[4]

---

3 In fact, in *Re A (conjoined twins)* [2000] EWCA Civ 254, the Court of Appeal decided that you could lawfully proceed in this scenario, killing "Mary" to save "Jodie".

4 The title of the Government response in 2012 to a consultation on a 2010 "White Paper, Equity and Excellence: Liberating the NHS"

"The role of the passive patient has gradually shifted into that of an active consumer of health care", as leading surgeon Samer Nashef put it[5].

Other structural and policy reforms embedded the same priorities and "customer focus" (in parallel with a wider trend towards integration between health and social care). For instance, the formerly separate systems for complaints in the NHS and in social care were merged in 2009, and the national guidance issued by the Department of Health (as it then was – it was rebranded the Department of Health and Social Care in 2017) was titled "a Guide to Better Customer Care". I know plenty of people in the healthcare system more used to working with "patients" than with "customers", who found this uncomfortable, and it does have a strong flavour of a service-on-demand and customer-is-always-right approach which I think can sometimes contribute to misunderstandings.

Whatever way the relationship is framed, though, trust and good communication are essential to avoid trouble.

Clinicians and Trust

Empowered consumers of health and social care, exercising their choice, driving improvements by spending their own health or social care budgets on their care where they want it. That's been the policy, and it depends on informing those consumers, for example by starting to publish more and more data[6] which, like anything, can have unintended consequences.[7]

5 "The Naked Surgeon", by Samer Nashef, Scribe (2015).

6 For example the outcome data for individual consultant surgeons from 2013.

7 In this instance, the argument could be that surgeons with the worst statistics may well be those regarded as the best in the business, whose daily bread is attempting the most challenging procedures which others would not countenance, and with a perverse incentive, now, for them to

But still, sources of information have flourished – such as “I Want Great Care”[8] and “Care Opinion”[9] – alongside the less focused output of the online commentariat and on social media.

This can play out through Dr Google, where the patient attends with a printout of their research and a pretty firm idea of what they think is wrong and what they think needs to be done about it.

Most clinicians I have spoken to about this would never say that increasing patient’s access to information is a bad thing. But it can add to the strain in consultation when a good chunk of the few minutes available has to be spent debunking myths from the internet, or explaining why a treatment on which the patient has become fixated is inappropriate, or why something else might best be tried first.

It will be interesting to see how the growing market for privately funded GP services, accessing primary care more generally as “on demand” may change this dynamic further still, especially with the events of the last few years driving a step change in the use of video consultation and other technology.

How long can a model survive of “the doctor will see you now” and the “doctor know best” when it comes to treatment options in a world of expectations set by Amazon Prime and TripAdvisor, and information democratised by Wikipedia?

In parallel with the drive towards consumerism and individual choice, the reputation of the medical profession has had quite a few setbacks in terms of both knowing best and acting in unquestioned good faith.

---

decline to even try these riskiest of operations, to the detriment of patients who might only have had that last roll of the dice – see “The Naked Surgeon”, cited above.

8 https://www.iwantgreatcare.org/

9 https://www.careopinion.org.uk/

We have seen horrifying examples of individuals from Harold Shipman[10] to Ian Paterson[11] causing devastation despite (and, in fact, enabled by) their white coats and medical qualifications. And scandals at Mid Staffordshire Hospitals[12] and Winterbourne View[13] have shown us that places of care can sometimes be anything but. Nursing, too, has not been exempt, as we have seen from Beverley Allitt[14] to Lucy Letby[15].

We feel less inclined to defer unquestioningly, leading to greater conflict and new battlegrounds.

Families feel obliged to be more rigorous about ensuring the quality of care (or more demanding, depending on your point of view); we increasingly see disputes arising over family or carers who insist on recording all care or carers, or seek to do so covertly (see the roaring trade in cameras embedded in bedside cuddly toys[16]).

---

10 A GP in Hyde, Greater Manchester, who was found to have killed around 250 patients in his care over a period of 23 years, mostly though not all elderly and frail, by injecting high doses of diamorphine.

11 A "rogue" breast surgeon, sentenced in 2017 to 20 years in prison for wounding with intent when carrying out operations without medical justification on 10 women, though the later inquiry found that more than 1,000 patients had unnecessary and life-changing surgery. https://www.gov.uk/government/publications/paterson-inquiry-report

12 https://www.gov.uk/government/publications/report-of-the-mid-staffordshire-nhs-foundation-trust-public-inquiry

13 https://www.bbc.co.uk/news/uk-england-bristol-20078999

14 A nurse convicted of murdering four infants, attempting to murder three others, and causing grievous bodily harm to a further six at Grantham and Kesteven Hospital in Lincolnshire in early 1991.

15 A nurse convicted of murdering seven infants, and attempting to murder seven others between 2015-2016, whose conduct is the subject of the Thirlwall Inquiry, which is ongoing at the time of writing.

16 There is some useful recent case law on this – see Chapter 7.

Conversely, we increasingly see care providers who want to exclude family from visiting, or control their behaviour, as staff face increasing challenge, if not abuse.

At an individual patient level, and perhaps especially in medical treatment for our children, we are less ready to allow a doctor the last word. We feel more ready to challenge, and to "battle" on behalf of a baby, who we characterise as "a fighter", especially if they outperform an initial gloomy prognosis (sometimes given by clinicians trying, in good faith, not to harmfully inflate expectations).

Even setting aside the criminal or reckless, just as the human fallibility of our clinicians is increasingly exposed, there's also a growing intolerance of error. Atul Gawande[17] writes that in earlier times we would face ill-health with trust in healers doing their best against an unknown and unknowable foe. A bad outcome was more in the lap of the gods than anyone's fault. Not so now. Collectively we know so much now about the medicine and the science that it is impossible for anyone to keep on top of everything. (In 2017, Robert Wachter wrote that the body of medical literature comprised around 24 million records and continued to expand at 2,100 articles per day[18]). Our reaction may be different because often the right diagnosis and treatment is no longer <u>unknowable</u>, though our individual doctor may be just as blameless.[19] Any failure comes to feel more human, more culpable. In tragedy, it can be human nature to identify someone to blame.

For all that, the level of trust in the clinical professions remains remarkable. One of my first jobs as a junior lawyer was on secondment to the Harold Shipman Public Inquiry, taking witness statements from the families of his potential victims. I remember my taxi into Hyde on

---

17 "Complications, A Surgeon's Notes on an Imperfect Science", 2003.

18 The Digital Doctor, McGraw-Hill, 2017 p118.

19 Growing use of AI in healthcare will of course put this into a different light again.

my first trip to the Shipman Inquiry. The taxi driver knew full well why I was there (having ferried a gaggle of young lawyers between train station and hotel over a period of months) and immediately said to me that what Shipman had done was terrible, to be sure, "*but he was a great doctor*". I find this less surprising now than I did at the time.

He explained what he meant was that Shipman was "an old-fashioned GP" – he "always had time for you", and "would come round to your house" to see you when other doctors were increasingly reluctant to do so; a slightly chilling thought in the circumstances.

People do still trust clinicians, at least much more than they trust anyone else. Even before the pandemic era outpouring of love for the NHS as a whole, in survey after survey over many years doctors and nurses always come out on top of the most trusted professions (judges sometimes do quite well in these surveys, by the way, but lawyers in general, well, less so). That trust is a precious asset, and it brings a heavy responsibility that it should not be used inappropriately.

But it does not always seem to always be readily appreciated by clinicians themselves, who are much more likely to tell me about feeling they are on the wrong end of a "compensation culture".

Communication, compensation culture, and how to not get sued?

It is true that the cost of clinical negligence compensation claims has grown enormously over the last 15-20 years[20], though this is largely due

20 Payments made under the main NHS Resolution compensation scheme, the Clinical Negligence Scheme for Trusts (CNST) in 2023/24 amounted to around £1.9 billion in damages, as well as around £500 million in claimants' legal costs, and around £150 million in the legal costs for the NHS defendants. In 2006/07, compensation payments had been around £300 million.

to the way that damages are calculated[21]. But the reality is that the number of clinical negligence claims have been falling since 2013/14[22], and even at their height, the number of claims is a world away from the frequency with which things go wrong.

The evidence base for the actual number of adverse incidents is scant. In 2000, a report titled "An Organisation with a Memory" (OWAM)[23] focused on patient safety and avoiding repetition of common errors, a particular tragedy which is difficult to avoid entirely in such a complex, vast and fragmented system. For these purposes, the key point made in OWAM was the sheer scale of adverse incidents (defined as "an event or omission arising during clinical care and causing physical or psychological injury to a patient"). Research by Professor Charles Vincent, a patient safety specialist at King's College London, estimated that there were around 850,000 incidents a year among acute hospital in patients[24], that one half of them were avoidable, and a third of them caused serious harm. Whichever way you look at those figures, a rate of compensation claims being brought of barely 10,000 claims pa even 25 years later can hardly be called a compensation culture.

---

21 A change in the way that large compensation claims are calculated for losses into the future, "the discount rate", in 2017 alone added around £360m to the bill. Happily, the rate has changed again in January 2025 in a way that should significantly reduce the levels of compensation paid, reflecting assumptions about better rates of return on investment of the awards of compensation today in respect of losses that are anticipated to arise in the future, such as future costs of care.

22 In 2023/24 NHS Resolution received 10,834 new CNST claims, up around 300 from the previous year, but down from the peak (11,634 claims) in 2013/14. Annual statistics – NHS Resolution

23 https://www.igt.hscic.gov.uk/KnowledgeBaseNew/DH_An%20organisation%20with%20a%20memory.pdf

24 Estimated at around 10% of admissions, and so presumably this figure can be scaled up in line with the increase in the number of hospital admissions to around double that (16.4m admissions in 2022/23).

This is not, by the way, to belittle or underestimate the experience of going through litigation (on either side) and there is powerful evidence of this in a paper which Professor Vincent also contributed to a few years earlier, showing the personal impact of litigation on clinicians.[25] They reported that of the clinicians who had faced a clinical negligence claim (whether won or lost), 79% felt distressed, 70% felt angry, 40% felt it affected their life, 34% lost confidence and 30% felt ashamed. Fully 19% reported wanting to give up medicine. I tried to keep this in mind when I was interviewing clinicians about just another routine case, as I might have seen it, when I was defending clinical negligence claims at the start of my career, mindful how easily you can slip into glibly reassuring them that the claim is against the NHS trust they work for rather than them individually, as if that relieves all anxiety.

But if it is fair to say that we do not typically rush to sue a doctor just because something goes wrong, what does drive the decision to sue? I have heard claimants' solicitors say time and again that patients and families are driven reluctantly to court as a result of the defendant clinicians' failure to be open, explain and (where appropriate) apologise. With the complaints process exhausted, they say, litigation is the last resort. The compensation available is not the motivating factor, though it is all the courts can offer, since they have no power to order the explanation or apology sought.

This is supported by a report by the Behavioural Insights Team, published by NHS Resolution in August 2018[26] analysing the

25 Impact of Litigation on senior clinicians: implications for risk management, Quality in Healthcare, 1997, 6, 7-13. https://qualitysafety.bmj.com/content/qhc/6/1/7.full.pdf. I am not aware of any research on the impact on clinicians of the much smaller group of cases that go to court about making a medical treatment decision, though we will look at some of these issues in Chapters 6 and 7.

26 https://resolution.nhs.uk/wp-content/uploads/2018/10/Behavioural-insights-into-patient-motivation-to-make-a-claim-for-clinical-negligence.pdf

motivation to bring a clinical negligence claim. This showed that nearly 90% of people who experienced an "adverse event" did not bring a claim. And of those that did litigate, only 6% said that their primary reason was to get financial compensation.

There is anecdotal evidence of patients and families coming to lawyers after a poor outcome from treatment, determined to sue a surgeon. In fact, after independent experts have reviewed the records, the surgeon appears to have been blameless (or, at least, not negligent), but the GP might have fallen short in the delay in making the referral for surgery. We often hear the patient will not have a word said against the GP, who they felt was marvellously sympathetic, and wants another opinion about the catalogue of failings they saw in the arrogant surgeon.

If you want to know how likely a doctor is to be sued, and why, look no further than the US medical practice insurance market. There, a bit of research was done in 1997 to help inform insurers set their premiums by better understanding which doctors were more likely to be sued (which is set out in Malcolm Gladwell's "Blink",[27] all about the power of first impressions).

Wendy Levinson[28] took recordings of hundreds of doctor / patient conversations. The doctors fell into two groups – one which had never been sued, and the other which had been sued at least twice. There were striking differences between the two groups. Those never sued spent longer with each patient (18.3 v 15 minutes). They were markedly better at the soft skills of communication; they used more orienting or signposting comments to explain the process and the structure of the consultation e.g. "first I'll examine you and then you can ask me

27 Little, Brown, 2005.

28 Wendy Levinson et al "physician – patient communication: the relationship with malpractice claims among primary care physicians and surgeons", Journal of American Medical Associations 277, no7 (1997): 553-599.

questions". When the patient was speaking, they were better at using "active listening skills" such as "minimal prompts" ("mm", "go on", "tell me more") and they were much more likely to use humour (appropriately) and to laugh. *There was no material difference in the amount or the quality of the clinical information conveyed.* It was not what they did, it was the way that they did it, as it were, and the rapport that this achieved with the patient appears to make them much less likely to be sued, regardless of the actual clinical outcome.

This was then taken further by another researcher, Nalini Ambady.[29] She took Levinson's recorded clips, shortened them to just 40 seconds of each doctor talking to patients, split into two 10 second chunks for each of two patients. And then *she blurred out the words being used, leaving only the tone of voice, rhythm and pitch*, which students were asked to rate for particular characteristics, e.g. warmth, dominance, anxiousness and hostility. Astonishingly, she found that you could accurately predict the doctors more likely to be often sued *based only on their tone of voice*. The ones sued regularly were the ones described as sounding "*dominant*".

Remember that being sued and being negligent are different things. Someone's willingness to litigate against you does not necessarily mean that you fell short of the expected standards on that particular occasion, or generally. But it is sobering that the evidence suggests that the best thing a doctor can do to avoid being sued is to make sure that the patient *feels listened to*, and not talked down to, in any consultation[30].

As such, communication (listening, not just talking), as much as clinical skills, should be the focus for attention to stay out of trouble and, more

29 Nalini Ambady et al "Surgeons' Tone of Voice: a clue to medical malpractice history", Surgery 132, no1 (2002): 5-9.

30 As Maya Angelou wisely said "… people will forget what you said, people will forget what you did, but people will never forget how you made them feel".

meaningfully, to ensure that patients get – and feel that they get – the best care as well as the best treatment.

And, sadly, listening skills are not always a clinician's strongpoint: One bit of research found that doctors typically interrupt patients within 12 seconds of the patient starting to speak[31].

Candour and contrition

While we are here, it might also be helpful to tackle one of the things that clinicians can be very reluctant to say: "sorry".

The phrase "duty of candour" is typically used to refer to the statutory obligations that were introduced by Regulations in the wake of the Francis Report into the Mid-Staffordshire Hospitals scandal[32]. Regulation 20(2) introduces a duty on any registered provider of health and social care to deal with a "notifiable safety incident" by giving an explanation and making an apology as soon as practicable.

This can cause confusion, as there are various strings attached to the definition of a notifiable safety incident – there must be an unexpected or unintended incident in the provision of health or care, which causes, or could cause, a certain level of harm. And human nature is such that we do not like having to make "an apology" if we do not feel that we have not done anything wrong.

To be fair, guidance from the CQC on how to interpret the criteria for a notifiable safety incident, has not always helped to make things clearer.

31 "What Patients Say, What Doctors Hear", by Dr Danielle Ofri, Beacon Press, 2017, at page 17.

32 Health and Social Care Act (2008) Regulated Activities Regulations 2014, Regulation 20.

But it is important to say that there is no part of the test for a notifiable safety incident that requires fault, or blame. It is simply an obligation to follow the process when a certain level of harm has been caused to a patient in our care.

Culture and habit though is that apologies feel like an admission of fault or blame, and it is important to get away from this idea in this context. As long this is properly understood, it becomes a bit easier to say "I am sorry that you came to harm in my care".

I also think that you should not get hung up on the niceties of the criteria for a notifiable safety incident, and certainly not interpret it too narrowly for fear of the obligation to make an apology. Alongside that statutory specific duty sits the more general Regulation 20(1) which says simply that registered providers of health and social care" must act in an open and transparent way with [patients]". No ifs and no buts, and that will generally be enough to answer any questions about the proper response to any situation, whatever the ambiguities of the "notifiable safety incident" criteria.

And alongside that as well, there is the professional duty of candour that rests on doctors and nurses as a result of the guidance from the GMC / NMC, which requires that:

> "Every health and care professional must be open and honest with patients and people in their care when something that goes wrong with their treatment or care causes, or has the potential to cause, harm or distress. This means that health and care professionals must:
>
> - tell the person (or, where appropriate, their advocate, carer or family) when something has gone wrong
> - apologise to the person (or, where appropriate, their advocate, carer or family)

- offer an appropriate remedy or support to put matters right (if possible)
- explain fully to the person (or, where appropriate, their advocate, carer or family) the short and long-term effects of what has happened.

Health and care professionals must also be open and honest with their colleagues, employers and relevant organisations, and take part in reviews and investigations when requested. They must also be open and honest with their regulators, raising concerns where appropriate. They must support and encourage each other to be open and honest, and not stop someone from raising concerns."[33]

And it is important to understand that making an appropriate apology is not an admission of liability[34], it is not likely to compromise any insurance cover, and it is not going to make a compensation claim more likely – in fact, quite the reverse.

The CQC's own guidance is clear that "saying sorry is not admitting fault"[35]. And the indemnifier of claims against the NHS (NHS Resolution) has also said that "saying sorry is always the right thing to do; it is not an admission of liability; it acknowledges that something

33 https://www.gmc-uk.org/professional-standards/the-professional-standards/candour---openness-and-honesty-when-things-go-wrong/the-professional-duty-of-candour

34 See the Compensation Act 2006 s2 which makes this clear, although there is a current proposal to amend this to make it clearer what is meant by "apology" to avoid any confusion – see https://assets.publishing.service.gov.uk/media/67a32d5108d82b458c553c5d/apologies-law-consultation-response.pdf

35 https://www.cqc.org.uk/guidance-providers/all-services/regulation-20-duty-candour

could have done better; and it is the first step to learning from what happened and preventing it from reoccurring".[36]

Crucially, the same document quotes the Chief Executive of NHS Resolution, Helen Vernon, saying that "we have never, and will never, refuse cover on a claim because an apology has been given".

This is not only right, it is savvy. The research by the Behavioural Insights Team into the reasons for people bringing compensation claims[37] found that seeking an apology was among the biggest factors in driving a compensation claim. People did not sue because they'd had an apology. They sued because they wanted one, and felt that they had not been given one, at least not a proper one. An apology that was perceived as half hearted, or insincere, would be likely to do more harm than good.

Research in America has also confirmed that, even in the most litigious society, "sorry works": lawsuits were fewer when an open and honest approach is taken, and appropriate apologies are given when harm has been done.[38]

An authentic and sincere focus on the harm that has been suffered in our care is the best way to make sure that an appropriate apology is given, without being mealey-mouthed about any issues of fault or blame, which are irrelevant to the duty of candour.

---

36 https://resolution.nhs.uk/wp-content/uploads/2018/09/NHS-Resolution-Saying-Sorry.pdf

37 https://resolution.nhs.uk/wp-content/uploads/2018/10/Behavioural-insights-into-patient-motivation-to-make-a-claim-for-clinical-negligence.pdf

38 S. S Kraman and G Hamm, "Risk Management: Extreme Honesty May Be the Best Policy", Annals of Internal Medicine 131 (1999): 963-67, cited in chapter 6 of Danielle Ofri MD, "What Patients Say, What Doctors Hear", (2017) Beacon Press.

Good communication is also fundamental to the law on consent, which is where we will begin, as soon as we are clear what options are actually on the table.

CHAPTER 2

CHOICES AVAILABLE

- Available options
- Assisting suicide
- DNACPR
- Resource allocation
- Discharge from hospital
- Compulsion

Introduction

The core of this book is about how patients (and doctors) make choices about medical treatment (and, by extension, when and how decisions should be made in the "best interests" of patients who "lack capacity" to make their own decision – each of which are technical terms explained in Chapters 4 and 5).

But it is important to be upfront about one key issue – just because you want a particular treatment, it does not necessarily mean it will be available to you. Subject to the NHS (or private) funding being available, the clinician decides what options are available to you, and *from those options*, if you are able to make your own decision, you can consent / refuse or choose. Our autonomy in this context extends only to making decisions among the options which are *actually available* to us. We can choose option B or option C, if offered, even if the strong medical advice is in favour of option A, or we can refuse them all. But we cannot demand an option D if it is not being made available to us. Essentially, if we have capacity to do so, we can choose from the menu of options, however unwisely, or walk away, but we cannot set the menu ourselves. This works on several levels.

Clinical Indication

For an individual clinician, it is well established that a patient cannot force treatment to be offered which is not clinically indicated. To exaggerate to absurdity, I cannot walk into my local hospital, fit and well, and demand a knee replacement operation. If a clinician recommends this for me, however, I can choose whether to accept it or refuse, or (perhaps) choose between different types of operation being offered or a conservative option. (The same goes, by the way for the admission and accommodation in hospital that might come with any investigations or treatment being offered – see below).

The leading case is the tragic situation of Leslie Burke,[1] who was 45 years old when his case reached the Court of Appeal in 2005. Mr Burke suffered from a congenital degenerative brain condition called spino-cerebellar ataxia, which confined him to a wheelchair. In time, as his condition inevitably deteriorated, he would come to need clinically assisted nutrition and hydration ("CANH" – putting nutrition and fluids directly into his stomach by a tube) to survive.

He objected to guidance issued by the General Medical Council (GMC) in 2002,[2] which put the decision about giving or continuing CANH in the hands of the doctors, without regard for what the patient wants. Mr Burke wanted CANH to be given whenever he needed it, and though

1 *Burke, R (on the application of) v General Medical Council & Ors* [2005] EWCA Civ 1003

2 "Withholding and Withdrawing Life-prolonging Treatment: Good Practice and Decision Making", GMC, August 2002.

there was no suggestion that he would not be given CANH in due course, he said that the GMC guidance was unlawful because it gave that decision to the doctors rather than to the patient. Mr Burke won the declarations that he wanted in the first instance in the High Court, but the Court of Appeal reversed this and upheld the GMC guidance as lawful:

> *"Autonomy and the right of self-determination do not entitle the patient to insist on receiving a particular medical treatment regardless of the nature of the treatment. Insofar as a doctor has a legal obligation to provide treatment this cannot be founded simply upon the fact that the patient demands it".*[3]

Just so, at a more mundane level, my GP is under no obligation to prescribe antibiotics for me, just because I want them. They must be, in the view of the clinician, clinically indicated.

It is the clinical indication, a gangrenous foot for example, as well as the surgeon's professional training and registration and the consent of the patient, that together make the amputation lawful which would otherwise be grievous bodily harm and likely to attract a lengthy prison sentence.

Consent of the "victim" in itself is no defence to such an assault, given the public interest in protecting people generally.[4] In a "healthcare" context, body modification carried out beyond the scope of proper

---

3 Paragraph 32.

4 The key case here, by the way, is one of the very few I remember from my law degree, and not only because it came out while I was at university. In *R v Brown*, House of Lords, [1994] 1 AC 212, a group of gay men who had been taking part in sado-masochistic activities – the phrase "genital torture" sticks in the mind – were exposed, as it were, by an unrelated police investigation. Though none of them had complained, they were successfully prosecuted for actual and grievous bodily harm under the Offences Against the Person Act 1861, their consent counting as no defence. https://www.bailii.org/uk/cases/UKHL/1993/19.html

clinical practice cannot be justified by a patient's consent alone. In May 2024, the self-styled "Eunuch-maker", Marius Gustavson, was imprisoned for life, with a minimum of 22 years, for a series of offences of grievous bodily harm with intent, for his practice of performing mutilating procedures, notwithstanding the consent of his victims; and equally three other men were sentenced for committing GBH on him with his own consent[5].

Subject to reform that may be imminent, at the time of writing, we have seen a similar point in the vexed law surrounding assisting suicide. Though suicide itself was decriminalised by the Suicide Act 1961, it remained a criminal offence to intentionally encourage or assist the suicide[6]. Time and again, the courts were asked by individuals to overturn what was said to be the discriminatory effect of this on those who may be unable to end their own lives without someone else's help, for example due to a disability, from Diane Pretty in 2001[7] through Debbie Purdy in 2008[8] and Tony Nicklinson in 2014.[9]

Though the courts always refused to change the law, insisting that this must be a matter for parliament, there was a victory of sorts after the Purdy case when it was held unlawful that the Director of Public Prosecutions had given no guidance at all on the circumstances in which the offence of assisting suicide would be prosecuted, for example in

---

5 https://www.bbc.co.uk/news/uk-england-london-68977469#:~:text=A%20self-styled%20%22eunuch%20maker%22%20who%20mutilated%20paying%20customers,counts%20of%20causing%20grievous%20bodily%20harm%20with%20intent

6 Suicide Act 1961 s2.

7 House of Lords [2001] UKHL 61 https://www.bailii.org/uk/cases/UKHL/2001/61.html

8 House of Lords [2009] UKHL 45 https://www.bailii.org/uk/cases/UKHL/2009/45.html

9 Supreme Court [2014] UKSC 38 https://www.bailii.org/uk/cases/UKSC/2014/38.html

taking a loved one at their insistence to Dignitas in Switzerland. In response, the DPP (Sir Keir Starmer QC by then, as it happens) published guidance in 2010, which has since been updated,[10] setting out the factors which might tend towards or against prosecution.[11]

For these purposes, the point is that wanting something does not necessarily mean that it must be made available to you, or even that giving you it would be lawful.

Resource allocation is not a best interests decision

Chapters 4 and 5 will explain capacity and best interests decisions more fully, but it is really important to get one thing straight here.

Lack of capacity, briefly, means that a patient is unable to make a decision for themselves, *when it is their decision to make*, obliging us to make a best interests decision for them *from the options which are available*. The decision what options to make available is not the patient's own decision to make, but a prior decision made by the clinicians or NHS. That remains true regardless of whether the patient has capacity to choose among them or if, instead, a best interests decision will be made.

Lack of capacity for any particular decision does not in itself entitle that patient to preferential access to resources. The Mental Capacity Act 2005 (the MCA) operates to prevent a patient who lacks capacity for any decision being disadvantaged as a result. It is not intended to give them a trump card or allow them to queue jump.

10 https://www.cps.gov.uk/legal-guidance/suicide-policy-prosecutors-respect-cases-encouraging-or-assisting-suicide

11 For example, one factor tending towards prosecution for assisting suicide is if the victim is in the care of the offender, who was acting in their capacity as a doctor, nurse or other healthcare professional.

"Best interests", defined by the MCA, is the legal test for how to pick among the available options for a patient who cannot choose for themselves. It is not appropriate, and obviously confusing, to talk about which options should be *offered* (as opposed to which of the available options should be *selected*) in terms of "best interests". For the clinician's decision what options to offer, the patient's "capacity" and "best interests" are totally irrelevant.

So, a case of a patient with a learning disability who cannot make decisions about his ongoing renal dialysis may raise the challenging legal question of whether it is in his best interests for dialysis to be forced on him, against his wishes, when he is non-compliant, because the dialysis is actually available. But it does not follow that he must immediately be offered a kidney for transplant because it would be in his abstract "best interests". There is a scarce resource and a waiting list limiting access to that. A best interests decision can only be made among options which are actually available now, just as the choice of a patient with capacity is limited in the same way.

The leading case is *MN v A CCG.*[12] MN was a profoundly disabled young man, in his early twenties at the time of the Supreme Court judgment in 2017. He was in a residential setting to meet his extensive care needs, but a dispute arose between his parents and the CCG funding his care. In essence, his parents wanted to have greater involvement in provision of his personal care and for there to be more frequent visits for MN back to the family home, arguing that these things were in MN's best interests. But these things required either more staff from the placement or more funding from the CCG, or both, which were not on offer.

Lady Hale gave the leading judgment in the Supreme Court, noting that the Mental Capacity Act only permits the Court of Protection to make a decision that the patient could have made for himself:

12 [2017] UKSC 22 https://www.supremecourt.uk/cases/docs/uksc-2015-0238-judgment.pdf

> *"[The court] has no greater power to oblige others to do what is best than P would have himself. This must mean that, just like P, the court can only choose between the "available options".*[13]

The point is perhaps even clearer in a clinical context in the case of AVS[14]. A 57 year-old man had become progressively unwell with Creutzfeldt Jakob's Disease, causing a serious brain injury and a very poor prognosis. He was thought to be in a persistent vegetative state. His brother – a solicitor as it happens – was insistent that an experimental treatment be given: a pump implanted under the skin in his chest delivering a drug – Pentosan Polysulphate) into AVS's brain, and he found a doctor willing to provide that treatment, at least for the first three months until the pump failed and was due to be replaced. There had been no benefit evident at all, and no clinician was willing to replace it to continue that treatment. AVS's brother brought the case to court arguing that the treatment should continue, in his brother's best interests.

The court rejected this argument strongly, a decision that was upheld in the Court of Appeal. Essentially, the court said, it is nonsense to try to frame this argument in terms of best interests unless of until it is actually an option that is available:

> *"It is trite that the court will not order medical treatment to be carried out if the treating physician/surgeon is unwilling to offer that treatment for clinical reasons conscientiously held by that medical practitioner...."*

> *"...[i]f there are clinicians out there prepared to treat the patient then the patient will be discharged into their care and there would be no*

13 At paragraph 35.

14 AVS v An NHS Foundation Trust [2011] EWCA Civ 7, https://www.bailii.org/ew/cases/EWCA/Civ/2011/7.html – strictly this was a decision to refuse permission to appeal, rather than a substantive judgment, but the reasoning was given in detail with the intention of setting a clear precedent.

need for court intervention. If there is no-one available to undertake the necessary operation the question of whether or not it would be in the patient's best interests for that to happen is wholly academic and the process should be called to a halt here and now."

Do not treat "best interests" as if a blank piece of paper or a blank cheque. It is a matter of choosing among the options that would have been available to the patient if he had capacity to make the decision for himself (see Chapters 4 & 5).

And as the philosopher Jagger noted, you can't always get what you want.

CPR / DNACPR

One area where this can all get especially blurry is the provision of CPR (cardio-pulmonary resuscitation).

A DNACPR[15] form is a document recording a decision that in the event of cardio-pulmonary collapse no attempt at CPR should be made. But whose decision is this, and why would it be made?

There are actually (at least) three different routes to a DNACPR:

1 A patient can decide that they don't want CPR

2 A doctor can decide that they wouldn't give CPR, because it wouldn't work; or

3 A doctor can decide that CPR could be done, but it is, on balance, best not to do it.

It really makes a difference which of these lines of thought lies behind any DNACPR notice, and it is unhelpful if this is not clear.

15 Do Not Attempt Cardio-Pulmonary Resuscitation.

Let's start with you, as the patient. If your heart stops, do you want every effort to be made to restart it? You may not have given this much thought, or it is possible you have a fixed and well-informed view already. But it is reasonably likely that any member of the public has a very distorted idea of the prospects of success, and what is really involved.

The likelihood of short-term survival from CPR for a cardiac arrest is said to be no better than 20%, even if it happens in hospital, even then with a likely slow decline and lots of collateral damage. The odds of longer-term survival neurologically intact are "abysmal".[16] For children the prospects are woeful, with just a 5% survival rate from CPR after cardiac arrest and a flat trace, and only 1% of those would avoid grave brain damage.

Outside hospital, of course, we fare even worse. Of around 30,000 cardiac arrests outside hospital in the UK each year where emergency medical services attempt resuscitation, only 1 in 11 patients in England (1 in 12 in Scotland) survive until discharge from hospital.[17]

But the public's impression of our chances is skewed by what we see. A study in 2018[18] reviewed 30 consecutive episodes of each of Grey's Anatomy, Holby City and Casualty broadcast between October 2012 and November 2013 and found that these contained 36 attempts at CPR,

---

16 "The Language of Kindness" by Christie Watson, Vintage, 2018, see p317. Oddly, she explains, if you're going to have a cardiac arrest anywhere, you should choose a Las Vegas casino, where there is a staggering 75% recovery rate from CPR, which she speculates may be due to the combination of high levels of staff training and very high levels of supervision to prevent cheating, so any collapse is spotted immediately.

17 https://www.bhf.org.uk/what-we-do/influencing-change/cpr-in-schools

18 "Cardiopulmonary resuscitation on television: are we miseducating the public?" Colwill M, Somerville C, Lindberg E, et al. Postgrad Med J 2018;94:71–75.

with a wildly implausible success rate (i.e. achieving spontaneous return of circulation) of 62%.

Still, even a small chance might feel well worth a go, if trying CPR does no harm. But again the reality is not always well known, or fully portrayed in the media.

As described by Rachel Clarke:[19]

> *"A crash team descends like a tempest, pumping the chest, shocking the heart, slugging in the adrenaline, doing whatever it takes to try to claw back a life interrupted. Resuscitation is violent, bone-crunching work. During CPR a dead body is essentially assaulted by a team of doctors who hope to achieve its resurrection. But if that hope is vain from the outset – perhaps because the patient is too elderly, frail and overwhelmed with illness ever to stand a hope of having their heartbeat restored – then the ending it inflicts is invariably ugly, brutal and devoid of dignity".*

Sometimes,

> *".... our heart stops because it is time for us to go. CPR in these cases is at best pointless, at worst a grotesque indignity".*[20]

And, she observes, there is more teaching on *how* to do CPR than on *whether* to do it, or how such decisions should be made.

So there are perfectly good reasons why a patient might well decide that they do not want CPR attempted in certain circumstances[21] and this, of course, must be respected. Normally, this would be recorded on a

19 "Dear Life", Little, Brown, 2020, p96.

20 Ibid, p108.

21 You may, perhaps, want to make an exception if the cardiac arrest happens in a Las Vegas casino, see note 16 above.

DNACPR form which would, you'd hope, be suitably prominent in your records to pre-empt any default to CPR, or else it'd be pretty worthless.[22]

However, as we've already explored, this doesn't work the other way – a patient cannot *demand* that CPR be given in future.

It is also open to the clinicians to take a view that any attempt at CPR would be futile (i.e. there would be little or no real prospect of success) and so they would be unwilling to do it. In that case a DNACPR form may be appropriate but it would be at the *doctors' initiative* rather than the patient's.

However, though this is squarely in line with the principle embodied in *Burke* above that a doctor cannot be forced to provide treatment against their judgement, a decision of this gravity cannot properly be made entirely unilaterally and without *consultation* with the patient.

Janet Tracey was 63 when she suffered a broken neck in a car crash, having recently been diagnosed with terminal cancer, and was admitted to Addenbrookes Hospital in Cambridge. She sadly died little more than two weeks later. In that time, a DNACPR notice was put into her records, withdrawn, and then reinstated, and when the family later sued the hospital trust there had to be a seven-day hearing with a number of witnesses to sift through the conflicting evidence about the extent of discussions with Mrs Tracey or her family about this in that period. The bottom line, the Court of Appeal later held,[23] was that the hospital had breached her rights[24] by "failing to involve her in the process" by which a DNACPR was instated. Though the court reiterated the point in *Burke*

22 There is a case of compensation being awarded for an attempt at CPR being made, against a patient's wishes, where the doctors ought to have known about a DNACPR form.

23 [2014] EWCA Civ 822

24 Right to private and family life under Article 8 of the European Convention of Human Rights

that it is not open to a patient to compel a doctor to provide treatment which is not felt to be clinically indicated, the patient should be "consulted" about a decision such as this, "unless … the patient will be distressed by being consulted and that distress might cause the patient harm".

Such "consultation" should not be misunderstood. It is more informing than asking. It does not empower a patient (or their family) to overrule the clinical decision, of course, but it does enable them to question it and, if appropriate, to seek a second opinion. This protects "the autonomy, integrity, dignity and quality of life of the patient".

A subsequent case has confirmed that the same duties of consultation with the patient or, where appropriate their family, apply where the patient happens to lack the mental capacity to make their own decisions about the treatment.[25]

So it is fairly clear where you stand if the doctor[26] won't do CPR, or if the patient doesn't want it. But this can gloss over a more difficult middle ground where the doctor might be prepared to try CPR, but thinks it is better not to.

Of course, the *Tracey* consultation requirement applies just as much here, and would hopefully flush out and challenge any assumptions being made by the clinician, for example about the patient's own values or views of their own quality of life. The capable patient might tell the doctor he's prepared to take the gamble and – as long as the doctor is prepared to spin the wheel – it is the patient's decision whether to do so.

Even more care may be needed, though, where it is a patient who lacks capacity to make their own decisions about the treatment and where the

25 *Winspear v City Hospitals Sunderland NHS Foundation Trust* [2015] EWHC 3250 (QB).

26 I am aware that resuscitation may often be decided or done by other clinicians, but with apologies to them I am trying to keep this simple.

clinician is making a decision for the patient that CPR is not in their best interests, weighing up the balance of the benefits and burdens. If this is what is being done, it must be done with a proper best interests decision-making process, compliant with the Mental Capacity Act 2005, and referred to the Court of Protection in the event of a dispute (see Chapters 5 & 7).

This is a very different place to be than a decision that the doctor is unwilling to do CPR due to futility, and simply has an obligation to "consult" with (i.e. inform) the patient. And it makes a big difference: No one can force a doctor to do something he thinks futile. But if doctor just thinks something is not in a patient's best interests, others can legitimately disagree, and the court can say he's wrong and that a DNACPR order based on best interests is inappropriate.

The court cannot order that CPR *must* be given, and ultimately the decision whether or not to do it falls to the clinician on the spot at the time it needs done, though it helps everyone if the merits of doing it have been given a bit of thought beforehand. Remember that DNACPR is about planning for the future. It can be because a clinician says that it would be futile, or because a patient with capacity to do so decides that they do not want CPR in some or all circumstances. Or it can be a best interests decision, following the MCA appropriately.

In some cases, though, the issues can be muddled when a DNACPR is put in place, especially if the result is recorded but not the reasoning, and if the clinicians (if at their behest) are unclear whether it is a case of futility or a (covert) best interests decision.

The best way to tease out the clinician's reasoning is to ask whether, if the patient had capacity to decide and wanted to take all the risks involved for the small chance of benefit, the doctor would be willing to provide the CPR. If they would, then it cannot be said to be "futile", and any DNACPR being led by the clinicians rather than the patient's own choice is really a best interests decision and ought to be seen as such, following the MCA appropriately.

As this is so often a cause of confusion, and at the risk of labouring these points, I'll recap into 5 different scenarios for an elderly patient, Betty, and her doctor, Dr David:

1. As a patient with capacity to make her own decision about this, Betty does not want the end of her life marked by attempts at CPR.

    - Fair enough – It's her life and her body.

    - She just needs to make sure that the right people know to ensure that her wishes are respected.

    - A DNACPR form, after discussion with her treating clinician / GP should do this, but an Advance Decision to Refuse Treatment (see Chapter 5) in the correct legal form is binding.

    - If that's what she wants, she should do an ADRT refusing CPR (in some or all circumstances) and make sure that her clinicians and family know about it.

2. Dr David thinks it would be futile to attempt CPR for Betty. It just won't work.

    - Fair enough – No-one (not Betty, not her family) can make him.

    - But it is best there are no surprises. Unless it is positively harmful to do so, David needs to consult with Betty (and/ or if appropriate with her family).

    - In this context that means making them aware of his view and his decision, and why. She or they can seek a second opinion.

- That consultation might, on reflection, suggest that the thinking is more along the lines of scenario 3 or 4.

- Dr David should document everything.

- And remember to keep this under review or time limited as appropriate, if the assessment of futility is based on things that might change.

3. Dr David thinks that CPR might be effective (in the sense of restoring circulation), but on balance it is not for the best, given the poor prospects and heavy burdens.

   - But Betty has capacity to make her own decision, *so it is up to her.*

   - Dr David should paint her an absolutely realistic picture.

   - But if Betty decides to take the heavy burdens for the small chance of limited benefit, well that's her decision, as long as Dr David is willing to offer it (and if not, why not, given it might work, and Betty is willing to take the risk?).

   - Alternatively, Dr David might find that the discussion prompts Betty to decide she does not want this and she may decide to bindingly refuse CPR as above (in scenario 1).

4. Or in the same scenario as 3, but this time Betty does <u>not</u> have capacity to make her own decision.

   - This then amounts to a best interests decision, and so Dr David must follow the MCA process.

- This means involving Betty herself appropriately, and others such as family to help inform the best interests decision (see Chapter 5).

- Any dispute about best interests can be referred to the Court of Protection (see Chapter 7).

5. Finally, imagine a different doctor, Dr Smith, attends when Betty has collapsed and Dr Smith has to make a decision about CPR on the spot.

    - If there is a valid and applicable ADRT refusing CPR that is binding then Dr Smith must not give CPR (unless she has reason to think that Betty has changed her mind, or that the ADRT is not valid, in which case she is covered while providing treatment if need be in the interim – see Chapter 5).

    - If there is a DNACPR based on Betty's capacitous wishes it should be treated like an ADRT.

    - If there is a DNACPR based on Dr David's view of futility, Dr Smith may well rely on it, but she is entitled to take her own view. If she thinks CPR is *not* futile, Dr Smith then gets into making a best interests decision whether to do it or not, in circumstances when this is obviously difficult.

    - If there is already a DNACPR based on a proper best interests decision-making process this should not be second guessed without good reason.

    - But the absence of both an ADRT and DNACPR form does not oblige Dr Smith to provide CPR. She must take her own reasonable view at the time on futility and, if not futile, on best interests. (By definition, by the time that a patient needs

CPR they will not be able to make their own decision about it, which is another good reason for planning ahead!)

You can see why it is helpful to be clear in any DNACPR about the *reasoning* as well as the decision, to minimise the uncertainty and the decision-making that must be done in a crisis when it could helpfully have been given some thought in advance.

I hope it should go without saying that the reasoning "DNACPR because learning disability" or "...old age" or "...dementia" is absolutely not ok.

And, for the reasons I have given, it would be hard to justify, either in legal or ethical terms, any sort of organisational policy that demanded that CPR must always be given to any patient unless a DNACPR is in place. Clearly, that decision on the spot should depend on the clinical situation and , as need be, an appropriate process of best interests decision making. It cannot be the case that CPR – if on offer – is automatically in someone's best interests just because a DNACPR decision has not been made.

Finally, the focus here has been on DNACPR, but it is worth noting that these important discussions about care planning, reflecting people's wishes, are often now dealt with in terms of the ReSPECT form[27], addressing a person's care overall, rather than being limited only to the issue of CPR alone, which seems to be a better way to do it.

Rationing

It is not just the case that an individual clinician is a gatekeeper of access to any and all healthcare your heart desires. There is also – within the NHS at least – a system level restriction, which you might call

27 https://www.resus.org.uk/respect

"rationing", but we are typically more comfortable putting in terms of resource allocation and prioritisation.

It has never been possible for the NHS to meet every healthcare need. As the demands on the service have grown over time, and the cost increased as a share of GDP accordingly, the tension between supply and demand has become more evident, and especially so in the last 15 years or so. On average, since 1948 the NHS has received an increase in funding of around 4% pa. Since 2010, in the era of austerity, that figure has been closer to nil, until the more recent boost around Covid. And while that represented a victory of sorts compared to the departments which faced swingeing cuts over that period, the very large reduction in funding of adult social care in that period has simply pushed further demand into the NHS.

This is not the place to get into the complexities of NHS structure, but it is significant that after the reforms in April 2013[28] the burden of determining what the NHS ought to provide was shifted. Previously the key bit of English legislation was the NHS Act 2006, s3 which provided that the Secretary of State must provide hospitals, doctors, nurses etc "to the extent that he considered necessary to meet all reasonable needs". After 2013 alongside the newly established National Commissioning Board (usually now known as NHS England) taking on certain national responsibilities, the burden of commissioning was put onto the new Clinical Commissioning Groups (replacing the previous Primary Care Trusts), which were obliged to ensure the appropriate provision in *their* view (not the Secretary of State's) or everything reasonably necessary to meet the needs of the people in their area (not nationwide). Pitched as enabling clinically led and locally focussed prioritisation (the more negative phrase for which is "the postcode lottery"), putting it largely in

28 Under the Health and Social Care Act 2012 reforms led by then health secretary Andrew Lansley.

the hands of 211[29] or so relatively small, new organisations to decide what NHS services ought to be commissioned.

Since the first edition of this book, CCGs themselves have been replaced in turn by Integrated Care Boards (ICBs)[30] which have inherited pretty much all their functions, since July 2022, on a larger footprint with 42 ICBs across England.

In the time that I have been working on this second edition (in the Spring of 2025), it has been announced that NHS England is to be abolished (or "merged" into the Department of Health and Social Care, depending on the framing), with its functions presumably to be split between going "up" into the DHSC and "down" into ICBs. But ICBs themselves have been ordered to cut 50% of their running costs in the next few months, predicted to drive mergers among the smaller of the 42 ICBs to create more economies of scale, pushing their number down towards half that. At the same time, there is likely to be a far-reaching reconfiguration of the ICBs' role and responsibilities, focussed on "strategic commissioning", and with many of their other current functions divested off to NHS providers or elsewhere[31] (TBC).

Alongside the continual churn of what a client has called "NHS re-disorganisation", one constant is that the strain between resources and demand has tightened, as we have all grown older, less healthy, and generally more demanding. At the same time, the public finances are tight, and there is real concern about the economy generally and the

29 Ever since then there have been mergers, in many cases to move them back towards the size of their predecessor PCTs.

30 Health and Care Act 2022 – https://www.legislation.gov.uk/ukpga/2022/31/contents

31 https://www.digitalhealth.net/wp-content/uploads/2025/05/Model-Integrated-Care-Board-%E2%80%93-Blueprint-v1.0.pdf

world around us, and especially the need to find more money to invest in defence.

In some ways the growing demand reflects the successes of the NHS (as well as wider social improvements). Maladies that used to inevitably kill us relatively quickly may instead now be beaten, or at least fought to a draw and leave us with many years of ongoing healthcare need, often living long enough to have several overlapping chronic conditions (co-morbidities) causing a new layer of complexity. On top of this, each ICB has an explicit statutory duty to carry out its functions "effectively, efficiently and economically",[32] and a duty to stay within its budget.[33]

On any view, juggling limited resources against ever greater demand is a thankless task, and the courts have generally been pretty sympathetic to the NHS about this when the issues have, occasionally, been tested.

One high profile example of this – in the mid 1990s, when I was first getting interested in such things – was the case of Jaymee Bowen,[34] a 10 year-old girl with leukaemia. Various treatments had already failed, and the health authority took a view that her prospects of success from further treatment could not justify the very high cost. Her parents challenged this decision, and the judge in the first instance hearing said that in these circumstances, with the life of a young girl in the balance, the health authority must "do more than toll the bell of tight resources. They must explain the priorities that have led them to decline to fund the treatment". But the Court of Appeal immediately overturned this:

> *'I have no doubt that in a perfect world any treatment which a patient, or a patient's family, sought would be provided if doctors were willing to give it, no matter how much it cost, particularly when a life was potentially at stake. It would however in my view, be shutting one's*

---

32 NHS Act 2006 s14Z33, as amended by the Health and Care Act 2022.

33 NHS Act 2006 s223GC, as amended by the Health and Care Act 2022.

34 Reported as *R(B) v Cambridge Health Authority* [1995] EWCA Civ 43.

eyes to the real world if the court were to proceed on the basis that we do live in such a world. It is common knowledge that health authorities of all kinds are constantly pressed to make ends meet. They cannot pay their nurses as much as they would like; they cannot provide all the treatments they would like; they cannot purchase all the extremely expensive medical equipment they would like; they cannot carry out all the research they would like; they cannot build all the hospitals and specialist units they would like. Difficult and agonising judgments have to be made as to how a limited budget is best allocated to the maximum advantage of the maximum number of patients. That is not a judgment which the court can make. In my judgment, it is not something that a health authority such as this Authority can be fairly criticised for not advancing before the court.'

Sadly, though the wide press coverage of the case brought an anonymous donor forward to pay for the further treatment, Jaymee died anyway, just a few months later[35].

The NHS can still come unstuck in court if the decision making is flawed. For example, it cannot be an irrational decision, or be undermined by bias or prejudice, or by taking into account factors it should not have (or vice versa). Human rights issues ought to be appropriately considered. In some cases, promises may have been made by the NHS which it can reasonably be expected to keep.[36] And in some circumstances human rights arguments for particular individual or groups of patients can add another layer, which is beyond the scope of this chapter. But at the end of the day, demand often outstrips resources

35 "Jaymee: The Story of Child B", Sarah Barclay, Viking, 1996 – published, poignantly, at a time when the cover could say "so far the treatment has proved successful and Jaymee is in remission".

36 For example the case of *Coughlan* (*R v North and East Devon Health Authority (ex parte Coughlan)*), [1999] EWCA Civ 1871, which is the leading case on the vexed question of where we draw the line between NHS funded care, which is free of charge, and social care, which is means tested, which is far too sticky to deal with here.

and it is usually perfectly ok for the NHS to say “no”, if it does so by a reasonable and proper process.

Typically, in our system, resource allocation tensions have been largely displaced into a mechanism of waiting lists, though there have also always been examples of particular treatments which are deemed to be non-core business for the NHS (most routine dentistry might be an example, or cosmetic surgery) driving patients for the most part towards private sector provision. In 1999, NICE[37] was established to provide national guidance, including explicitly considering the cost / benefit of new technologies or medication, and to bring some consistency in approach. Even so, you may still find that the scope of NHS provision for you individually may depend on the approach of the ICB in whose area you happen to be registered with a GP, or where you live.[38]

Discharge from Hospital

Just as we have no right to demand particular treatment, so we have no right to demand admission to hospital, and indeed no right to stay in hospital once deemed medically fit for discharge.

This is no small issue – according to the Nuffield Trust, in May 2024 over 12,000 people were in hospital in England who no longer needed to be there, down slightly from a peak of over 14,000 in January 2024. A great many of those are desperate to leave hospital, but are unable to do

37 The National Institute of Clinical Excellence, in 2013 given an extended remit to include social care interventions and renamed as the National Institute for Health and Care Excellence, though still abbreviated as NICE.

38 Note that the rules about which ICB is actually responsible for commissioning your care are messy and complex in places, and again warrant more unpicking than can be done here – not least because all the reform mentioned above is likely to move these goalposts again shortly.

so while there are delays in finding the right social care or other support after discharge.

For a small number of cases, a patient who is medically optimised may simply refuse to leave. Here, the cliché that "possession is nine tenths of the law" has some basis – it is very much easier not to admit a patient than it is to make an inpatient leave against their wishes.

But the law is clear that there is no right to reside in a hospital bed, other than by the hospital offering it to you on the basis of clinical need, and there are various legal powers available to hospitals which need to take steps to secure that a patient leaves.

For instance, the Criminal Justice and Immigration Act 2008 s119 makes it a criminal offence to cause a nuisance or disturbance on the premises of an NHS hospital. There is an exception only if they are there to receive medical treatment, which would not apply to someone who has been declared to be no longer in clinical need of the bed. It has not yet been properly tested in the courts whether simply refusing to leave hospital in itself is sufficient to be considered a nuisance or disturbance, but I have certainly seen cases in which someone's behaviour does amount to this. As well as s119 of that Act making this a criminal offence, s120 provides for a power to remove someone from the premises who is committing that offence, which can be exercised by a police officer or by someone authorised by the Hospital, and which allows for the use of reasonable force, if necessary, except only if doing so would endanger the person's physical or mental health.

One problem is that this power includes no authority to take a patient to another particular place – say a care home, or back to their own property – but only to remove them from the NHS premises.

In the great majority of cases, though, it is sufficient to write a formal letter to a patient who is reluctant to leave setting out that they have no right to reside and are expected to leave in a reasonable timescale, referring to these powers, and – perhaps – to the fact that if court proceedings are needed then the trust may seek to recover its legal costs from the (former) patient.

Some cases are more complex, and it is open to the hospital trust to make an application to the court, which is typically framed in terms of possession proceedings as if this is a property dispute. Such court cases are rare, and there are only a handful of reported judgments – for example in University College London Hospitals NHS FT v MB, seeking possession of a hospital bed in the early days of the pandemic[39], and most recently in *Northampton General Hospital v Mercer*, which set out some broad principles for such cases[40]

In *Mercer*, the patient had been medically fit for discharge after only 11 days of the admission, and had then remained in hospital, refusing to leave, for more than 18 months. The judge considered the various arguments in public and private law that an individual might have to successfully oppose such an application by the hospital. The judge was clearly sympathetic to the hospital's position, opening the judgment with "bed-blocking in NHS Hospitals is a huge problem". Helpfully, he says that a hospital bed or room – even if occupied long-term – is probably not to be considered a "dwelling" requiring a court order for eviction under s3 Protection from Eviction Act 1977, but he appreciates why a hospital might prefer to seek a court order for possession or an injunction in cases where some force might be needed to remove someone from hospital against their will.

With respect to the learned judge in that case though, I would caution against one part of the judgment in the Mercer case, where he considers the question of her "capacity to consent to discharge from hospital". Apart from the fact that this was academic here, as there was no doubt

39 [2020] EWHC 882 (QB) https://www.bailii.org/ew/cases/EWHC/QB/2020/882.html

40 [2024] EWHC 2525 (KB) https://www.bailii.org/ew/cases/EWHC/KB/2024/2515.html

about the patient's capacity, the more fundamental problem is that leaving hospital is not a matter of consent. It is not the patient's decision whether to leave – they must leave once the bed is no longer being offered to them. The only question for the patient is where they go, not if they go; they cannot stay in hospital.

As such, the proper question is whether they have capacity to make a decision about their destination on discharge, and – if they cannot make that decision – then a best interests decision needs to be made among the available options. But staying in hospital is not an available option, and does not become so just because someone lacks capacity to (or refuses to) make the decision about where to go on discharge.

Sometimes, there may be a dispute about where a patient should be discharged to, or perhaps the proposed discharge in their best interests would be very much against their wishes, as might be the case with someone who only wants to go back to their own home for whom residential care is now thought to be necessary. In those cases, if the patient cannot make that decision for themselves, it may be necessary to make an application to the Court of Protection for a decision among the available options[41], and for this to be done with the urgency necessary to reflect the need to get that patient out of a hospital bed that they no longer need, while there are so many others who do.

Compulsion

The focus of this chapter has been on getting access to resources that a patient (or a family) want, and how this is managed.

41 At times, there may be additional complication from the possibility that the situation after discharge might amount to a deprivation of that person's liberty, which may need prior court approval – for more on this see http://www.lawbriefpublishing.com/product/deprivationofliberty/

But, for completeness, there is another side to this coin, which has also been highlighted by recent events – to what extent can treatment be forced on someone unwillingly?

In normal times, this is largely an issue for the Mental Health Act 1983, which is beyond the scope of this book but in broad terms provides for treatment without consent of a person's mental disorder in certain circumstances, alongside a raft of procedural safeguards for that patient's rights. It does not allow treatment of their *physical* health, unless it is directly linked to the mental disorder for which they are being sectioned[42], for example in some cases of treatment for the physical consequences of a person's eating disorder.

Other than for mental health treatment, the Mental Capacity Act 2005 (see Chapters 4 & 5) can be used to make best interests decisions about physical medical treatment, including against a patient's wishes, when they lack capacity to make the relevant decision for themselves.

Apart from that, for a patient with capacity but at risk of spreading an infectious disease as a result of non-compliance with treatment there are (rarely used) powers under the Public Health (Control of Disease) Act 1984 together with the Public Health (Infectious Disease) Regulations 1988.[43] Under sections 37 and 38 of the Act a local authority can ask a justice of the peace for an order to remove a person suffering from one of the specified diseases to hospital and to detain them there if, broadly, proper precautions cannot be taken or are not being taken, causing serious risk of infection to other persons. The Act contains no time limits on detention.

---

42 Mental Health Act 1983, s63.

43 Applying to England, Wales and Northern Ireland and only to specified diseases including cholera, plague, smallpox, typhus, AIDS, anthrax, leprosy, rabies and tuberculosis.

Even so, of course, this was nothing next to the swingeing, draconian powers included in the Coronavirus Act 2020, rushed through parliament in just a few days in response to the pandemic.

The Coronavirus Act provided for an enormous range of issues, from emergency registration of health and social care professionals, through to food supply, postponing elections, banning events and the use of video links in criminal trials.

Schedule 21 confered wide "powers relating to potentially infectious persons" exercisable by the relevant authorities in England, Wales, Scotland and Northern Ireland. Those could include a public health official compelling someone suspected of being infectious with coronavirus to go somewhere specified for up to 48 hours, to undergo screening and assessment, including providing biological samples and, if need be, to remain isolated for up to 14 days or impose restrictions for up to 14 days on their movement, activities or contact with others. The 14-day period could be extended in certain circumstances.

Those were not normal times.

Key points

- Patient choice is limited by what is actually being offered. You can't always get what you want.

- Available options can be restricted by what is clinically indicated (or futile), by affordability (in the NHS, at least), or what the clinicians are willing to do.

- Decisions about what options are available are for the NHS organisations or individual clinicians to make, and not for the patient, and so the patient's "capacity" and "best interests" are not relevant (I'll explain capacity and best interests more in Chapters 4 and 5). This means that any challenge to this decision-making is a matter of public law (i.e. judicial review), not for the Court of Protection.

- Decisions about DNACPR in particular need clarity, especially about the different possible reasons for any such decision. It can be a patient deciding that they do not want it. Even if it is purely the clinician's decision not to offer CPR as it would be futile, it brings a duty of consultation with the patient and/or family as appropriate. But sometimes a clinician's DNACPR is really a best interests decision that ought to be recognised as such and the Mental Capacity Act followed accordingly (see Chapters 4 and 5).

- You have no more right to remain in hospital once the bed is no longer being offered to you than you have a right to insist on being admitted in the first place.

- Our decisions (and best interests decisions on our behalf) can only be made among the options that are being offered to us, on the basis of clinical judgement (and, in the NHS, funding and availability).

CHAPTER 3

CONSENT[1] – ADULTS MAKING CHOICES

- My body, my life
- *Montgomery* (via *Bolam* and *Sidaway*) and practicalities
- Bending the rules for autonomy (causation and wrongful birth cases)
- Consumerism, rhetoric and reality
- Common language and assumptions

My body, my life

Once a treatment option is being offered to an adult – it is clinically indicated and (NHS or privately) funded – the consent of the patient makes it lawful to carry it out.

Giving treatment *without* consent is only lawful if there is another legal framework to rely on, such as the coercive treatment of mental disorder using the Mental Health Act (which is outside the scope of this book), consent on behalf of a child by someone with parental responsibility or the court (see Chapters 6 and 7), or the use of the Mental Capacity Act

1 This topic is covered in more detail by Lauren Sutherland QC in another book in this series, but is so essential to the law around medical treatment that I ought to set out the essentials, but recommend her book if you want to know more.

to make a best interests decision for someone who lacks capacity to make the relevant decision (see Chapters 4 and 5).

Otherwise, treatment of an adult patient without consent is an unauthorised invasion of someone's bodily integrity and can lead to a civil action for damages and, at least in theory, to criminal liability for assault. No harm needs to have been caused by the intervention, and good intentions is no defence. The classic statement of this, albeit in anther jurisdiction, is by Cardozo J:

> *"Every human being of adult years and sound mind has a right to determine what shall be done with his own body; and a surgeon who performs an operation without the patient's consent commits an assault."*[2]

As well as potential civil and criminal liability, other sanctions can be enforced by the Care Quality Commission (the regulator of health and social care providers), whose Fundamental Standards make it an offence, with an unlimited fine, for a provider to give treatment or care to an adult without consent.[3]

Treatment can be refused by a patient with capacity to make that decision, even if the consequences are fatal. In one leading example in the case law in 2002[4], "Ms B" was a 44 year-old woman of Jamaican ancestry with a successful career as a social worker. Sadly, she became paralysed from the neck down and dependent on mechanical ventilation after a haemorrhage on her spine. She asked for the treatment to be withdrawn so that she could die, but the doctors refused. On her application to the High Court, she argued that the ongoing ventilation without her consent

---

2 *Scloendorff v Society of New York Hospital* 105 NE 92 (NY, 1914)

3 Or, of course, some other proper legal authority such as the Mental Health Act or Mental Capacity Act – Health and Social Care Act 2008 (Regulated Activities) Regulations 2014: Regulation 11.

4 *Re B (adult: refusal of medical treatment)* [2002] EWHC 429.

amounted to an unlawful trespass to her person and must therefore stop. The judge agreed. Finding that she was "competent to make all the relevant decisions" (this was before the Mental Capacity Act 2005 – see chapter 4), the judge held that notwithstanding the principle of the sanctity of life:

> *"the right of the competent patient to request cessation of treatment must prevail over the natural desire of the medical and nursing profession to try to keep her alive".*

Outside the use of some clear legal framework, such as the Mental Health Act, for example, there is no power to force treatment onto an adult patient who refuses it and has capacity to make that decision. And while there may be more reason to err on the side of caution in the assessments that are made, and the advice / support that is sought around the decision-making, no such power arises just because the consequences of not giving / not continuing such treatment are grave.

It is easier, perhaps, to rationalise not starting treatment than it is to withdraw it, where treatment has already started, but it is the patient's ongoing consent that makes it lawful, and if that consent is withdrawn, there is no lawful basis for the treatment to continue.

In September 2007, Kerrie Wooltorton was admitted to Norfolk and Norwich University Hospitals having drunk 350mls of anti-freeze, but stated clearly that she did not want any treatment, other than to keep her comfortable, but she had come to hospital because she did not want to die alone. She was assessed to have capacity to make that decision, and so no treatment was given, other than keeping her comfortable until her death 4 days later. The press covered this a little hysterically, as if it were some kind of "physician assisted suicide", or even "euthanasia", but it was simply an extreme example of the patient's capable refusal of treatment being respected. As the coroner said at the inquest, in which he did not criticise the hospital at all, it would have been unlawful for the clinicians to treat her against her wishes.

The idea of consent is absolutely fundamental to medical treatment,[5] and so it is important to understand how to obtain it properly, which brings us to Sam's story.

Sam Montgomery

Sam Montgomery was born at 5.57pm on 1 October 1999, at Belshill Maternity Hospital, near Glasgow. The problem was that his head had been delivered 12 minutes earlier but his shoulders got stuck, trapping his umbilical cord and depriving him of oxygen. In the words of a medical expert at the later trial, it was "every obstetrician's nightmare".

The hypoxia caused cerebral palsy affecting all 4 limbs, as well as left sided Erb's palsy (damage to the nerves of his shoulder from the obstetrician pulling it free); he was eventually awarded £5.25million in compensation to pay for the care he needs for life as a result of his injuries.

I say "eventually", because he was nearly 16 years old by the time the claim brought on his behalf was upheld in the Supreme Court, in March 2015. His case is now the leading judgment setting out the law on consent, and in particular the information that must be given to a patient for them to make a proper decision about their treatment.

The essential elements of consent are that it is

1. freely given,

---

5 A rare but topical counter-example is the introduction of deemed consent for organ donation under the Organ Donation (Deemed Consent) Act 2019, which came fully into force in England and Wales on 20 May 2020. Even then, of course, it only has effect as a default position after a patient's death and the patient's expressed wishes in life have precedence.

2. properly informed,[6]

3. and that the patient has the mental capacity to make the decision.

Sam's mother, Nadine Montgomery, argued that her consent to the vaginal delivery approach was not valid, as she had not been properly informed of the risks.

In particular, Mrs Montgomery should have been told, she said, about the higher risks of the delivery in her case, because she was of "small stature" ("five foot nothing", as she says) and had maternal diabetes, which together increased the risk of shoulder dystocia (the shoulders getting stuck, as they did) to 9-10%. Only in very rare cases would the shoulders getting stuck cause a serious injury, but if that did happen the outcome could be catastrophic. The only alternative, in the face of those risks, would have been to opt instead for a caesarean section which would, in fact, have avoided all Sam's injuries.

Sam's claim for compensation was defended, and the case went through the Scots courts and then ultimately up to the Supreme Court[7], where it would fundamentally change the law.

(It may be appropriate to pause here and reflect how invidious it is to refer to "*Montgomery*" or the "*Bolam* test" as if the key legal principle we take from the court judgment can obscure the individual human being and, all too often, human tragedy at the centre of the case and giving it their name. Perhaps, this is just the nature of the common law system, with the law built case by case, but it is arresting to find yourself speaking to an audience about "the *Montgomery* approach" with Nadine

6 Though it is often used, personally I have always had a problem with the phrase "<u>informed</u> consent": as opposed to what – "<u>un</u>informed consent"?! Being properly informed is an essential element, so it is meaningless, I think, to talk of "informed consent". There is no other kind.

7 The final appeal court for England, Wales and Scotland. Until October 2009 this was the judicial committee of the House of Lords.

Montgomery in the room or referring to "*Ferreira*" as if it's just a case or a legal principle, when to Luisa Ferreira it is her sister's death. I sometimes wonder what Catherine McFarlane thinks of the House of Lords case all about the fact her parents did not intend her to be born, or what the five daughters of Victoria Gillick – who must now be my age or older! – make of their name being attached to the test for the ability of children to make medical treatment decisions, but we'll get to all those later).

The Baggage of Bolam and Sidaway

Clinical negligence law centres around something called the *Bolam* test, from a case in the 1950s in which Mr Bolam sued Friern Barnet Hospital. He had been referred for electro-convulsive therapy (ECT) as a treatment for depression. As a matter of clinical best practice, to avoid physical injuries when ECT was given, some practitioners at that time used to give the patient some muscle relaxant drugs. Others used to strap the patient to the bed. Some did both, and some (including Mr Bolam's treating clinician at Friern Barnet) did neither.

During his convulsions in ECT, Mr Bolam broke both hips (and I can only presume that this did not do much for his depression either). When the compensation claim came to court, the judge explained to the jury[8] that the doctor is not negligent if "he has acted in accordance with a practice accepted as proper by a responsible body of medical men skilled in that particular art".[9]

This became known as "the *Bolam* test" and sets what is called the standard of care a patient can expect, and therefore what constitutes breach of that duty. It got a lick of paint in a 1998 case[10] in which the

8 We don't have juries in these cases nowadays in England, though I gather that they can still be used in Scotland.

9 *Bolam v Friern Barnet Hospital* [1957] 1 WLR 582

10 *Bolitho v City and Hackney Health Authority* [1997] UKHL 46

House of Lords[11] added that the particular practice accepted as reasonable by a responsible body of doctors had to be able to withstand logical analysis, not just be any old clinical habit, however widespread. But essentially it leaves the standard of care expected as a matter of practice set by the medical profession itself.

For the purposes of the law on consent, though, the next crucial step was in 1985 in a case about spinal surgery[12]. Mrs Sidaway was advised by her neurosurgeon to have cervical cord decompression as treatment for her pain in her neck, right shoulder and arms. He did not tell her about the inherent risk of the procedure, of less than 1%, that the operation could cause paraplegia. She decided to have the operation, and was one of the very unlucky ones who ended up paralysed. There was no evidence that the procedure had been performed negligently, but she argued that she should have been told of the risk and, if she had, she would not have had the surgery and so the injury would have been avoided. When her case reached the House of Lords they held, by a majority,[13] that her claim should fail. The question of whether or not she should have been told of a particular risk depended on whether a reasonable body of medical opinion would have decided not to tell her i.e. applying the *Bolam* test not just how the procedure should be performed, but also to the question of what information must be given to the patient to get their consent.

In effect, this seemed to establish that a patient was only entitled to know what a reasonable doctor thought that they ought to be told. Indeed, one doctor acting as an expert witness in the case argued "giving the full details may drive a patient away". No doubt, he said, if a patient asked

---

11 Then the most senior court in the land, abolished and replaced by the Supreme Court in October 2009.

12 *Sidaway v Board of Governors of the Bethlem Royal Hospital* [1985] AC 871.

13 Lord Scarman, rather ahead of his time, gave a dissenting minority opinion which is substantially echoed in the Montgomery judgment, some 30 years later.

questions the doctor would answer, but in terms of a clinician volunteering information about the risks to an ordinary patient:

> *"The only effect that mention of risks can have on the patient's mind, if it has any at all, can be in the direction of deterring the patient from undergoing the treatment which in the expert opinion of the doctor it is in the patient's interest to undergo".*

I say "ordinary" patient as, with quite some chutzpah, Lord Diplock explained in his judgment that there is one special, superior category of patients who are entitled to a discussion with the doctor on more equal terms:

> *"But when it comes to warning about risks, the kind of training and experience that a judge will have undergone at the Bar makes it natural for him to say (correctly) it is my right to decide whether any particular thing is done to my body, and I want to be fully informed of any risks there may be involved of which I am not already aware from my general knowledge as a highly educated man of experience, so that I may form my own judgment as to whether to refuse the advised treatment or not."*

So, doctor knew best (unless the patient happened to be a judge!).

Progress in practice

Rather than the judiciary, it was clinicians themselves, through their professional bodies, who really moved things on in the years after *Sidaway*, with ever greater emphasis on a patient-centred approach, while the law lagged behind professional practice.

For example, the BMA handbook of Medical Ethics, 1984:

> *"no influence should be exerted through any special relationship between a doctor and the person whose consent is sought... Doctors*

offer advice but it is the patient who decides whether or not to accept the advice.... The onus is on the doctor carrying out the procedure to see that an adequate explanation is given"

"successful relationships between doctors and patients depend on trust. To establish that trust you must respect patient's autonomy – their right to decide whether or not to undergo any medical intervention"

"patients must be given sufficient information, in a way they can understand, to enable them to exercise their right to make informed decisions about their care"

Seeking Patients' Consent: the Ethical Considerations, GMC 1998:

"when providing information you must do your best to find out about the patients' individual needs and priorities. It is for the patient, not the doctor, to determine what is in the patient's own best interests"

Association of Anaesthetists of Great Britain and Ireland, Consent for Anaesthesia, 2006:

"what would this patient regard as relevant when coming to a decision about which of the available options to accept?"

Consent: Patients and Doctors Making Decisions Together, GMC 2008:

"For a relationship between doctor and patient to be effective, it should be a partnership based on openness, trust and good communication..."

"The exchange of information between doctor and patient is central to good decision-making. How much information you share with patients will vary, depending on their individual circumstances. You should tailor your approach to discussions with patients according to:

- *their needs, wishes and priorities*

- *their level of knowledge about, and understanding of, their condition, prognosis and the treatment options*

- *the nature of their condition*

- *the complexity of the treatment, and*

- *the nature and level of risk associated with the investigation or treatment".*

Good Medical Practice, GMC, 2013:

> *"give patients the information they want or need in a way they can understand … respect the patient's right to reach decisions with you about their treatment and care"*

Whether these documents drove or reflected prevailing clinical attitudes over time, it is fair to say that they were some way ahead of the law, at least until 2015.

The latest version is the GMC Guidance "Decision Making and Consent", in effect from November 2020[14] setting out seven "principles of consent":

1. All patients have the right to be involved in decisions about their treatment and care and be supported to make informed decisions if they are able.

2. Decision making is an ongoing process focused on meaningful dialogue: the exchange of relevant information specific to the individual patient.

14 https://www.gmc-uk.org/professional-standards/the-professional-standards/decision-making-and-consent#

3. All patients have the right to be listened to, and to be given the information they need to make a decision and the time and support they need to understand it.

4. Medical professionals must try to find out what matters to patients so they can share relevant information about the benefits and harms of proposed options and reasonable alternatives, including the option to take no action.

5. Medical professionals must start from the presumption that all adult patients have capacity to make decisions about their treatment and care. A patient can only be judged to lack capacity to make a specific decision at a specific time, and only after assessment in line with legal requirements.

6. The choice of treatment or care for patients who lack capacity must be of overall benefit to them, and decisions should be made in consultation with those who are close to them or advocating for them.

7. Patients whose right to consent is affected by law should be supported to be involved in the decision-making process, and to exercise choice if possible.

Montgomery v Lanarkshire – Supreme Court (2015)

Back to Sam's case in 2015: Mrs Montgomery said that if she had been told of the increased risks of shoulder dystocia, due to her height and diabetes, and offered a caesarean section, she would have taken it, and Sam's injuries would have been avoided. Indeed, the evidence of the treating obstetrician was that

> *"if you were to mention shoulder dystocia to every [diabetic] patient.. then everyone would ask for a caesarean section and it is not in the maternal interests for women to have caesarean sections."*[15]

Sam's claim failed at first in 2010, and again on appeal in 2013, as those lower courts were bound to follow the House of Lords' judgment in *Sidaway*, and so applied the *Bolam* test to the question of the information given to Mrs Montgomery. As the claimant, Sam had not established that no responsible body of medical opinion would have not mentioned that increased risk, and so it was not negligent that this clinician didn't do so.

On a final appeal in 2015, though, Sam was successful, as the Supreme Court moved on from *Sidaway*, 30 years earlier, and brought the law into line with the changing world, as well as clinical best practice:

> *"Since Sidaway ... it has become increasingly clear that the paradigm of the doctor-patient relationship implicit in the speeches in that case has ceased to reflect the reality and complexity of the way in which healthcare services are provided, or the way in which the providers and recipients of such services view their relationship. One development which is particularly significant in the present context is that patients are now widely regarded as persons holding rights, rather than as the passive recipients of the care of the medical profession. They are also widely treated as consumers exercising choices: a viewpoint which has underpinned some of the developments in the provision of healthcare services".*[16]

Referring to the ready availability now of clinical information on the internet, for example, they continued:

> *"It would therefore be a mistake to view patients as uninformed, incapable of understanding medical matters, or wholly dependent upon*

15 [2015] UKSC 11, para 13

16 Para 75, Per Lords Kerr and Reed.

a flow of information from doctors. The idea that patients were medically uninformed and incapable of understanding medical matters was always a questionable generalisation, as Lord Diplock implicitly acknowledged by making an exception for highly educated men of experience. To make it the default assumption on which the law is to be based is now manifestly untenable"[17]

The Supreme Court held that the question what information a patient should be given should no longer be determined by what a reasonable body of doctors consider that they ought to be told. Quoting from an Australian High Court Case[18] they said:

"whether the patient has been given all the relevant information to choose between undergoing and not undergoing treatment is a question of a different order. Generally speaking, it is not a question the answer to which depends upon medical standards or practices".[19]

Instead, they decided that a doctor is under a duty to take reasonable care to ensure that the patient is aware of any "*material*" risks involved in any treatment, and of any reasonable alternatives.

So what is "material"?

The Supreme Court explained that information relating to a medical treatment decision is "*material*" if:

- A reasonable person in the patient's position would be likely to attach significance to it; or

17 Para 76.

18 *Rogers v Whitaker*, (1992) 175 CLR 479.

19 Paragraph 71.

- The doctor is or should reasonably be aware that the particular patient would be likely to attach significance to it.

So, the test of materiality is a mix of objective and subjective elements, but crucially both parts are *from the perspective of the patient*, rather than the doctor. It no longer matters what "the reasonable doctor" would tell the patient about the proposed treatment. The patient is entitled to hear what *the reasonable patient* would want to know AND what the doctor knows (or ought to) that *this particular patient* wants to know.

The clichéd examples often given are of the small risk of loss of vision in one eye being hugely more significant to the individual patient already blind in the other eye; or a tiny risk of injury to vocal cord function being much more significant to a professional singer.

A particular patient facing surgery who had read Samer Nashef's "Naken Surgeon"[20], might like to know when the proposed surgeon last had a holiday, for example.

And the focus should not be, as it often is, only on the *risks* of treatment. The *benefits* and the *alternatives* should be explained fully as well, on the same basis.

Reasonable alternatives

The patient is also entitled to know about reasonable alternative or variant treatments, though not necessarily things which are so far-fetched as to be wholly hypothetical.[21] The intention is to enable patients to make

20 Scribe, 2015. Mr Nashef, a leading cardiac surgeon, writes beautifully about decision making and risk, and shares data to suggest that a surgeon is twice as likely to kill you if it is their last day before a holiday than if it is their first day back.

21 *A v East Kent Hospitals NHS Foundation Trust* [2015] EWHC 1038 (QB). http://www.bailii.org/ew/cases/EWHC/QB/2015/1038.html

their own decision, and that means knowing not just the points that the doctor would make to persuade them to "do the right thing", but a full picture of the risks and benefits involved in each option, and of having no treatment at all.

That said, a more recent case brings the *Bolam* test back into play on the question of whether an alternative is reasonable or not. Neil McCulloch[22] died on 7 April 2012, having suffered a cardiac arrest at home. His family claimed that this was caused by clinical negligence in that his doctor had not discussed with him a treatment option (non-steroidal anti-inflammatory drugs or NSAIDs – eg Ibuprofen) that might have helped. They argued that the duty in Montgomery obliged the clinician to discuss any reasonable alternative treatment option.

The Supreme Court rejected this. Identifying appropriate treatment options is a matter of clinical expertise and judgement, and so it is appropriate to look at this through the lens of the *Bolam* test – would a responsible body of medical opinion have offered those options?

Once the reasonable options are set, by clinical judgement, the clinician's role shifts, and they are obliged to give the patient the information about each of those options for the patient to make an informed decision for themselves, weighing the information that is important to them, and not just being steered to the clinician's preference:

> *"As the BMA point out, "the doctor's duty is not fulfilled by 'bombarding' the patient with every possible potential treatment for every potential diagnosis, however mainstream or fringe, however simple the case may be, and however likely any given treatment might be to bear fruit. If it obstructs patient understanding, providing too much information may be as unhelpful as providing too little." To require a doctor to outline the risks of all possible alternative*

---

22 McCulloch v Forth Valley Health Board [2023] UKSC 26 https://caselaw.nationalarchives.gov.uk/uksc/2023/26

> *treatments, even those considered not to be reasonable, is unlikely to be in the patient's best interest and may impair good decision making".*[23]

Therapeutic exception

There is a limited therapeutic exception, by which the court in *Montgomery* recognised that a doctor should be entitled to withhold information if he reasonably considers that its disclosure could be seriously detrimental to the patient's health.

This leaves an element of paternalism, perhaps, but sets the bar considerably higher than the doctor simply thinking it best not to tell a patient something that they might not want to hear, or might deter them from the course that the doctor thinks best:

> *"it is not intended to subvert [the general principle] by enabling a doctor to prevent the patient from making an informed choice where she is liable to make a choice which the doctor considers contrary to her best interests".*[24]

Some practicalities

Since *Montgomery* only brought the law up to date with good practice, it ought not, perhaps, to have had a huge impact.

But implementing it robustly does have obvious, practical implications:

- A clinician must start from the patient's perspective – what would a reasonable patient want to know?

---

23 *McCulloch*, op cit, at para 73, per Lords Hamblen and Burrows, giving the unanimous judgment of the Supreme Court.

24 Paragraph 91.

- And she must also know *this individual patient*: how else can she possibly be satisfied that information which is material *for this patient* has been discussed?

- As such, consent cannot be a one size fits all process determined by the particular procedure proposed, but must be bespoke to each patient. Pre-printed literature about the "standard" risks or benefits of something may have a place in supporting good communication, but it cannot do the whole job – see below.

- It is *not about percentages*. The most frequent question I am asked by clinicians about this is whether there's an obligation to tell a patient about a risk of [X]%. X can vary, but my infuriating answer is always: "it depends". Even the tiniest risk may be material to a particular patient in some circumstances.

- So, logically, consent must be *a discussion* in which the clinician gets to know the individual patient and their particular concerns and values. It must be as much about the clinician asking questions and listening as about giving information.

- This reinforces the point that consent is a *process* that occurs over time, not in an instant. Consent is not simply a signed form. As anyone will tell you, "if it is not written down it didn't happen" but the signed form is no more than a bit of evidence, rather than consent in itself. It is much better to have a detailed note setting out a *Montgomery* compliant discussion and that the patient decided to proceed with treatment X than a signed "consent form" which includes none of that detail. A signed form, without the reality of that proper process behind it, is no more than a facade.

- Equally, of course, that discussion needs to be appropriately documented to record what has been communicated fully. What was the patient told? What did they ask about? What was important to them? If you just write the word "consent" and a tick, it may be hard to show that this has been done properly.

- This all takes time. The second most common question I get asked, usually shortly after my disappointing answer to the first one, is "when am I supposed to find the time to do all this then!?". Fair enough, perhaps, but in this context the courts do not start with the practicality of the clinician's day in mind, but the patient's rights. And it can be very time consuming indeed to be involved in litigation to prove that you did it right if you didn't, or if you didn't write it down so it's not easy to show that you did. For clinicians under pressure to get through appointments at a pace that makes it difficult to have the idealised discussions the judiciary envisage, they might mention to their management the potential consequences of not treating patients with consent, as set out at the start of this chapter.

If this feels like a counsel of perfection and setting unrealistic expectations of the consenting process in the real world, remember that it is only the law catching up with the approach expected by professional good practice for years.

Persuasion, paternalism and maternalism

Consent is not about *persuading* a patient to your point of view and preferred treatment.[25] It is better to frame the process as collaborative, in which clinicians offer options and information, and the patient makes a decision.

The language can be important. I was upbraided once at an ethics committee meeting when speaking about the patient's "compliance" with treatment, and I was told that this had unwelcome connotations of a

25 I have seen training on consent given under the title of "Getting to yes!" – which I think needs to be treated with some care.

passive recipient of treatment, doing what they were told. Instead, I was told, the preferred term was "concordance", to convey better the idea of an agreement, a collaborative project between the clinician and the patient.

Doctors sometimes tell me that some patients, especially older patients, will simply want to defer the decision to "whatever you think best, doctor". It could be, perhaps, quite cold and unsupportive for this to be pushed back to the patient, straight bat, as the doctor sets out the options and insists that the patient alone must choose. I am not sure that the law requires that exactly. But there does need to be some care, all the more so with those who are especially vulnerable and dependant on the doctor's views, that this is not used to unduly steer the patient to a paternalistic intervention.

The reality of sickness of course may often be of frailty, anxiety, uncertainty, and dependency. The model of individual autonomy may break down, and we may feel unsupported if left entirely unguided with a range of options before us and a load of complex information.

A colleague told me about an approach of "maternalism":

> *"Maternalistic physicians are not dictating to our patients what to do, but rather guiding them gently to what we think is best. We give our patients autonomy but never make them feel alone or unsupported in their care. We reassure them that no matter what they decide, we will be there for them. We care for the patient as a whole, not just an illness, but as a person with faults, weaknesses, with their own interests and goals, with human hopes and fears. We acknowledge our patients as the unique individuals they are, and we love them all the same. Even if they don't do what we, as maternalistic physicians, think is best for them".*[26]

26 https://www.huffpost.com/entry/maternalism-in-medicine, 1 April 2015.

In respecting patients' autonomy, perhaps we do need some caution to avoid ditching paternalism so thoroughly that we leave patients feeling uncared for.

But for now, autonomy tends to be king, and two other interesting lines of cases also show the courts willing to stretch the law to reflect this.

Bending the rules on causation – *Chester v Afshar*

The first of these arises, again, in the context of clinical negligence, on the issue of causation of injury. Here it is important to understand that the fundamental purpose of the law of negligence is not to punish the wrongdoer, but rather to compensate the person who has suffered a loss as a result of a breach of the duty of care that they were owed.

As such, glib as it is to put in in these terms, to some extent there is "no harm no foul". This is because, however outrageous or extreme the degree of the breach of duty it would not typically attract compensation if it did not cause an injury. Think of the careless driver weaving all over the road but who – miraculously, perhaps – does not hit anyone or anything, and causes no injury. He might well be in trouble with the police or lose his licence, but there'd be no claim for compensation as a result of negligence. No one has suffered a loss to be compensated. On the other hand, a significantly less culpable act could still be negligent and could incur liability for a colossal amount of compensation if it happened to cause a grave injury.

This is the "but for" test, and in the medical context, the classic case is *Barnett.*[27] Mr Barnett was a night-watchman and attended hospital feeling unwell early in the morning on New Year's Day. The doctor on call decided not to trouble himself to assess Mr Barnett in person, but seems to have come to a view, over the phone from the doctors' lounge, that Mr Barnett ought to sleep it off. This was substandard care, and a

27 [1969] 1 QB 428.

breach of the duty of care owed to the patient by reference to the *Bolam* test. Mr Barnett later died, and his widow sued for compensation, but Mrs Barnett recovered nothing because in fact his problem was arsenic poisoning[28] and, even if the doctor had seen him as he should, this could not have been treated in time to save his life, and "but for" the breach of duty of care, he would still have died anyway. The breach of duty did not cause the death.

There may, of course, be other consequences for the clinicians at fault in such cases – for example accountability at an Inquest, the regulatory functions of the GMC / NMC, or in extreme cases perhaps the police. Broadly speaking, though, compensation is calculated according to the principle of putting the person back into the position that they would have been in had there been no breach of duty, and sometimes a breach of duty makes no difference to the outcome.

In the context of negligent failure to properly obtain a patient's consent, then, where is the compensatable injury? One approach was to put the onus on the patient to prove that if he or she had been appropriately warned of the material risks of a particular procedure, as they should have been but were not, then they would have refused it. That is evidentially hard, because such claims are often brought only after a complication of the procedure has occurred, appearing to taint the claimant's evidence with the benefit of that hindsight. In addition, they may have had very significant symptoms for which that treatment was recommended, so the claimant must persuade the court that they would have chosen to go on suffering those symptoms untreated. And on that basis, even if such a claim were established, compensation for any injury caused by the treatment would need to be quantified as if any *benefit* of the procedure that the claimant had, but now says would have been refused, would also have been lost. It's a minefield. But one landmark case on causation, a

28 Caused innocently, as I recall, from the teapot or crockery he used.

full decade before the *Montgomery* judgment, showed the growing emphasis on the autonomy of the patient.

Miss Chester sought treatment from a neurosurgeon, Mr Afshar, for longstanding back pain. Much like the facts of *Sidaway*, he advised surgery, but did not tell her, as he should have, of a 1-2% risk of paralysis which, in fact, she suffered. She sued for his negligence in failing to warn of that risk, but in her evidence she did not go so far as to say that if she had been given that warning she would have refused the surgery altogether, only that she would have considered further. She might have had the surgery another time, she said, but then the risk of paralysis would have been just the same.

Her case reached the House of Lords in 2004[29] and by a majority of 3:2 she won. The dissenting minority judges talked about the importance of the "but for" test and her failure to establish that the injury suffered would in fact have been avoided. For the majority, though, the fundamental principle was the patient's autonomy, and that the surgeon's duty towards the patient in this respect would be "drained of its content" if not enforced in this way when it has been breached.

So the highest court in the land bent the usual rules about the need for negligence to have *caused* an injury or loss, because of the importance of respect for autonomy.

Another line of cases raises a related issue about whether what has obviously been *caused* by the negligence (a failure of a sterilisation or a vasectomy, leading predictably to the birth of a child) can properly be framed as an *injury or loss*, so as to justify a claim for compensation.

---

29 *Chester v Afshar* [2004] UKHL 41
https://www.bailii.org/uk/cases/UKHL/2004/41.html

Autonomy: Can the birth of an unplanned child be an injury?

In 1989 George McFarlane had a vasectomy. Told that sperm samples confirmed infertility, he and his wife stopped using contraception. But Mrs McFarlane became pregnant again, and their fifth child, a healthy but unintended girl named Catherine, was born on 6 May 1992. In 1997 they brought a claim compensation for:

- Pain suffering and the inconvenience of the pregnancy and birth, claimed at £10,000; and
- The financial costs of raising the unplanned child, claimed at £100,000.

The claim failed. The judge (Lord Gill, himself a father of six) told them that "*the privilege of being a parent is immeasurable in monetary terms, and so the benefits of parenthood transcend any patrimonial [i.e. financial] loss*".[30]

Though the couple won on appeal, the case then went up to the highest court – the House of Lords (now called the Supreme Court) and they lost the claim for the financial costs, though the modest claim for pain and suffering of pregnancy and childbirth was allowed. Five judges heard the case, and in essence all agreed (though they all gave slightly different reasons) that a healthy child was a blessing and as a matter of policy this must be held to outweigh any financial cost.[31] (I must say that I have always found it a bit rich, pun intended, that a law lord – earning £269,530 in 2024[32] – should impose that view on a couple who have decided for themselves not to have the "blessing" of a fifth child, perhaps out of a sense of financial responsibility in very different circumstances.

30 *McFarlane v Tayside Health Board* [1998] SC 389.

31 *McFarlane v Tayside Health Board*, House of Lords [2000] 2 AC 59.

32 https://assets.publishing.service.gov.uk/media/66e830f5e4b40ed591881b73/Judicial_Salaries_2024_to_2025.pdf

As a judge said in an earlier similar case in a lower court: however beloved, "every baby has a belly to be filled and a body to be clothed")[33]

A few years later, the law was tested by a similar claim with a twist – what if the child was disabled, rather than healthy? In *Parkinson v St James and Seacroft NHS Trust*[34] a sterilisation had been negligently performed on Mrs Parkinson, as result of which her unintended fifth child, Scott was born. He happened to have profound behavioural difficulties, thought to be caused by autism. A claim was brought for the costs of raising him, and in this case the Court of Appeal (three judges, each – unhelpfully – justifying their decision with different reasons) allowed the claim for the additional costs associated with Scott's disability, though the "basic" costs of raising any child were disallowed as a result of the decision in *McFarlane*. (Here, though I far from begrudge the Parkinsons the much needed financial support they won, I do find it uncomfortable that the idea seems to be that a "healthy" child is a blessing[35] transcending any possible costs of raising the child, but that the same is not said of a disabled child).

The third in the trilogy was a further twist – a disabled mother of a healthy child. In *Rees v Darlington Memorial Hospital NHS Trust*[36] Katrina Rees had a genetic condition that left her severely visually impaired. She feared that this would make it very difficult for her to raise a child and, for this and other reasons, she had a sterilisation in 1995. The procedure was performed negligently, and she gave birth to a son, Anthony, on 28 April 1997. He seemed to be a healthy child, and so the question was whether her claim for compensation ought to be dismissed

33 Pain J in *Thake v Maurice* [1984] 2 All ER 513.

34 [2001] 3 All ER 97.

35 The word "healthy" is said 55 times in the House of Lords' judgment in *McFarlane*.

36 [2002] 2 All ER 177.

like the healthy child case of *McFarlane*, or (partially) successful like the disability case of *Parkinson*?

Again, the case went to the House of Lords, this time with 7 judges, rather than the usual 5, and again unhelpfully with little consensus between them. The decision, by a majority of 4:3, was that Mrs Rees could not recover the costs of raising Anthony, not even the additional costs relating to her own disability. *McFarlane* prevailed: a healthy child is still "a blessing", even to a disabled mother. But, instead, she was awarded £15,000 as a "conventional sum"[37] for the injury to her autonomy, to "afford some measure of recognition of the wrong done",[38] in addition to the compensation for undergoing the pregnancy and birth.

Lord Millett expressed the basis for this award most clearly. It is not to treat the birth of a healthy child in itself as an injury, but "for the denial of an important aspect of their personal autonomy, viz the right to limit the size of their family".[39]

The striking point from all this, for these purposes, is in *Rees* and in *Chester*, the courts ultimately framed the claimants' loss in these cases terms of injury to their *autonomy*, attracting compensation in itself; the emphasis is on the importance of people being able to determine for themselves how their lives should be lived.

37 Like the damages awarded in some cases for bereavement, a fixed sum which is acknowledged cannot really compensate for the loss, currently £15,120, since 1 May 2020, under the Damages for Bereavement (Variation of Sum) (England and Wales) Order 2020. Of course for claims today, that £15,000 needs to be uprated by inflation since that 2002 decision.

38 Lord Bingham

39 *Ibid* at 1023. In fact, Lord Millett had suggested exactly this, albeit with a lower figure of £5,000, in *McFarlane*, and been ignored by the other judges.

For completeness, in *Shaw v Kovac* in 2017[40] the Court of Appeal held that where full compensation had already been paid for the injuries caused by negligence, including negligent failure to obtain appropriate consent, then the injury to autonomy as a result of that particular failure should not give rise in itself to a distinct head of damages, like the conventional award in *Rees*.

For these purposes, though, patient autonomy is consistently coming out on top in the case law where it is weighed against clinical paternalism, and we'll see much more of this in the next few chapters.

Consumerism & choice, rhetoric & reality

The emphasis on autonomy is reinforced by the policy and language of health and social care: the empowered consumers, spending their personal budgets and enforcing their rights under the NHS Constitution, reflecting a wider trend in society and values. But at times it conflicts with other values – justice, and non-maleficence – in ways that continue to give us trouble.

It is not as simple as always giving people what they want, despite the rhetoric of patient choice etc; the NHS is not just a supermarket or service industry. We have already seen that you cannot demand, for example, something not felt to be clinically indicated, or something too expensive for the NHS to fund or, in any circumstances (for now), assistance with your suicide,[41] however much you want it.

And there are circumstances in which a patient's exercise of their own choice conflicts with other rights or values. An "unwise" decision to refuse beneficial treatment must be respected, regardless of the patient's

40 [2017] EWCA Civ 1028. http://www.bailii.org/ew/cases/EWCA/Civ/2017/1028.html

41 In contrast to the clinicians being bound by Kerrie Wooltorton's capable refusal of treatment, as above.

reasons. But what if their choice is apparently or explicitly based on the race or gender of the proposed clinician? Do we feel more amenable to it if a refusal to be seen by a doctor of a particular gender appears to be driven by cultural sensibilities? How far should we go to accommodate a patient who wants treatment, but not to be treated by a "foreign" doctor?[42]

If the right of a patient with capacity to choose to refuse treatment is absolute and can be exercised for good reason, or no reason at all, what right do we have to look behind someone's reasons (good or bad – and in whose opinion?) for such a refusal?

The NHS is a massively diverse place,[43] and there are duties owed to individual staff as well as to the patients. Reasonable adjustments to allow for cultural sensibilities as to the gender of a clinician are likely to be accommodated. But in accepting a patient's refusal to be treated other than by a clinician of their preference there may come a point at which it becomes an undue distortion of the efficiency of the work or fair allocation of resources, or even a pandering to prejudice that fails in the NHS's duty towards the staff involved. The "customer" is not always right.

Similarly, there cannot be a reasonable expectation or demand that treatment may only be given by the most expert of clinicians. We must all share some responsibility for the necessary opportunity for training and clinical development, for the sake of us all, much as we might prefer that we ourselves are only treated by the most established experts. Similar issues arise around the deployment of physicians' associates, for example.

42 Around 1 in 8 NHS staff are not British, with more than 200 different countries represented.

43 I do remember fondly the evening I spent at the annual staff awards dinner of a major NHS trust at which a nationally recognised diversity and inclusion programme was celebrated and the two colleagues who led it were brought on stage, only for the bloke to be given a bottle of whiskey while the lady was handed a bunch of flowers.

That said, as always, openness and transparency are vital. If a patient has asked whether the procedure will be performed by Professor Jones and is promised that it will be, there may be no valid consent given for the procedure that is actually undertaken by another, more junior clinician.

The information given to the patient is the key, and since *Montgomery*, we have had a string of further compensation claims, trying to expand the guidance on whether and what patients should be told about the risks, benefits and alternatives in various factual scenarios. Case by case, we are feeling our way towards a better understanding of how the test needs to be applied in practice. But there will always be cases which bring new challenges.

Common language

One further challenge is that, if we are to rely as the basis of "informed consent" on a discussion between doctor and patient, reflecting what the patient wants to know, as much as what the doctor wants to tell her, we need to know that *they are both speaking the same language,* and I am not only thinking about reasonable use of interpreters across the more obvious language barriers.

The judgment in *Montgomery* makes it clear that the test of "materiality" of risk is not reducible to a simple matter of percentages. But a fascinating bit of research in the Lancet in 2002 showed the chasm between what a clinician typically means by certain customary terms of probability or risk, and how it is usually interpreted by a layman:[44]

44 "Recommended qualitative descriptions with EU assigned frequency bands and participants' estimates from the pilot study", The Lancet vol 359, March 9, 2002, p853.

Descriptor	Medical usage	Man in the street (n200)
"Very common"	More than10%	65%
"Common"	1-10%	45%
"Uncommon"	0.1-1%	18%
"Rare"	0.01 – 0.1%	8%
"Very rare"	Less than 0.01%	4%

So if a clinician says "common" thinking of something between 1-10%, his patient might well be thinking of 45%.

There is a real obligation on clinicians to not just articulate risks and benefits, but to make sure that they are well understood, even when using what may feel like ordinary language. (And remember that we are just not very well accustomed to understanding risk, living in a world where the odds of winning the national lottery are 1 in 45,057,474,[45] but it is advertised under the slogan "it could be you!").

I tend to like the clinicians who can really contextualise effectively: "I've done 800 of these procedures and X has only happened once", as well as really explaining in concrete terms the often massive range of possible outcomes if the particular risk eventuates. A "bleed" can mean many things. What are we really talking about, and what would it mean in practice?

Such a discussion is critically important, in fact, not only to enable the patient to optimise their decision-making, but also as we have seen to give the doctor the best chance of not being sued (see Chapter 1).

45 https://www.national-lottery.com/lotto/prizes

Pre-printed material?

Discussion is the crucial word here, but we have to be realistic about the pressures on time and resources available to treating clinicians. It is entirely understandable to have handy pre-printed information about the typical risks and benefits of particular treatment options, and indeed some companies specialise in producing this material to a very high standard[46]. But – for at least two reasons – it is really important that this is understood to be material that supports the discussion, not something that replaces it.

The first reason is that, logically, we cannot satisfy the *Montgomery* requirement of giving the patient the information that is important to them as an individual solely by giving them something that is produced for everyone. The material might help, of course, and a patient might want something to take away and reflect on. But it cannot negate the need for a discussion about what it important to them individually, to give the clinician a chance to tailor / supplement that general information.

The second reason is that it is unrealistic to rely on giving written information to a patient alone as, on the whole, we simply lack the literacy for that to be good enough. There is a reason why the most popular newspapers are said to be aimed at a reading age of around 9 years. The National Literacy Trust reports that 18% of adults aged 16-65 (or 6.6 million people) can be described as having "poor literacy skills"[47].

46 See for example Eido healthcare https://www.eidohealthcare.com/

47 https://literacytrust.org.uk/parents-and-families/adult-literacy/

In the healthcare context specifically, research[48] has found that 43% of the adult population (aged 16-65) lack the literacy skills to cope with typical written information about their health. This is not an issue of older patients struggling to cope: this is the working age population, and the figure for 16-44 year-olds is even higher: 57%. Split by income, the figure rises to 96% for the lowest income group. For that part of the population, a leaflet really might not be worth the paper it is written on. We are even worse at numeracy, by the way, with 61% of adults lacking the ability to make sense of the data relating to our healthcare decisions.

Doctor doesn't know best?

A further nail in the coffin for "doctor knows best" is a bit of research by the King's Fund[49] which exposes the misplaced assumptions that clinicians can make about their patients:

> *"...there are breathtaking gaps between what patients want and what doctors think they want. For example, doctors believe that **71 per cent** of patients with breast cancer rate keeping their breast as a top priority. But what is the actual figure reported by patients? **Seven per cent**". (emphasis added).*

Perhaps we should put this a little more fairly.

Doctor *does* know best, of course, *if the question is a medical one*: What treatments are possible? What might work best? How would it work? How long would it take? What are the risks and benefits?

48 "A mismatch between population health literacy and the complexity of health information: an observational study", British Journal of General Practice, June 2015, G Rowlands et al.

49 King's Fund, "Patient Preferences matter", May 2012. https://www.kingsfund.org.uk/sites/default/files/field/field_publication_file/patients-preferences-matter-may-2012.pdf

But not so much on questions that are best left to us, the patient ourselves, which are not simply medical: Is it right for me? Are the risks worth taking? Can I live with it if we don't try? Can I live with it if we do?

We might find that there are fewer disputes if we more readily recognise that the "decision" about medical treatment has those two sides – the clinicians' expertise what to offer (subject to, potentially, limited resources), and the patient's expertise in their own life, in deciding what is right for them.[50]

Assuming, of course that the patient can make the decision for herself (ie "has capacity"), as we'll see next.

Post-script – Sam and Nadine

Just before we move on, though, I am delighted to be able to bring Sam and Nadine's story more up to date.

Sam Montgomery is now 25 years old and graduated with a BSc in Software Engineering from University of Strathclyde. Nadine describes him as "highly intelligent" and says though he has difficulties with his speech which means it is not always easy for him to make himself understood, "he surely does!"

Sam has a sister, 2 years younger, born by elective caesarean section. At the time of writing, she is due to deliver her own baby shortly, by planned elective Caesarean section.

---

50 I am not the first to make this point, of course. Emma Hill, editor of the Lancet, for example wrote "Every patient is an expert in their own chosen field, namely themselves and their own life", in "Smart Patients", The Lancet 15 (2014): 140-141.

As well as being excited about a grandchild, Nadine Montgomery has completed a law degree at Strathclyde University and is now working in Glasgow as a solicitor in clinical negligence for Levy and McRae. Birthrights, a human rights in childbirth charity, announced Nadine as their first ever patron in 2019. In this role, Nadine continues to champion women's autonomy and consent in childbirth, supporting their communications and campaigns and training for healthcare professionals. Nadine was further honoured to become an Ambassador for the unique charity Baby Lifeline in 2020 and has joined forces with their team to improve safety in maternity care. Nadine was nominated as Rising Star of the Year at the Scottish Legal awards in 2024.

Nadine was recently delighted to have been awarded an Honorary Fellowship of the Association of Surgeons of Great Britain and Ireland which is the highest honour the Association can confer. Although Nadine's main focus is to ensure patient safety, she was nonetheless honoured to have been recognised in this way, and to know that her continued contributions are recognised. "*Out of our own tragedy, we find our life's purpose*", she told me.

Nadine has done me a great favour in reading and improving this chapter for me, for which I am very grateful.

Key points

- For an adult patient with capacity to make the relevant decision, treatment without consent is unlawful (unless you can rely on another legal framework, such as the Mental Health Act). Such a patient can refuse treatment for good reasons, bad reasons, or no reasons at all.

- The options available to the patient can properly be limited by resources, or by the doctors' judgement of clinical appropriateness (subject to the *Bolam* test). But out of those which are reasonably available to the patient it is not OK for the doctor to tell the patient only about the option/s the doctor thinks best.

- In 2015 the Supreme Court judgment in *Montgomery* brought the law on consent to medical treatment up to date with clinical best practice and GMC guidelines, focussed on information material to the patient, not what the doctor thinks is important.

- Time and again, the courts have put an emphasis on the importance of respecting autonomy, sometimes bending the usual rules to award compensation.

- At times, though, respect for autonomy must be balanced against other values, including duties towards staff, and the principles and law on available options set out in the last chapters.

- Communication is key; evidence shows that there are risks in making assumptions, whether about the interpretation of subjective language about risks, or about what clinicians might expect to be most important to a patient. And it is deeply risky to rely on providing written information alone.

- Consent is a process of communication and agreement. It must be voluntary, informed and given with capacity to make the decision. A signed consent form can be evidence of this but is not an end in itself. Evidence of what has been discussed and agreed is important, of course, should you ever have to defend the decision making in future, but the substance is more important than the form.

CHAPTER 4

CAPACITY PART A – ABLE TO MAKE THIS DECISION

- "Decisions, decisions"; and "because, because…"
- Excluded decisions
- Autonomy v paternalism in the MCA
- Capacity and insight
- Relevant information
- Understanding (and believing), retaining and using / weighing
- Executive function
- Unwise decisions
- The diagnostic test
- Inherent jurisdiction
- Fluctuating capacity
- Communicating a decision
- Empowering P
- Practicalities

The balance between autonomy and paternalism is a thread through many of our challenges in this area. The Mental Capacity Act 2005 (the MCA) encapsulates this perfectly. At its core are the questions of how we support people to make their own decisions where possible, how we make best interests decisions to protect people who cannot, and (crucially) how we tell the difference. (The MCA itself uses "P" as shorthand for the person who may lack capacity. Often the lawyers and judges do likewise, as will I, though I'll sometimes use a name for a change, and to add a bit of humanity).

The MCA is a carefully crafted bit of work. There was a lot of thought and consultation, and a long period of implementation, and I think it is a great bit of law. It is well-written, coherent, and largely self-explanatory; we can readily see what it is trying to do, and how it goes about it; it has a clear Code of Practice[1], in plain English, with clear examples.

The Code of Practice is intended to be guidance and cannot in itself make or change the law. The obligation on those dealing with the MCA in a professional capacity is to "have regard to" the Code[2], and so it is ok – necessary, even – to depart from the Code where it is appropriate to do so. One very significant problem – at the time of writing – is that the Code of Practice (2007) is *long* overdue an update. As you will see, there has been a lot of case law since it was published, and some of it shows that the Code was wrong in places.

(One reason for the delay with this update is that when a draft new Code of Practice was published for consultation in the Spring of 2022, it was not only an update on the MCA but also dealt with the proposed (at the

---

1 https://assets.publishing.service.gov.uk/government/uploads/system/uploads/attachment_data/file/497253/Mental-capacity-act-code-of-practice.pdf published 2007.

2 MCA s42(4).

time) reforms to the law on deprivation of liberty[3]. Though that consultation closed on 14 July 2022, the government has not yet published or responded to the outcome of the consultation, no doubt partly due to the change in government in 2024, and partly due to the uncertainty of the prospects for the reforms on DoL. The impact of this, sadly, is that we are left dealing with a Code of Practice that is less helpful than it could be, and in some places is misleading, or flat wrong. Even if the DoL reforms are not coming any time soon, an updated MCA Code of Practice is essential and urgent).

Decisions, decisions

The MCA provides a legal framework for making decisions about almost everything – from the trivia of everyday life like what to wear, or eat, and management of our finances and property, through to some of the most important decisions of our life – where we live, who we have contact with, and whether or not we have vital but risky medical treatment.

In fact, pretty much the only issue entirely excluded from the MCA is the compulsory treatment of mental disorder without the patient's consent,[4] which is the province of the Mental Health Act 1983 (as amended).

So the one thing I do not like about the MCA is the title. I would not have called it the *Mental* Capacity Act (it started life as the Mental Incapacity Bill, which I think would have been even worse!). I think the word "mental" here is unhelpful and adds nothing.

---

3 For more on this see – A Practical Guide to the Law of Deprivation of Liberty, Law Brief Publishing (2024), http://www.lawbriefpublishing.com/product/deprivationofliberty/

4 MCA s28.

But – and I think the "mental" in the title is at least partly to blame for this – I have known clinicians treating physical health conditions flatly refuse to engage with the MCA, saying it is a matter for a psychiatrist.

I remember asking a very eminent physician about his assessment of a patient's capacity to make his own decision about the complex cocktail of medication being prescribed. He explained to me slowly but impatiently that he can't comment on "mental issues" because those (tapping his head) are for a psychiatrist. If it were a heart problem he told me, gesturing helpfully to his heart, he'd refer to "a car-di-olo-gist".

That is just plain wrong. As I explained to him, if he cannot give a view on the patient's capacity to make the decision about the treatment he proposed, then he cannot be confident that the patient has given valid consent. (I do appreciate that I will be jaundiced by disproportionate exposure to the clinicians who need support and advice about cases, either because they are less familiar with the legal framework, or because it is an especially sticky one. No one ever phones the lawyers to say it's all good. But I have sometimes found that clinicians have got a stronger sense of the need for consent than they have of the niceties of the MCA).

There may be a useful role for a psychiatrist to give a view on a patient's mental condition, of course. But the treating clinician knows the information relevant to the treatment decision that needs to be made, has a responsibility to get consent, and (since there is no consent without capacity), cannot simply abdicate responsibility for assessing a patient's capacity entirely.

So, I love the MCA but I would drop the word "mental" from the title.

And if it were up to me, I would also drop the word "capacity"! My suggestion would be to call it instead the "Making This Decision Act", and I'll explain why.

The MCA is not about making *decisions in general*, and I think that the use of a fairly abstract noun like "capacity" lures us towards saying something meaningless (and dangerous) like "Doris lacks capacity" FULL STOP.

"Capacity" in the MCA is defined as the ability to make the particular decision which needs to be made. So, to lack capacity for, say, a decision about having an amputation, the patient must be unable to make that decision. This is defined as being unable to understand, or retain, or weigh up the information relevant to that decision, or (and this is less common, given the scope of support that can be offered) unable to communicate a decision made. That's called the "functional test".

The inability to understand / retain / weigh up the information must be because of a (temporary or permanent) impairment or disturbance in the functioning of the mind or brain, sometimes called the "diagnostic test" (more on this later). The input of a psychiatrist might be helpful here to consider if there is such a condition and its impact on decision-making, but clearly the psychiatrist does not know as well as the surgeon the information relevant to the decision for an amputation, for example, the risks and benefits, the options, and the consequences of refusing the treatment altogether.

And this is why, if someone asks for your view about "capacity", you are best to reply "for what decision?". And why it is meaningless to say that someone "lacks capacity" without reference to the decision in question. Unless or until the decision, and the actual available options, are identified, it cannot be possible to assess whether or not the patient can understand or retain or weigh the information relevant to the decision, because you cannot know what the information is!

We all get casual at times, but it helps to have an alarm bell whenever you see or hear the word "capacity" followed by a full stop. It means nothing unless we are clear that we are looking at the patient's capacity to make a decision about this medication, or about that surgery, or about their admission to hospital or their residence on discharge. Each decision has different information which is relevant to it, and the fact that someone cannot make one decision does not mean that they cannot make any other. It is perfectly plausible that someone may lack the capacity to make a decision about complex chemotherapy options, for example, but be able to make a simpler decision about more straightforward treatment.

On balance, I think we do better to use the word "decision" much, much more often than the word "capacity". For starters, this unavoidably focuses on the right starting point – what is the decision that needs to be made, and what are the actual options available, to identify the relevant information to meaningfully assess capacity.

Using "decision" also helps to avoid another huge bear trap by making sure we focus on the actual available options, and what is actually the patient's decision (as we have saw in Chapter 2). So, if Bob has a terrible disease and needs surgery, the surgeon may offer procedure A, or B. Each has risks and benefits, and Bob – if he has the capacity to make the decision for himself – can choose A, or B, or if he wishes can decline treatment altogether for his own reasons, good, bad or indifferent. That is what autonomy, and capacity, means.

But suppose Bob cannot make that decision for himself because his dementia means that he cannot understand or retain or use or weigh the information relevant to the actual treatment options (i.e. he "lacks capacity" for that decision). Then a "best interests decision" must be made for Bob. We will get to the detail of this later, but for now let me emphasise that *Bob's treatment options are the same whether he has capacity to make the decision for himself or a best interests decision must be made for him*. It might be in his best interests to have operation A or operation B, or perhaps to have no treatment at all. But you can't say that he should have operation C instead. The surgeon is not offering that to Bob, and the decision what treatment options to offer is the surgeon's decision, not Bob's. Bob can't make the surgeon offer something he is unwilling to do, whether because it is not clinically indicated, or because it is not available as a matter of practicality or funding or whatever. Bob's decision is to choose among the actual options made available to him by the clinicians' decision, and a best interests decision on his behalf is no different.

This seems trite, but (along with the role of, ahem, "next of kin" – see next chapter) I cannot tell you how often this is the root of confusion and trouble in medical treatment disputes.

"Best interests" does not trump resource allocation or clinical decision-making about available options. It is not a queue jump card for stuff that would not have been available to the same patient if he had capacity to make the treatment decision for himself.[5]

For the reasons set out in Chapter 2, a judicial review can be brought to argue that other options ought to have been offered, but because *what to offer* is not the patient's own decision, it cannot be a matter of best interests or up to the Court of Protection.

But time and again cases are unnecessarily difficult because they start in the wrong place, asking what's in Bob's best interests as if in the abstract, on a blank piece of paper, without first properly identifying the decision or the available options.

Instead:

- Start with what is Bob's situation and what does he need?

- What is to be made available to him, whether limited by clinical judgement, or (reasonably, or else you may be challenged in judicial review) by resource allocation?

- That identifies the options, and therefore the information relevant to the decision, and it is only at this stage that you can sensibly assess whether Bob has capacity to make this decision for himself, and if so to take his consent, if he gives it.

5 See *MN v ACCG*, [2017] UKSC 22, discussed in Chapter 2.

- If Bob cannot make that decision for himself, as he cannot understand / retain / use or weigh up the information relevant to the decision, because of a mental disorder, then a best interests decision should be made, from among the same available options.

I strongly recommend using the word "decision" as much as possible, and am much more comfortable when I can see the word "decision" used in the paperwork far more frequently than the word "capacity".[6]

"… because, because"

Perhaps under the undue influence of having just seen Wicked (more than once) at the time of writing and having some of the older tunes from the Wizard of Oz in my head, one further tip for getting the MCA right occurs to me since the first edition.

We will come back to each bit in more detail below, but having advocated the use of the word "decision", you could do worse as a way to ensure MCA compliance than to think "decision, because, because".

For example – Bob cannot make a <u>decision</u> about his proposed amputation of the gangrenous leg <u>because</u> he cannot understand (or retain, or use/ weigh, as the case may be) the information relevant to the decision, <u>because</u> of his dementia.

Boom! You are MCA compliant for the assessment of capacity: thinking about the particular decision that needs to be made, and then the person's ability to make that decision (the functional test) and – if they can't – both the mental disorder (the diagnostic test) and the causative nexus between them.

---

6 Though here I am, with a full stop after "capacity" breaking my own rule already!

Of course, it might be that your assessment is that Bob can make his own decision about the amputation. But if you come to the view that he cannot, then framing it in terms of "decision, because, because" will make sure that you are on solid MCA ground.

Excluded decisions

Pausing here, some decisions are described as "excluded" from the scope of the MCA. This is easy to misunderstand. MCA s27-29 provides that no best interests decision can be made for a list of things where this would be inappropriate – e.g. marriage, sex and some other aspects of family relationships, or voting – but it is not true to say that these decisions are outside the scope of the MCA. Whether the person has the capacity to make those decisions for themselves will still be governed by the MCA, but if they lack capacity then that's the end of it, and there can be no best interests basis to go ahead with those decisions.

(It's beyond the scope of this book, but obviously that opens a can of worms where someone lacks capacity to consent to sex, alongside the provisions of the criminal law that sex without consent is an offence[7], where such relationships may be happening between "assenting" adults, e.g. with learning disabilities, or married couples with dementia in a care home. If Betty now lacks capacity to consent to it, then any sexual contact is unlawful, even with her husband of 40 years, and there is a dilemma for the carers how to balance the degree of interference in her life to prevent that happening, against the restrictions, harm and upset that may cause for instance if she is then prevented from having unsupervised contact with her husband, or anyone else that she wants to).[8]

7 Sexual Offences Act 2003.

8 A (male) consultant psychiatrist once challenged me about this, arguing that the wife had given "irrevocable consent" to sex by virtue of the marriage ceremony, but let's not even go there.

Autonomy and paternalism – the 5 key principles, and the role of the court

Having got the long winded but, I think, important bit about "decisions, decisions" (and because, because) off my chest, let me make one more point – about the theme of autonomy and paternalism – by way of preamble.

The MCA is sometimes enthusiastically used as a tool of paternalism, the mechanism by which we are allowed to intervene in someone's life to make sure that they are kept safe, they get the treatment that they need (whether they want it or not), and we (health and care professionals and their enablers) fulfil our duty of care towards them. This plays out in lots of ways, which we will get to shortly.

But the MCA is as much, or more, about *autonomy*, and we forget this at our peril. Look at the five core principles of the MCA, which are set out in section 1 ("s1"):[9]

1. A person must be assumed to have capacity unless it is established that he lacks capacity.

2. A person is not to be treated as unable to make a decision unless all practicable steps to help him to do so have been taken without success.

3. A person is not to be treated as unable to make a decision merely because he makes an unwise decision.

4. An act done, or decision made, under this Act for or on behalf of a person who lacks capacity must be done, or made, in his best interests.

9 As a piece of legislation, it is unusual, and refreshing, that key principles are set out at the start.

5 Before the act is done, or the decision is made, regard must be had to whether the purpose for which it is needed can be as effectively achieved in a way that is less restrictive of the person's rights and freedom of action.

Note that the first 3 are obviously all about autonomy; about respecting people's right to live their lives as they wish, and helping them to do so.

And in fact so is number 5. This "least restrictive" principle is commonly misunderstood, so I'll tackle it here. It does <u>not</u> say (as often misrepresented) that we must do *the least restrictive thing* (and if you find yourself arguing with someone who says that X must be done for Bob because "it is the least restrictive thing" remind them of this). It says, when making a best interests decision where someone does lack capacity for that decision, ask yourself if there is a less restrictive way to meet their best interests. The best interests principle is king, once someone lacks capacity. The least restrictive thing (let people with dementia and no road sense wander freely across the roads?) may not be in their best interests. But we should meet their best interests in the least restrictive way possible, and test our thinking on best interests by asking if there is a less restrictive way that best interests can be achieved.[10] Why? Because of respect for their autonomy.

And even the most overtly paternalistic bit – that we must decide or act in someone's best interests when they cannot decide for themselves – is to be applied in a way, the Act goes on to say, that is steeped in respect for autonomy: can the decision be delayed until they can decide for

10 The Code of Practice gives an example of a young man with severe learning disabilities with sudden and unpredictable epilepsy. He cannot make his own decision about his care, and it is in his best interests for there to be an intervention to prevent him hitting his head and suffering serious injury, but it is less restrictive to provide a protective helmet than it would be to achieve the same end by imposing constant, close supervision.

themselves?[11] P must be involved in the decision-making as much as possible;[12] P's wishes and feelings, values and beliefs must be appropriately taken into account in assessing his best interests.[13] Why? Autonomy.

And yet, the empowering ethos of the MCA has not really been delivered in practice, perhaps as result of engrained cultures of "paternalism in healthcare and risk aversion in social care".[14]

Whenever a patient refuses treatment in a way that raises concerns about an alarming outcome, the first reaction is often a "best interests" meeting. I have seen plenty of those without there yet being a scrap of evidence that the patient lacks capacity to make the decision for themselves. Often partway through the "best interests" meeting, the note will record a discussion about the need to assess capacity (but how can we even discuss "best interests" before lack of capacity to make the decision is established?!).

I am yet to see a note of anything called an "empowering decision-making" meeting, with the focus on enabling P's exercise of their own autonomy.

This "protection imperative" instinct, as Mr Justice Baker called it in one case[15] is understandable in some ways, and not just because keeping people safe and doing the right thing for them is what drives a lot of good people to work in the health and social care sector. We make the beartrap

---

11 MCA s4(3).

12 MCA s4(4). I hate seeing in the notes "If Bob has capacity ask him what he wants". No! Ask him anyway, because what he wants matters, capacity or not.

13 MCA s4(6).

14 House of Lords post legislative scrutiny committee on the implementation of the MCA, March 2014.

15 *CC v KK* [2012] EWCOP 2136.

a bit easier to fall into by often aligning responsibility for the MCA within an organisation with other roles, such as safeguarding, which also have a strong paternalistic streak. And we make the consequences of positive risk taking deeply unappealing. Not only could P come to harm if we do not intervene when they unwisely refuse our treatment or care, but the family, the coroner, the regulator, the press can be unforgiving. In the public sector, especially, heads may roll where things go wrong. And in the private sector such incidents can be business critical.

The "protection imperative" means that we can find ourselves setting the bar too low to find lack of capacity so we can intervene, or find ourselves tending towards the safest option when making a best interests decision.

I once saw a High Court Judge, speaking at a conference, explain his sympathy for this. He said that the court can provide comfort where a public body may be unsure about a patient's capacity or uncomfortable about the risky path it thinks is right, in the patient's best interests. A judgment of the court to resolve this would be transparent, and accountable, based on arguments on either side of the case, including representation for P himself, and it can be appealed to a higher court. And, he said – and this bit a little smugly – if a "right but risky" best interests decision made in good faith by a judge went horribly wrong, "to sack a High Court Judge needs a vote of both houses of parliament, and it's not happened since 1689!" It may be that the strength of judicial job security means that the court can offer some help, and I'll say more about the role of the court in Chapter 7.

Capacity

The need for assessment of legally-binding decision-making ability long predates the MCA 2005, of course. Something called the Court of Protection also existed before the MCA was implemented in 2007, but it was really about dealing with the property and finances of "lunatics and idiots", as the less than politically correct language of the time had it, especially where they were rich enough for this to be worth worrying about.

Decisions about medical treatment for adults rarely came before the courts and were all dealt with under the inherent jurisdiction of the court, rather than any legislation. For example, in 1994 the court had to consider an application by a hospital for an order authorising it to force an amputation of a gangrenous foot on a patient who was refusing.[16]

Mr C suffered from paranoid schizophrenia and was sent to prison for stabbing his landlord, where he developed gangrene in his right leg. He was given only a 15% chance of survival without an amputation but he flatly refused, saying he'd rather die with two legs than live with one. The court decided that his refusal was competent and should be respected as, although his schizophrenia impaired his thinking, he understood and retained the relevant information, believed it,[17] and had arrived at a clear choice. This despite the fact that Mr C apparently thought that he was himself a world class vascular surgeon and that he could dismiss the opinions of the treating clinicians accordingly.

But, and I love this bit, deluded about his own clinical credentials or not, having been allowed to refuse the amputation he beat the odds and survived the gangrene anyway, another reminder about the risks of prognostic overconfidence[18].

---

16 The well-known case of *Re C (adult: refusal of treatment)* [1994] All ER 819.

17 The explicit reference to *belief* in the information relevant to the decision is one distinction between the test applied in *Re C* in 1994 and the later statutory version in the MCA in 2005 – and see below for a more recent treatment of this issue.

18 In NR [2024] EWHC 2400 (Fam), Poole J had reason to revisit an earlier decision in which he had agreed to a Trust's application that withdrawal of life sustaining ventilation would be in the best interests of a 4 year-old boy, who went on to defy all medical expectation and to

The reason to mention this case is that the statutory test adopted for capacity when the MCA arrived some 20 years later will look very familiar – can P make their own decision, by which we mean: can they (1) understand, (2) retain, and (3) use or weigh the information which is relevant to make the decision, and then (4) communicate it.

Obviously all reasonable efforts should be made to support P to communicate a decision made – see below. More prosaically, aiding communication is about all appropriate support being given to help P engage with the process fully, whether in making his own decision, assessing his capacity, or involving him or eliciting his views for a best interests decision.

We'll unpack the rest of it – understand, retain, and weigh – a bit, and I'll use some real cases as examples. First though, I'd flag up the need for some care to avoid too readily falling into taking a false proxy for the rigorous statutory test.

The MCA makes clear, needlessly I'd hope, that extraneous factors such as age or appearance are not to be taken as establishing a lack of capacity, and nor should any particular diagnosis.[19] But we do commonly see reference to (lack of) "insight" used as a ready stepping-stone to saying P lacks capacity.

The test for capacity to make a particular decision depends only on his ability to understand, retain and use or weigh the information relevant

survive without it, prompting the judge to retract other declarations about ceilings of care, and to reflect that "medicine is a science of uncertainty", quoting Sir William Osler – https://www.bailii.org/ew/cases/EWHC/Fam/2024/2400.html

19 MCA s2 – any "condition or his, or aspect of his behaviour which might lead others to make unjustified assumptions about his capacity".

to that decision and not on any particular "insight" on P's part into his own mental health in general or need for treatment of his mental health.[20]

As Nathan Filer explains in his superb book "This Book Will Change Your Mind About Mental Health",[21] "insight" can be a very elastic term, and is all too temptingly used for someone who does not agree that they have the (mental health) condition we think they do or need the treatment that is thought to be best for them. By (circular) definition then, it should not be used to identify those who we can force into physical healthcare treatment in their best interests.

As Filer wryly observes, if a patient is not objectively judging their own situation and abilities entirely accurately, they are in good company. Referring to our innate and apparently universal "illusory superiority", Filer describes an experiment in which doctors were asked to assess the extent to which the generous hospitality of certain drugs companies affected their prescribing habits. Fully 61% said that they were themselves entirely unswayed by such influence, but they thought that only 16% of their colleagues would have the same integrity.[22] We all lack insight to some extent.

Helpfully, the courts have recently clarified this for us in CT v London Borough of Lambeth. In that case, a judge had found that CT – a man in his 50s who had a complex psychiatric history, including "post-traumatic stress disorder, suspected antisocial personality disorder,

---

20 Issues of treatment of the mental health would be more a matter for the MHA.

21 Faber & Faber 2019.

22 Filer, see previous footnote, at p44 FN3. This is of course the same phenomenon that prompts 80% of us to say that we are above average drivers, 95% of teachers to consider themselves as above average teachers, and – closer to home – I suspect that many cases inappropriately go to trial because each side's lawyers are very likely to imagine themselves smarter than the other side. https://en.wikipedia.org/wiki/Illusory_superiority

dysexecutive syndrome and polysubstance use", as well as cognitive impairment following a head injury at the age of 12 – lacked capacity for decisions about his residence and care. But one of the reasons that the judge reached that conclusion was that CT lacked insight into his mental health condition, and the judge felt that this was part of the essential information relevant to the decisions that CT faced. The Official Solicitor appealed on CT's behalf, and Mrs Justice Theis agreed:

> *"Insight is a clinical concept, whereas decision making capacity is a legal concept. Capacity assessors must be aware of the conceptual distinction and that, depending on the evidence, a person may be able to make a particular decision even if they are described as lacking insight into their general condition."*[23]

Be very careful not to use "proxies" for the legal test for capacity. If you say that someone lacks "insight", this is wholly irrelevant to the question of their capacity to make a particular decision, unless you go on to explain how that lack of insight (if caused by a mental disorder) means that they cannot understand, or retain, or use or weigh the information relevant to that decision. Which means that any comment about "insight" in itself doesn't really get us anywhere in MCA terms, and is probably best avoided.

It is the information relevant to the decision at hand that must be understood, retained and used / weighed up, so (having started in the right place – what is the decision and what are the options?) what is the relevant information?

What is the relevant information?

This will depend on the nature of the decision, of course, but will typically be the same information that would be part of a discussion to

[23] Per Mrs Justice Theis, in *CT v London Borough of Lambeth* [2025] EWCOP 6 (T3). https://www.bailii.org/ew/cases/EWCOP/2025/6.html

obtain consent: the options, risks and benefits of each, and the consequences of making no decision at all.

Crucially, it is not necessary to understand every little detail of the information to constitute capacity to make the decision, a broad overview is enough. And it must be actually made available to P before it can really be said that their understanding etc has properly been tested. A good example is the case of *CC v KK.*[24]

KK was an 82 year-old lady who suffered from Parkinson's and vascular dementia. She had been living at home with social services support, but there was increasing concern over her vulnerability and susceptibility to falls. Over 7 months she used the "lifeline" emergency call service nearly 1,100 times before she was admitted to a nursing home at the end of July 2011. KK consistently objected to staying there and said that she wanted to go home, so the case came to court to determine if she lacked capacity to make that decision for herself, as the professionals thought, and if so whether it was in her best interests to stay in the nursing home, against her wishes.

The judge, Mr Justice Baker, found that she had capacity to make the decision for herself. It appears to have made a difference that he heard oral evidence from KK herself, rather than relying on written evidence about her. He described her as "clear and articulate" and "betraying relatively few signs of the dementia which … afflicts her". She was realistic about her care needs and accepted that she needed some support. She may not have been able to weigh every detail, but she understood in broad terms, and that was enough.

Crucially, the judge was very critical of the fact that the local authority making the application had not really considered what support would be available for her if she went home, and on this basis the judge felt that she couldn't really be said to have failed to understand, retain or weigh

24 [2012] EWCOP 2136. https://www.bailii.org/ew/cases/EWHC/COP/2012/2136.html

up the information relevant to the decision. She hadn't been given the information relevant to the decision because, in honesty, the local authority had decided that she ought to stay in residential care and not explored any alternative, never mind tested her understanding of the options.

Another example of setting the bar too high, perhaps as a result of the "protection imperative", is my favourite case (at least since I had children myself). In *A Local Authority v A*[25] two adults, each with a severe learning disability, were in a sexual relationship, and the local authority felt that a long-term contraceptive implant should be fitted to the woman to prevent pregnancy. The local authority argued that while the couple each had capacity to consent to the sexual relationship, for instance they knew that it could lead to pregnancy, they didn't have capacity to make decisions about contraception because, among other things, they *did not know what it would be like to raise a child.*

Mr Justice Bodey found that this was not a reasonable element to include in the test for capacity. It was enough that they understood the nature and effect of various contraceptive options. Requiring that they understand what it would be like to raise a child would be setting the bar far higher for them than most couples could pass even without mental disability. Before you've had one, *nobody* has a clue what it is like to raise a child![26]

---

25 [2010] EWHC 1549 (Fam) https://www.bailii.org/ew/cases/EWHC/Fam/2010/1549.html – from the days when anonymisation routinely left little more than an alphabet soup of case references. These days cases are more likely to name the public bodies at least, which does make recognition a bit easier – see Chapter 7.

26 Or as the judge put it "…it is unrealistic to require consideration of a woman's ability to foresee the realities of parenthood, or to expect her to be able to envisage the fact-specific demands of caring for a particular child not yet conceived (let alone born) with unpredictable levels of third-party support. I do not think such matters are reasonably foreseeable…"

Before any assessment of someone's capacity to make a particular decision, it is really important to have a proper think about what the information relevant to that decision is. Logically, this can make it quite tricky to assess capacity when the options available have not yet been identified. How can you sensibly assess someone's ability to understand / retain / use or weigh information relevant to the decision without being able to say what the choice is, or the pros and cons of each of the specific options?

The growing body of case law now helps us a little with some kinds of decisions[27]. So, for instance, in *S v Birmingham Women's and Children's NHS Trust*, HHJ Hilder (sitting as a High Court Judge) set out that for a decision about a termination of pregnancy the relevant information would be:

a. What the termination procedures involve for P ('what it is'), and the options available;

b. The effect of the termination procedure / the finality of the event ('what it does');

c. The risks to P's physical and mental health in undergoing the termination procedure ('what it risks');

---

27 On this, I commend the work of 39 Essex Chambers, keeping and updating a summary of some of the case law on discrete issues as a guidance note on their website – https://www.39essex.com/sites/default/files/2024-06/Mental%20Capacity%20Guidance%20Note%20-%20Relevant%20Information%20for%20Different%20Categories%20of%20Decision%20May%202024.pdf

d. The possibility of safeguarding measures in the event of a live birth.[28]

So, now we have the information relevant to the decision, we must consider whether P can understand, retain, and use or weigh it in making a decision.

Understand (and believe)

We have already seen in the *CC v KK* case above that it is important not to set the bar too high in terms of the level of understanding for someone to be considered able to make their own decision about something. Few of us are truly expert in the issues on which we each have to make decisions in daily life, and we are not routinely treated as unable to do so. A broad understanding of the salient information is enough.

You may recall that in the *Re C* case, above, the test for the patient being able to make the decision for himself included that he "believes" the information that is relevant to the decision. Belief had no place in the legislation when the test was codified into the Mental Capacity Act, which simply needs the person to be able to understand, retain, and use or weigh the information relevant to the decision (and to be able to communicate their decision). And the Court of Appeal has now set us straight on this.

The case of Sudiksha Thirumalesh was especially tragic, and it attracted a lot of press attention. Sudiksha was only 19 years old and had an incurable genetic disease which left her desperately ill. The treating clinicians wanted to move her onto palliative care in order to provide some relief for her symptoms, but Sudiksha refused this. Though she was in multi-organ failure, Sudiksha continued to communicate through a voice box to insist that she would not accept the medical opinion that

28 [2022] EWCOP 10, and see also Re H (An Adult; Termination) [2023 EWCOP 183.

there was no longer anything more to be done, and she was insistent on seeking active treatment, including an experimental therapy that was not available in the UK. In her own words, Sudiksha wanted to, at least, "die trying to live".

The hospital trust applied to the Court of Protection, where Mrs Justice Roberts held[29] that she lacked capacity for the relevant decisions, and therefore that decisions about her treatment could be made in her best interests, including a palliative care plan. In the event, no such decisions were actually made, as she died only a few days after that decision.

But on the point of principle – that it was wrong for the judge to have treated her as unable to make the decision simply because she did not accept the clinicians' opinion about the reality of her situation – her family was granted permission to appeal to the Court of Appeal.

In essence, Roberts J had found that Sudiksha could not make the decision for herself because of her "complete inability to accept the medical reality of her position, or to contemplate the possibility that her doctors may be giving her accurate information". This is really tricky ground. If this is right, does positive thinking or optimism get to a point where it disqualifies us from making our own decisions? What role is there for hope?

The appeal was successful. The Court of Appeal held[30] that Roberts J had been wrong. The statutory test for capacity does not include belief in itself. If the patient does not accept or believe information about the proposed treatment, then it might well be that they cannot understand or use / weigh it, but they are not the same thing, and (as with the "insight" issue above) the actual statutory test is what should be applied.

---

29 [2023] EWCOP 40 – https://www.bailii.org/ew/cases/EWCOP/2023/40.html

30 [2024] EWCA Civ 896 – https://www.bailii.org/ew/cases/EWCA/Civ/2024/896.html

To establish a lack of capacity for a particular decision, it is not enough to show that P does not accept the information that they are being given, or even that they do not believe it.

The test is, simply, as set out in the MCA. And given the risks there would be in allowing any easy confusion between disagreeing with your doctor and being unable to make the decision for yourself, perhaps that is just as well, if we are to preserve our right to make a decision that others might consider unwise without it being necessarily indicative of a lack of capacity.

How long must P retain the relevant information?

Another memorable Bodey J case tackles this tricky point in the context of capacity to marry.[31]

AK was not a lucky man. In 2006, aged 50, he suffered severe brain damage in a fall. After that, while still significantly disabled, he was in a relationship with a woman, BK, which he ended. Tragically, in 2008, he then suffered a further catastrophic brain injury when he was hit by a bus, leading to a permanent placement in a neuro-disability unit and a large compensation claim against the bus company. BK, his ex-girlfriend, then felt the time was right to rekindle their relationship. In November 2010, under the pretence of taking AK out from his residential home to an event organised by a brain injury charity, in fact she took him to a registry office where they married. The registrar was not aware of any concerns, though clinicians had previously expressed a view that he would lack the capacity to marry. AK's family were appalled and the Court of Protection had to pick the bones out.

One of the arguments ingeniously made on behalf of BK was that even if AK did not have capacity for the decision to marry at some times, he

31 *A local authority v AK* [2012] EWCOP B29, https://www.bailii.org/ew/cases/EWHC/COP/2012/B29.html

certainly knew what he was doing at the time of the ceremony, and so it should be held valid – "The fact that a person is able to retain the information relevant to a decision for a short period only does not prevent him from being regarded as able to make the decision" (MCA s3(3)).

The judge was having none of it: "The reference to the retention of information for 'a short period' in s3(3) of the Act cannot seriously be interpreted to mean, in the context of the lifetime commitment of marriage, for so short a period as AK is able to recall whether he is married at all, or reliably (when he does remember) to whom".

A fleeting window of decision-making capacity, if that is truly what happens, is risky to rely on if you are dealing with a decision (such as serious medical treatment, or marriage) from which there will be long-term consequences.

The judge's scepticism of AK's capacity was no doubt compounded by the transcripts of professionals' discussions with AK about his marriage which are, unusually, appended at length to the judgment, and include AK's explanation that one of the key advantages of being married, in his mind, is that you get "holiday pay".

Use or weigh the information

It is important to appreciate that requiring P to use or weigh the information does not mean that they must use it in the same way as you or I would, or give it the same weight as we would. The point is to focus on the decision-making, not the decision that they make, and of course, the things that are important to P in making their decision is matter for them.

But there is a difference between giving things a different weight than we would (and so making a different decision) and not being able to weigh them at all.

For example, in TS (2021)[32] the court dealt with an 81 year-old man who was assessed to need a pacemaker fitted for his heart block. He was detained under the Mental Health Act for a delusional disorder – for many years he had thought that he was being persecuted by public bodies and officials, going so far as to cover his windows at home with foil to prevent neighbours looking in. He believed that his heart problems were caused by the police and council, and he did not want the pacemaker fitted until that abuse had stopped. Having identified the heart problem, the antipsychotic medication that he needed could not be given safely until the pacemaker was in place.

The applicant trusts applied to the Court of Protection, and Mr Justice Poole agreed that TS lacked capacity for the relevant decision – "*His ability to weigh up the advantages and disadvantages is distorted by a paranoid belief that the authorities are persecuting him*" – and approved a detailed care plan providing for the pacemaker to be implanted, albeit against TS's wishes, in his best interests.

Though we might understandably take more care with assessment of capacity when the decision being made has grave consequences, it does not necessarily follow that the "level of capacity" is higher or that P is less likely to be able to make it.

For example, in SB, the court had to deal with a decision about the termination of a pregnancy which had already reached its 23rd week.[33] The fetus and the father had no distinct rights, and it was a question whether the mother, SB, had capacity to make the decision for herself and, only if she did not, what was in her best interests.

32 [2021] EWCOP 41 https://www.bailii.org/ew/cases/EWCOP/2021/41.html

33 The legal limit for termination of pregnancy is 24 weeks (save in cases of preventing "grave permanent injury" to the mother, or risking her life, or if substantial risk of serious handicap for the child) – Abortion Act 1967 s1.

SB[34] was 37 years old, well-educated and well-travelled, and had met her husband around 2 years earlier, in which time she had a previous termination of pregnancy at around 19 weeks. She had suffered from bipolar disorder for around 8 years, which was sometimes controlled with medication. She had been detained under mental health legislation in the past. For the first few months of the current pregnancy, SB gave every appearance of wanting and loving the baby. Perhaps for that reason, the judge speculated, she stopped taking medication for her bipolar disorder, and her mental health deteriorated. She developed paranoid beliefs that her husband no longer wanted the child and wouldn't support her. She arranged a termination of pregnancy, which was only missed due to problems travelling to the clinic. Before she could do any more, she was detained under the MHA after she threatened her husband with a knife.

SB continued to insist that she wanted the termination, and so the detaining mental health trust applied to court for a decision. The evidence of the treating psychiatrist, supported (albeit a little more cautiously) by an independent expert, was "100% clear that she does not have capacity to take the decision" about the termination. But – in another lesson about the risks of undue certainty – the judge disagreed.

Mr Justice Holman held that, with all due respect to the psychiatrists, ultimately the court would determine capacity, and in appropriate cases could depart from the experts' view.

He accepts that aspects of SB's thinking, such as the paranoia about her husband's perceived lack of love or support may be influenced by her deteriorating mental health, but she had other reasons for her decision, such as the fact that she wouldn't want a child while detained under the MHA. He was influenced by the fact that she'd had a previous termination, with no regrets, and knew what was involved. What the MCA requires is the ability *to make a decision*, and:

34 *Re SB (termination of pregnancy)* [2013] EWCOP 1417. https://www.bailii.org/ew/cases/EWHC/COP/2013/1417.html

> *"It seems to me that this lady has made, and has maintained for an appreciable period of time, a decision. It may be that aspects of her reasons may be skewed by paranoia. There are other reasons which she has and which she has expressed. My own opinion is that it would be a total affront to the autonomy of this patient to conclude that she lacks capacity to the level required to make this decision. It is of course a profound and grave decision, but it does not necessarily involve complex issues. It is a decision that she has made and maintains; and she has defended and justified her decision against challenge. It is a decision which she has the capacity to reach".*

Clearly the judge was appalled at the idea of ordering that a woman protesting that she does not want a baby should be made to continue the pregnancy against her wishes. So many of these cases are intensely specific to their own facts, making it dangerous to extrapolate from them too readily. But the point that a decision can have grave consequences without necessarily being complex in terms of the information to understand, retain and weigh is an important one; so is the idea that a flaw in the reasoning, e.g. an element of paranoia or delusions, may not necessarily taint the whole decision-making process or cost the person their autonomy in full. We should not try too hard to find a fault with the thinking, or then, if we do find one, to conclude that the person's decision-making is null.

In the best interests chapter next, we will see that autonomy still does matter, even if capacity is lost.

Executive function

In the last few years, there has been a lot of attention on the issue of "executive function", I think as a result of it coming to be very regularly mentioned in safeguarding adult reviews. But – like "insight" – it needs to be treated with some care if it is not to cause trouble.

As I understand it, executive function is an umbrella term for a set of cognitive skills controlled by the frontal lobe, including planning and organisation, flexibility, social behaviour, emotional control / impulsivity, and motivation. Often it is said of those who may have problems with this, perhaps as a result of an acquired brain injury, that they come across as plausible when they discuss their decision-making, but they will "talk the talk, but not walk the walk". It is sometimes described as the "frontal lobe paradox", where someone seems to be very capable of making decisions when assessed, but they struggle in real life.

It is easy to see how this can readily be conflated with inability to make a decision in accordance with the MCA, but it is not quite the same thing. Like insight, executive function is a clinical concept; mental capacity (per the MCA) is a legal concept. There is no such thing as lacking "executive capacity"!

Where someone is apparently able to make the decision but not able to implement it, though, we have a real problem. Do we say that the MCA is only interested in those who cannot make the decision, and so someone with executive function problems inhibiting their implementation of the decision is, without more, simply someone with capacity to make that decision for whom there can be no best interest decisions. Or do we say that someone who can make but cannot enact their decisions is just as vulnerable and in need of the protection of best interests decision making as someone who cannot make the decision at all, tempting us to stretch the legal tests for capacity so we can bring them into its protection?

There is no easy answer, and the Code of Practice (the 2007 version in force) gives us no help at all. It just was not an issue in contemplation at the time. The draft updated Code of Practice to the MCA that was out for consultation in 2022 does try to grapple with this in places, but of course it is not in force, and in any case doesn't really do much more than rehearse that this is tricky:

> *"another common area of difficulty is where a person with an acquired brain injury gives coherent answers to questions, but it is clear from*

> *their actions that they are unable to give effect to their decision. This is sometimes called an impairment in their executive function. If the person cannot understand (and/or use and weigh) the fact that there is a mismatch between what they say and what they do when required to act, it can be said that they lack capacity to make the decision in question. However, this conclusion can only be reached when there is clear evidence of repeated mismatch between what the person says and what they do. This means that in practice it is unlikely to be possible to conclude that a person lacks capacity as a result of their impairment on the basis of one single assessment".*[35]

This is not in force yet, and even then is only guidance. There is no proposed amendment to the MCA itself, and this guidance relies on a fairly expansive interpretation of the legislation, making the issue of enacting the decision into part of the information relevant to making the decision.

That is not much use if you have an urgent need to assess someone's capacity to make a particular decision right now, without the luxury of an ongoing review of their actions. But of course you can look at the period of time leading up to now, as well as the situation right now. And you can challenge the person for their explanation for any pattern of behaviour that contradicts their apparent decision. And you can make sure that you consult with others who know P about these things, getting the most rounded view of their capacity to make this decisions that we can.

But it is clear that this carries an increased risk of losing sight of some of the fundamentals here. Which of us hasn't said we will do something and done something else, maybe even repeatedly (think new year's resolutions perhaps!)? Which of us hasn't told a professional what we think they want to hear, while firmly intending to do something else? We know that an

---

35 At paragraph 4.38 – https://assets.publishing.service.gov.uk/media/62962d1f8fa8f50395c0a054/draft-mental-capacity-act-code-of-practice.pdf

unwise decision is not proof of a lack of capacity. What about someone making "wise" decisions but apparently unable to enact them?

As with insight, we need some care to stick to the law – problems with executive function might mean that they cannot (because of that mental disorder) understand / retain / use or weigh the information relevant to a particular decision. But that diagnosis alone should not be mistaken in itself for a lack of capacity, any more than any other diagnosis should.

Unwise decisions and capacity

We sometimes see a case in which an adult is said to lack capacity for a medical decision now, when they are refusing essential treatment, only to get their medical records and see that over the previous months or years they have had other treatment on many occasions for which the notes say that they "consented", i.e. they were either assessed or assumed to have capacity for those decisions.

Now of course capacity is decision and time specific and it is entirely possible that the information relating to those earlier medical treatment decisions was less complex than in the current case, and so they were able to understand, retain and use or weigh it to make a decision then, but are not able to for the decision now. Or that they have had a decline in their cognitive function since that earlier treatment, with the same effect. Alternatively, there is an argument that capacity to consent and to refuse can properly be treated differently; that the consequences of *refusing* treatment, especially where this is likely to be life changing or ending, may be harder to understand fully than the lesser consequences of consenting.

But it would be generous to think that this principled reasoning was always the basis. The reality must sometimes be that capacity simply isn't considered as carefully when there is compliance which can readily be mistaken as consent.

We have moved on, mostly, from any erroneous discrediting based on the *identity* of the decision-maker, for example diminishing the autonomy of patients with particular characteristics or diagnoses. But we still have a way to go before moving the focus, as the MCA demands, fully on to the decision-making *process*, rather than on the decision *made* (e.g consent or refusal of the treatment proposed).

The only explicit reference to the nature or quality of the decision (as opposed to the decision-making process) in the Act is that an unwise decision does not establish a lack of capacity to make it. It is, though, perfectly legitimate for an unwise decision to prompt particular attention to assessment of that person's capacity. As much as there are examples of heavy handed paternalism interfering with autonomy in the name of good intentions, there are also cases of dereliction of duty where "no" is taken too readily for an answer, misunderstanding or misapplying the assumption of capacity to leave people who may lack capacity without the protection of a proper MCA process, including best interests decisions where appropriate. In the context of denial of appropriate treatment to patients with a learning disability in particular, Mencap produced a powerful report on this called "Death by Indifference" in 2016.[36]

This is not "damned if you do and damned if you don't". It is the quite proper obligation that a clinician must assess the capacity of the individual patient in front of them to make each decision that is being made (not least because without capacity there can be no consent) and it can be just as dangerous to the patient for a clinician to accept any refusal unquestioningly as for them to try to overbear it presumptuously.

If the potential practical or legal implications of trying to deliver treatment for a refusing patient seem too daunting, which I can fully understand, then seek advice and support, and the sooner the better. Delay or denial of the issue is very unlikely to serve either the patient or

36 https://www.mencap.org.uk/sites /default/files/2016-06/DBIreport.pdf

the clinicians well, and the Court of Protection is there to help, not to punish anyone for finding it difficult or getting it wrong.

One recent example was the case of the woman with the "sparkly" lifestyle,[37] which attracted media attention in late 2015[38], no doubt due to the judge's description of her

> "... *life characterised by impulsive and self-centred decision-making without guilt or regret. [She] has had four marriages and a number of affairs and has, it is said, spent the money of her husbands and lovers recklessly before moving on when things got difficult or the money ran out.*
>
> *"She has, by their account, been an entirely reluctant and at times completely indifferent mother to her three caring daughters. Her consumption of alcohol has been excessive and, at times, out of control ... In particular, it is clear that during her life C has placed a significant premium on youth and beauty and on living a life that, in C's words, 'sparkles'."*

Now aged 50, a diagnosis of breast cancer had prompted an overdose which only achieved kidney failure leaving her facing a life on dialysis, which she deplored. She refused treatment, and the trust brought the case to court seeking authority to treat her against her wishes, if need be, in her best interests on the basis that she lacked capacity for the decision.

Her refusal of the life-saving treatment itself was presented by treating psychiatrists and independent experts as, perhaps, a personality disorder which caused her to close her mind to the possibility of a future including

37 *King's College Hospital NHS Foundation Trust v C* [2015] EWCOP 80. https://www.bailii.org/ew/cases/EWCOP/2015/80.html

38 https://www.theguardian.com/uk-news/2015/dec/02/court-grants-impulsive-self-centred-mother-permission-to-die

the treatment proposed. C's family, and the Official Solicitor[39] acting on her behalf, submitted that she had capacity, and this was simply an unwise decision.

The judge said:

> *"That C considers that the prospect of growing old, the fear of living with fewer material possessions and the fear that she has lost, and will not regain, 'her sparkle' outweighs a prognosis that signals continued life will alarm and possibly horrify many.... C's decision is certainly one that does not accord with the expectations of many in society. Indeed, others in society may consider C's decision to be unreasonable, illogical or even immoral within the context of the sanctity accorded to life by society in general. None of this however is evidence of a lack of capacity. The court being satisfied that, in accordance with the provisions of the Mental Capacity Act 2005, C has capacity to decide whether or not to accept treatment, C is entitled to make her own decision on that question based on the things that are important to her, in keeping with her own personality and system of values and without conforming to society's expectation of what constitutes the 'normal' decision in this situation (if such a thing exists). As a capacitous individual C is, in respect of her own body and mind, sovereign".*

It was, in short, her own decision, however unwise. As he quoted from an older case:

> *"An adult patient who...suffers from no mental incapacity has an absolute right to choose whether to consent to medical treatment, to refuse it or to choose one rather than another of the treatments being offered... This right of choice is not limited to decisions which others might regard as sensible. It exists notwithstanding that the reasons for*

39 A public official often acting as litigation friend to the patient in medical treatment cases, explained a little more in Chapter 7 and see the Glossary.

making the choice are rational, irrational, unknown or even non-existent."[40]

Having found that C could make her own decision in this case, the court did not have to deal with the Official Solicitor's further argument that even if C couldn't weigh up the information properly to make a valid decision, this was not *caused by* an impairment of or disturbance in the function of her mind or brain, which is the essential "diagnostic" element of the test for capacity, and is easily overlooked with the focus usually heavily on the "functional" elements of understanding, retaining and weighing up the information.

Caused by an impairment or disturbance in the mind or brain

The inability to make the decision must be "*because of* an impairment of or disturbance in the functioning of the mind or brain".[41] It is not enough to establish the jurisdiction of the MCA or the Court of Protection to make a best interests decision if P cannot understand, retain or use or weigh the relevant information to make a decision without that causative link from an "impairment of or disturbance of the mind or brain".

The sequence is important[42]. The first question is whether P can make the decision for themselves (the functional test) and then, if they can't, whether that is because of a mental disorder. The reason for this sequence is that doing it the other way round (asking first if there is a mental disorder, and then asking whether they can make the decision) risks too readily drawing an inference from the mere existence of the mental

40 Per Lord Donaldson in *Re T (adult: refusal of treatment)* [1993] Fam 95 at 102.

41 MCA s2(1).

42 See the Supreme Court judgment in A Local Authority v JB [2021] UKSC 52 – https://www.bailii.org/uk/cases/UKSC/2021/52.html

disorder that P cannot make the decision; what might be called "diagnostic overshadowing".

The impairment or disturbance can be temporary or permanent,[43] and can include the effects of alcohol or drugs, as well as e.g. dementia, a learning disability, brain injury or a mental health disorder.[44] It does not matter if there is no specific diagnosis[45], or the correct diagnosis is disputed, only that there is a mental disorder.

It is not enough that (1) P has an impairment of or disturbance in the function of the mind or brain and that separately (2) P cannot make a decision as they cannot understand or retain or weigh up the relevant information (or communicate a decision). The inability to make a decision must be ***because of*** the impairment or disturbance in their mind or brain.[46]

Without both the mental disorder, and that causative link, we may need to find other ways to intervene to protect a vulnerable adult, if need be, as the MCA would give no jurisdiction.

Inherent Jurisdiction and safeguarding

One alternative route to intervention for an adult, if the MCA is not available because P has capacity for the relevant decision, is the inherent jurisdiction of the High Court. This is still used for children and was used for adults until the MCA 2005 came into force in 2007.

Typically this is used where P has decision-making ability but their exercise of it is distorted or undermined by an external influence such as

43 MCA s2(2).

44 The MCA Code of Practice gives a list of examples in para 4.12.

45 North Bristol NHS Trust v R [2023] EWCOP 5

46 *PC & NC v City of York Council* [2013] EWCA Civ 478.

coercion or bullying. The focus, then, of any court order is not on determining P's best interests, but on removing that external influence to allow P to make their own decision freely.

For example, if an elderly couple are being unduly pressured by their son to force them to sell their home for his benefit, then the local authority may ask the court to intervene not on the basis of lack of capacity or best interests, if they do not lack capacity for that particular decision, but under the inherent jurisdiction to make orders to restrain the son from his bullying behaviour and let the parents make their own decision.[47] This could, of course, also raise questions of the criminal law e.g. coercive or controlling behaviour,[48] and no doubt ought to be referred to safeguarding professionals.

One rare but powerful example of the use of the inherent jurisdiction in the health and care context was the case of Meyers.[49] The local authority made an application to the High Court, concerned for the wellbeing of Mr Meyers, a 97 year-old blind man who was found to be living with his son in what was described as "deeply squalid conditions". Mr Meyers had capacity to make his own decisions about his care and residence, but was found to be under undue influence from his son which disabled him from truly exercising his autonomy. Mr Justice Hayden said:

> *"I instinctively recoil from intervening in the decision making of a capacitous adult. However well motivated the state may be in seeking, paternalistically, to protect people from their own unwise decisions, it is a dangerous course which has the potential to threaten fundamental*

47 *A City Council v DL*, [2012] EWCA Civ 253, https://www.bailii.org/ew/cases/EWCA/Civ/2012/253.html

48 Serious Crime Act 2015 s76, which criminalises coercive control between partners, ex-partners, or family members, as long as the victim and perpetrator are living together at the time of the offence. It carries a maximum sentence of 5 years imprisonment.

49 Southend v Meyers [2019] EWHC 399.

> *rights and freedoms … the inherent jurisdiction is not ubiquitous, and should be utilised sparingly".*

Nonetheless,

> *"here Mr Meyers' life requires to be protected and I consider that ultimately the state has an obligation to do so".*

It is easy, when framing issues in terms of human rights, to focus readily on their right to privacy and family life, and overlook other rights, including their right to life, and to protection from inhuman and degrading treatment. Making an order that prohibited Mr Meyers from living with his son, Hayden J concluded:

> *"the treatment of Mr Meyers has not merely been neglectful but abusive and corrosive of this dignity. To the extent that the Court's decision encroaches on Mr Meyers' personal autonomy it is, I believe, a justified and proportionate interference".*

Having full decision-making capacity is, by the way, no barrier to an appropriate safeguarding referral where there are concerns about a vulnerable adult, e.g. in cases of self-neglect as much as abuse by a third party.

Fluctuating Capacity

Capacity which comes and goes is often a huge practical problem. I am, however, instinctively a little wary of the haste with which the label of "fluctuating capacity" is applied. In my experience, it can be tempting to conclude capacity is "fluctuating" without really getting to the bottom of what particular decision needs to be made, when it needs to be made, and the obligation to enhance and support P's capacity as much as possible (see below).

Sometimes, "fluctuating capacity" is a misleading label, reached for too readily where we mean that there is a disagreement about someone's capacity, often with distinct group of professionals taking contrary views.

In some cases, it may be that "fluctuating" really means that Bob has capacity for some decisions but not others; or that he would not have capacity to make a particular decision at all times. Well yes – we all function better at some times than others, though there can be exaggerated examples of this for instance in "sundowning" when the behaviour of patients with dementia can become more difficult to understand in the late afternoon or early evening.

Most decisions can allow a little flexibility in when they need to be taken, which can often accommodate this. There is an obligation[50] to take "all practicable steps" to help P towards capacity. And to consider whether a decision can possibly be deferred until P regains the capacity to make it for themselves.[51]

It is perfectly appropriate to consider it in terms of a patient making a decision for themselves in the morning, when they are able to make a decision, what medication they will have in the afternoon, when they may not. Or a patient may wish to make an Advance Decision to Refuse Treatment.[52]

I would also hesitate to use the term "fluctuating capacity" for a patient who, for a few days, lacks capacity to make decisions about certain medical treatment due to a urinary tract infection, or a post detox delirium. It is clearer, perhaps, to say that P lacks capacity at that time for those decisions; to defer, until P can make them, such decisions as can

50 MCA s1(3).

51 MCA s4(3).

52 See chapter 5 and MCA s23.

appropriately be deferred; and to make in P's best interests the decisions that must be taken now.

For that reason, a bit of mythology that I have heard – that there must not be an assessment of capacity for someone suffering short lived delirium or the effects of an infection – is clearly nonsense. There will be some decisions that can wait until P has recovered the ability to make them himself, but for others there is no such time and best interests decisions must be made now. There can be no basis to make such a best interests decision unless there has first been an assessment of P's capacity to make that decision for himself.

In my experience, cases in which capacity truly fluctuates are rare, and certainly much rarer than the usage of the term suggests.

In some cases, a patient with capacity to do so may be able to consent (or not) at the outset of a course of treatment to the predictable steps involved, including some that may need to be taken while the patient is not able to take those decisions, for instance in a period of unconsciousness post-operative recovery after elective surgery (sometimes called "advance consent", as if there is any other kind!).

In those few cases where a treatment plan will cover a period in which P's capacity to make the relevant decisions will genuinely come and go the courts have jurisdiction to make clear to the clinicians what would / would not be lawful, in P's best interests, in the period that they lack capacity.[53]

Going a little further, in July 2019 the Court of Protection gave a hospital trust authority to proceed, if need be, with obstetric care in the best interests, but against the wishes, of a patient (who was 35 weeks pregnant and had paranoid schizophrenia and emotionally unstable personality

53 MCA s15(1)(c). See for example *Royal Borough of Greenwich v CDM* [2018] EWCOP 15. http://www.bailii.org/ew/cases/EWCOP/2018/15.html

disorder) who had capacity at the time the application was made, but was anticipated might later lose capacity for decisions about her obstetric care, in the strain of the situation as she went into labour.[54] The MCA may, perhaps, have been stretched a little to accommodate the approach sought, but the court accepted that it was better to have a clear plan approved by the court in advance than to wait for a perfectly foreseeable crisis to occur and then have to resolve any issues in an emergency.[55]

A similar situation came before the courts on an urgent basis on 30 August 2019, when a patient "R" was 39 weeks and 6 days into her first pregnancy. She was detained by a mental health trust, which applied to court jointly with the neighbouring hospital trust that was responsible for her obstetric care. R had a diagnosis of bipolar affective disorder with psychotic episodes. Like the previous case, all agreed that R had capacity for decisions about her obstetric care at the time, but in labour there was a risk of substantial deterioration in her mental health such that capacity might be lost; there was a risk of needing a caesarean section which she might resist, risking harm to herself and her baby. Mr Justice Hayden dealt with the case at an urgent hearing, making declarations the same day that the appropriate obstetric care should be given as need be, in the event that capacity for those decisions was lost in labour.

In the event, the baby was born a few days later without the need for a caesarean section, and R was co-operative throughout. But since the court had authorised a very intrusive intervention against the wishes of someone who, at the time the court considered it, had capacity for her own decisions and was, unfortunately, unrepresented in the proceedings,

54 *United Lincolnshire Hospitals v CD* [2019] EWCOP 24. https://www.bailii.org/ew/cases/EWCOP/2019/24.html

55 In contrast, perhaps, see the Cardiff Vale case in Chapter 7.

the judge explained the decision in some detail and offered some guidance for future cases in a later full written judgment.[56]

The judgment recognises the artificiality of using the MCA in these circumstances to anticipate a loss of capacity in future, but says that in any case this decision is certainly within the court's power under the wide-ranging inherent jurisdiction of the High Court.

But the judgment also includes an important general observation:

> *"The right of all individuals to respect for their bodily integrity is a fundamental one. It is every bit the right of the incapacitous as well as the capacitous."*[57]

The law, though, can be a blunt tool to deal with situations in which capacity for a decision genuinely comes and goes. In Somerset NHS FT v Amira[58], Mr Justice Mostyn commented that he thought that the court had no jurisdiction at all to make anticipatory declarations, and that MCA s5-6 should simply be used instead. That was only a comment in passing[59], since the judge found that in fact she had lost capacity for the relevant decision, and so the question of the court's lack of power to make declarations in anticipation of the loss of capacity was academic. But, respectfully, it is not clear that is right, and as we have seen there are plenty of other cases where this has been done.

---

56 *GSTT and SLAM v R* [2020] EWCOP 4 http://www.bailii.org/ew/cases/EWCOP/2020/4.html

57 Paragraph 48, and see Chapter 5.

58 [2023] EWCOP 25.

59 "Obiter", as lawyers say, meaning that it is a bit of judicial thinking out loud, and not an essential part of the reasoning for this decision, and therefore no part of any potential precedent.

In Leicestershire County Council v P[60] Mrs Justice Theis had to deal with a lady in her 50s who had been traumatised by experiences in her early life and was now diagnosed with Dissociative Identity Disorder. It did not matter that there was some disagreement over the diagnosis and others thought it was complex PTSD causing the disassociations. The problem was that when she disassociated, whatever the cause, she was thought to lack capacity for certain decisions. The judge held that there is a power to make anticipatory declarations, but that it was not appropriate to do so here. P in this case had something like 50 different identities, and it was hard to discern when she was disassociating and therefore when capacity for some decisions might be lost. As such, there is no practical use in making declarations of what would be in her best interests in that scenario, if the professional carers supporting her could not reliably know when that was happening and the best interests decisions could be triggered.

Conversely, in *Oldham MBC v KZ,*[61] the same judge, Mrs Justice Theis, decided that it was appropriate to make anticipatory declarations. In that case, KZ was a 20 year-old man who was profoundly deaf, and as a result of deprivation of language in childhood[62], he lacked capacity to make some decisions when he became dysregulated. In this case, the judge was happy that it was appropriate to make anticipatory declarations about his best interests, as this happened relatively rarely, and it was very clear to the carers when he became agitated and capacity was lost.

An alternative approach the courts have used is to take a "longitudinal view" of capacity. In A Local Authority v PG[63], Mrs Justice Lieven rejected anticipatory declarations as unworkable in practice for PG,

---

60 [2024] EWCOP 53.

61 [2024] EWCOP 72 (T3).

62 The judge explained that this meant that he was unable to deal with certain cognitive processes for which language is essential, in a way that had similarities in effect to a learning disability.

63 [2023] EWCOP 9.

whose capacity for decisions about care and contact was thought to fluctuate. Instead, it was more realistic to take the "longitudinal view" that on balance PG lacked capacity for those decisions, treating them in effect as ongoing, or "macro decisions", for which she lacked capacity often enough for it to be expedient to treat her as lacking capacity all the time. This is, plainly, the triumph of pragmatism over principle. The court is asserting that it can make best interests decisions for someone even though – at times – they have capacity for that decision, in a way that is difficult to reconcile with the legislation that only gives the court jurisdiction when P lacks capacity. But what are we to do?

These situations are difficult in practice, and it is always wise to get legal advice at an early stage.

Communicating

For completeness, one aspect of the test for capacity has been neglected so far. Even if P can understand, and retain, and use or weigh the information relevant to a decision, they would still be considered to lack capacity for that decision if they are unable to communicate the decision, because of a mental disorder.

I suppose this might be thought to be a factor in cases where a patient is unconscious, or in a Prolonged Disorder of Consciousness, for example, but it is not often the only issue. I cannot think of a case in which inability to communicate alone has been the decisive factor in determining that a patient cannot make a particular decision.

That is at least partly due to the extent to which technology and support can be used to enhance and enable communication in many circumstances. I am thinking of the man who wrote a book using only a blink to select letter by letter from an alphabet chart, which was the only movement he could make in what was otherwise a locking in syndrome after a stroke[64]. I would need some convincing that inability to communicate alone is the reason for a patient's lack of capacity to make a particular decision.

Empowering

Assisting a patient to communicate their decision is just a part of the broader principle that no-one should be treated as unable to make a decision for themselves unless "all practicable steps" have been taken to help them to do so without success.[65]

As I have said, I would love to see clinicians as readily hold an "empowering decision-making" meeting where professionals strain to think of ways to better help Bob to be able to make the decision for himself, rather than any concern about their capacity leading straight into a "best interests meeting" or decision.

Such empowerment and support can be very practical and common sense – using accessible language, and considering whether P functions better at a particular time or day, or with the greater comfort / confidence of a particular environment, or with support. Involvement of speech and language therapy can be very helpful. Support can also include materials in audio or visual / pictorial form, role playing or recognition of their particular communication needs, language or culture, with interpretation as need be.

For example, in the KZ case just mentioned above, though KZ had a cochlear implant he preferred to use British Sign Language. The initial assessment that found that he lacked capacity for some decisions was carried out by a psychiatrist, reliant on the manager of KZ's placement to act as BSL interpreter, when they had only BSL level 1 training. Mrs

64 The Diving Bell and the Butterfly by Jean-Dominique Bauby.

65 Mental Capacity Act 2005 s1(3), and see the Code of Practice para 2.6.

Justice Theis' judgment says that where any assessment of capacity is done for someone who is a deaf BSL user, this must be done by someone who is both suitably qualified in BSL themselves and who is familiar with the deaf community, failing which it should be explained to the court why this was not possible.

We should be given every chance to make our own decisions, before being treated as unable to do so.

Some practicalities

- The MCA Code of Practice Chapter 4 on capacity is very helpful, clear and full of practical examples, albeit in great need of an update.

- If you find yourself in a "best interests meeting" and it is not entirely clear (1) what is the decision that has to be made and what options are available, and (2) that P has been assessed to lack capacity for that decision, then it may be better to discuss those two points before getting onto any discussion about "best interests", and perhaps suggest that the meeting is called something else.

- Remember the "empowering ethos" of the MCA. If you are waiting for P to lose capacity so that you can intervene in a way that you know they would oppose then you are likely to be at risk, and you should take some urgent advice.

- The assessment of capacity should be proportionate, and sometimes it makes sense for related decisions to be rolled together and capacity for them assessed as a whole, e.g. the decision about surgery and the decision about the anaesthetic. Be careful not to take the "decision specific" nature of the test for capacity to logical but absurd extremes. Sometimes decisions do need to be seen as a whole.

- Assessment of capacity is a matter of clinical judgement, and though we might find that a judge says that we were all wrong, clinicians should not expect their lawyers to second guess their views on capacity to make a decision about medical treatment, but only to help ensure that the correct legal framework is applied.

- Just as a clinician taking consent should ideally be someone who will (or who could) perform the procedure, so that they know all the information to be given, the same applies to the clinician assessing capacity for that procedure. It should not be routinely outsourced to a mental health specialist, though it can be perfectly appropriate to seek specialist input on whether or not there is an "impairment or disturbance in the functioning of the mind or brain" and on the causative link between that and the inability to make the decision. Testing whether someone understands, retains and can use or weigh the information relevant to a decision about treatment is usually best done by someone who themselves knows the information relevant to that decision.

- Don't be paralysed by uncertainty. Lack of capacity only needs to be established on the balance of probabilities,[66] and though of course lack of capacity should not be concluded lightly, delay in agonising about it can sometimes cause more harm. And remember that MCA s 5 offers a good deal of leeway – you will have a general defence to any liability which could arise from any lack of proper consent if you reasonably believe that P lacks

66 More likely than not – not "beyond reasonable doubt", which is the standard of proof for criminal cases.

capacity for that particular decision, and that you are acting in their best interests (see Chapter 5).

- Remember that showing your working (writing down why you think that P lacks capacity for that decision, not just that they do, by reference to the statutory test) will help enormously if your assessment and actions come under scrutiny later.

- Don't settle for, or be fobbed off with, "fluctuating" capacity without being very clear when it fluctuates, why, what has been done to support P, whether the decision can only be made when capacity is lacking, and if so why?

- As the facts change, it is OK to change your mind, and it is OK to accept that you got it wrong before. To some extent assessment of capacity is subjective, and in plenty of cases perfectly reasonable clinicians disagree, experts disagree, and even – when cases are appealed through the courts system – judges can disagree. It is much harder to defend an intransigent view in the face of changing facts, continuing to fight from the trench you have dug, than it is to explain that you've changed your mind and why.

- Where assessments of capacity conflict, greater weight may often be given to the assessment of those who know the patient best.

- And be reassured that the MCA is relatively new still, and while the case law produced by the Court of Protection is helping to form an increasingly detailed picture of how it should work, there is still plenty of blank space to fill in; we are all feeling our way a little. We don't yet have hundreds of years of cases in this area, as we do in others, and so there are only a handful of judgments on some issues and the picture can start to look very different when a new case comes along. This means that the case law is evolving quite quickly, and it is important to try to stay on top of it.

Key points

- "Capacity" is specific to the particular decision that needs to be made, and so you cannot sensibly assess *capacity* until you define the *decision* and know what the options actually are. Using the word "decision" much more than the word "capacity" will help.

- Take care not to let concern about someone tempt you to conflate your views on their best interests with your views on their capacity, or to intervene too readily. Take care not to inadvertently impose too high a bar on P's level of understanding. Take care not to find yourself using something else ("insight"? "executive dysfunction"?) as a proxy for the correct legal test.

- The Court of Protection exists to resolve any dispute or uncertainty and, in some cases, to offer reassurance when you are fairly sure of the right thing but it is deeply uncomfortable to do.

- If a patient has capacity to make a decision, then his decision (however unwise) is final, and there is no jurisdiction under the MCA or for the Court of Protection to intervene. In rare cases, the inherent jurisdiction can be used to intervene to protect someone whose decision-making is compromised by undue external influence.

- The ethos of the MCA is as much, arguably more, about autonomy and empowering people to make their own decisions as it is about protecting them by ensuring decisions are made in their best interests. Try to keep this balance in mind, and don't be too slow to seek support and advice as need be.

CHAPTER 5

CAPACITY PART B – BEST INTERESTS AND WHO DECIDES

- Advance Decisions to Refuse Treatment
- "living will", LPAs and "next of kin"
- Collaborative best interests decision-making
- IMCAs
- Who is the decision-maker?
- "Best interests" is and isn't...
- Respecting incapacitous autonomy
- Deception and covert medication
- Proportionality, restraint and deprivation of liberty
- Life and death and withdrawal of treatment
- Futility v best interests

So, a patient lacks capacity to make a decision for herself, despite "all practicable steps" to support her, and it cannot reasonably be deferred until capacity can be recovered. A "best interests decision" must be made.

But what does "best interests" mean? And, just as important, who decides?

ADRT

The first thing to consider is that the patient herself may have made the relevant decision, in advance, planning ahead before losing capacity.

The law formalises this as an "Advance Decision to Refuse Treatment", in MCA s24-26. I strongly recommend that you call it by its full name, or at least abbreviate to "ADRT", because that helps to avoid forgetting the RT bit, which is important.

Just as a patient with full decision-making capacity can only consent to, refuse or choose between options actually being offered to them, so a patient who plans ahead for a time after losing capacity for a decision about medical treatment is in no better a position. Trying to consent to something long in advance is fairly nebulous and hypothetical, and entirely contingent on actually being offered that treatment when the time comes. On the other hand, if you are clear in your own mind that, in particular circumstances, you would not want certain treatment then you can say so now, and it can be taken as binding.

A good example is a patient making a capacitous choice not to endure attempts at CPR in their last few moments, documented in a DNACPR form.[1]

Putting this into a legally binding ADRT understandably brings some formalities and safeguards. An ADRT:

- can only be made by a patient over the age of 18.
- Will only apply to the treatment it specifies.

1 Though, in other cases, a DNACPR form could also be done – with appropriate consultation of course – because a clinician would be unwilling to do CPR anyway, as explained in Chapter 2.

- Will not be relied on if the patient still has capacity to make the relevant decision at the time (of course), nor if since it was made they have acted in a way that is inconsistent with it, including the appointment of an LPA to make decisions about that treatment (see below).

- Can be withdrawn at any time (verbally or impliedly by actions, not necessarily in writing).

- If it applies to life sustaining treatment (but not otherwise[2]) it must explicitly say so, and must be in writing and witnessed.

Where an ADRT is valid and applicable to the treatment decision that needs to be made, the ADRT has the effect of a capacitous and binding refusal by the patient. If you reasonably rely on an ADRT you reasonably think is valid and applicable you will incur no liability if you turn out to have been wrong. But to err on the side of caution, no liability is incurred if you treat someone in the interim if in doubt while the existence or validity of an ADRT is established, in the Court of Protection if need be[3].

---

2 But of course the problem with an ADRT made only verbally, as well as being limited to relating only to non-life sustaining treatment, is the evidential challenge of establishing exactly what was said and meant, or making the treating clinicians aware of it. It is always a good idea to write stuff down.

3 In *Barnsley NHS Foundation Trust v MSP*, [2020] EWCOP 26, 1 June 2020, the court found that an Advance Decision to Refuse Treatment was not binding, as it did not comply with the formalities required to apply to life-sustaining treatment, but was nonetheless such clear evidence of the patient's wishes that his very clear decision ought to be given effect, in his best interests. This attracted significant media interest as it involved a man in his thirties having life-sustaining treatment withdrawn as he did not want to live with a stoma. http://www.bailii.org/ew/cases/EWCOP/2020/26.html

In September 2021, the Court of Protection heard an urgent out of hours application by University Hospitals of Birmingham NHS FT,[4] who were dealing with Mrs W, a lady of 80 years of age who had been a Jehovah's Witness for most of her adult life, and was now in a "perilous condition" in hospital with severe anaemia after internal bleeding due to an ulcerated gastric tumour. A blood transfusion would reduce her risk, and she would be likely to survive another 5-10 years. Mrs W now lacked capacity for decisions about her treatment due to advanced Alzheimer's dementia, but in 2001 she had made an ADRT to refuse blood or blood products, even if her life was in danger. The question was whether this ADRT was valid.

In a hearing by phone, between 11.45pm and 3.25am, Mr Justice Poole heard that though the ADRT had been made before the MCA 2005 came into effect, it was in a form that complied with all the procedural requirements of the MCA, and appeared to be binding. But the Court also heard that she had subsequently appointed all four of her children as LPAs for health and welfare, without telling them about the ADRT. Mrs W had also been in hospital since then and had been insistent that she did not want a DNACPR to be imposed. In the current admission – albeit after her capacity to make the decision for herself had been lost – she seemed to have agreed to have blood products if her life was at stake.

In the circumstance, the judge held that her ADRT was not binding, given the actions since it was made that called into doubt whether it had remained her fixed decision, and declared that it would be in her best interests to have the bloods to save her life if need be.

Another case since the first edition of this book is illustrative. In *JH*[5], Mr Justice Hayden dealt with a 43 year-old man who had a diagnosis of "Asperger's Syndrome (now recognised as Autistic Spectrum Disorder)"

4 Re PW (Jehovah's Witness: Validity of Advance Decision) [2021] EWCOP 52 https://www.bailii.org/ew/cases/EWCOP/2021/52.html

5 NHS Surrey Heartlands ICB v JH [2023] EWCOP 2 – https://www.bailii.org/ew/cases/EWCOP/2023/2.html

and a phobia of hospitals that seemed to be related to the extensive investigations and treatment he'd had since childhood into constant gastrointestinal pain and discomfort that plagued him all his life. He was "profoundly anxious and entirely unprepared to attend hospital", and now rarely left the house, restricting his nutrition to at best occasional high calorie drinks and mineral water. The GP who visited him at home every couple of months considered him "visibly undernourished and emaciated". At the time of the application, on 20 December 2022, there was a real concern that JH would not survive the Christmas period.

JH had made an ADRT in December 2017 refusing a raft of interventions and treatments.

The judge heard evidence from JH directly, and had "no doubt at all that the content of the [ADRT] is the authentic voice of JH himself". There was no evidence to displace the assumption of capacity that he could made the ADRT when he did. Perhaps because the judgment was given in a hurry, and out of hours, it is not entirely clear whether the judge was holding that JH had capacity at the time of the application to make decisions about his treatment (the ADRT of course only coming into effect when that capacity is lost), though he does say that JH had capacity to conduct the litigation himself. It may be that the question was really what should be done – should the ADRT be respected – if JH continues to deteriorate and his capacity to make those decisions about treatment is inevitably lost at some point.

Though Hayden J remarks that JH is "an interesting and engaging man", and comments on his enthusiasm and talent as a musician, such that "with all this going for him, one might think JH would cling to life with all his might". But

> *"ultimately, he simply cannot accept the type of intrusive investigations contemplated here, even if such investigations ultimately improved the quality of his life and extend its duration. Refusing these procedures may not be a decision that many of us would consider to be right, but as I have said, that is not what falls into question here. The court is*

required to protect JH's capacity to take decisions for himself both those that may be, objectively, ill-advised, as well as those that might, more generally, be regarded as wise".

Though the ADRT was apparently declared to be valid and binding (unless of course JH were to change his mind before that treatment were needed), a focus only on the validity of the ADRT itself would have missed the point:

"...had I found that JH lacked capacity, either in December 2017 or indeed, at the time of this hearing, I could not have contemplated a situation in which the envisaged investigations could have been forced upon him. The strength of his feelings, the consistency with which they have been held, for so many years, and his obvious distress at the contemplation of such an intrusive investigative process would, in my judgement, be brutally corrosive of JH's autonomy. It would both compromise his dignity and cause him great personal trauma. It could not be reconciled with any concept of "best interests" in the manner required by the MCA".

Of course, there is no use in an ADRT if the clinicians don't know about it or follow it. In a 2018 case,[6] an ADRT was not followed as a result of poor communication, and the judge (Mr Justice Hayden) said:

"... the medical profession must give these [ADRTs] the utmost care, attention and scrutiny. I am confident the profession does but I regret to say that I do not think sufficient care and scrutiny took place here. The lesson is an obvious one and needs no amplification. Where [ADRTs] have been drawn up and placed with GP records there is an onerous burden on the GP to ensure, wherever possible, that they are made available to clinicians in hospital. By this I mean a copy of the

6 NHS Cumbria GGC v Rushton [2018] EWCOP 41 – NHS Cumbria CCG v Rushton [2018] EWCOP 41 (21 December 2018)

> *decision should be made available and placed within the hospital records with the objective that the document should follow the patient".*

Just squeaking into this second edition, Mr Justice Poole went a little further in another interesting judgment on an ADRT, in the context of allegations of bad faith and forgery[7].

AB is a 43-year-old man who has been in a prolonged disorder of consciousness since a cardiac arrest on 5 May 2024, kept alive by artificial nutrition and hydration (CANH). Only 4 months later, in August 2024, AB's fiancée drew to the trust's attention a "living will" document which set out AB's wishes, apparently made just before his collapse. His fiancée issued court proceedings in November 2024, mainly to try to enforce AB's apparent wishes in the living will to restrict the family's access to him.

The document also included AB's refusal of life-saving treatment in various situations, including if he were to have suffered a brain injury like this, though at that stage the trust did not consider it was valid and applicable.

AB's family disputed the document altogether, saying that it had been faked by his fiancée, or at least had been coerced by her, and so did not represent his true wishes.

Mr Justice Poole held that the document was valid and applicable to his current treatment, assuming it was authentic and freely given. There will need to be another hearing to determine that, listed later in June 2024, with evidence from witnesses, though the Court refused to allow permission for the independent expert evidence on handwriting and linguistics that the parties sought. The judge said that such a challenge to

7 Re AB (ADRT: Validity and Applicability), [2025] EWCOP 20 (T3) – 10 June 2025 – https://www.bailii.org/ew/cases/EWCOP/2025/20.html

an ADRT would not lightly be allowed, but there were some reasons to doubt it the authenticity in this case.

In the meantime, the judge made some observations about ADRTs generally that might be helpful:

- As Hayden J had said, there is little value in having an ADRT if clinicians don't know about it – an ADRT should be shared with the GP, and the patient's friends and family should be told to share it with clinicians asap.

- Told that there is an ADRT, the clinicians should see a copy of it, not rely on a summary by phone, for example.

- It should not simply be assumed that an ADRT is valid, unless there are doubts. "It would be wise for clinicians presented with an apparent ADRT proactively to make enquiries – with family or friends of P if possible – to discover whether there is any evidence that might call into question the validity of the ADRT".

- "If there is unresolved doubt or an ongoing dispute about the validity, applicability and/or authenticity of an ADRT, then it is likely that an application to the Court of Protection will be required." And that application should be made by the Trust, and done promptly.

- "MCA 2005 s26(5) allows treatment to be given "while a decision as respects of any relevant issue [relating to an apparent ADRT] is sought from the court" but that is not a reason to delay seeking a decision from the court."

The T is important as well as the R. It is Refusal of *Treatment*, and an ADRT does not permit a patient to bindingly refuse in advance basic care, such as accommodation, shelter or food[8].

Of course, someone can also put in writing or express verbally what they would positively want to happen in a particular scenario, and of course a clear note of exactly what Doris would want in any given scenario is hugely helpful when it comes to giving proper weight to her own wishes in making a best interests decision. But personally, I find the use of terms like "living will" or "advance decision" for this sort of thing potentially confusing.

In some cases, a patient can give consent for a course of treatment just before losing capacity (such as a patient going into surgery warned of the risks of particular complications or aftercare required and consenting to the appropriate treatment if need be), and their consent may extend to a number of steps into the future, taking place after loss of capacity, where these have been predictable enough to be discussed with the patient in a *Montgomery* compliant way beforehand (see Chapter 3).

Otherwise, the only legal effect of a patient's expression of wishes for treatment in the future is that they must be taken into account in any future best interests decision-making process. That is not insignificant, as great weight is quite properly often put on the patient's wishes, but they may not be decisive and it shouldn't be sold to people that they will. And, of course, a patient wishing for treatment in the future can no more compel a clinician to offer a particular option in future than they can in the present (see Chapter 2).

---

8 In contrast, of course, clinically assisted nutrition and hydration via a PEG feed, for example, could certainly be refused by an ADRT – see for example Rushton v Cumbria CCG [2018] EWCOP 41. https://www.bailii.org/ew/cases/EWCOP/2018/41.html

There are some resources about how to make an ADRT, as well as appointing an LPA, in the Appendix at the end of the book.

Lasting Powers of Attorney

There have been various forms of power of attorney in the past, focussed on managing property and money. Prior to the MCA, an Enduring Power of Attorney (EPA)[9] could be appointed for dealing with your finances.

But the MCA introduced new "Lasting Powers of Attorney" (LPA)[10], and provided for these to come in two flavours: property & affairs, or health & welfare (which would include medical treatment).

A property & affairs LPA can run while the donor has capacity for those decisions, simply allowing the convenience of sub-contracting that work. Health & welfare LPAs only come into effect when the donor has lost capacity for the relevant decision themselves. Granting an LPA to my partner does not entitle her to allow doctors to treat me against my wishes while I can still make that decision for myself!

The donor of an LPA must have capacity to make the LPA at the time it is made. Obviously, there is a limit to how far a clinician today faced with an LPA can be expected to play Poirot about the state of the patient's mind years ago when the LPA was granted to assess if it is kosher, especially if the patient today has lost capacity for the particular treatment decision that needs to be made, perhaps as a result of deterioration in their dementia, for example. But you might reasonably raise an eyebrow when presented with an LPA purportedly granted by a patient who lacks capacity now for a medical treatment decision as a result of a profound and long-term learning disability.

9 Enduring Powers of Attorney Act 1985

10 MCA s9-14.

And, of course, because an LPA is simply someone bestowing certain decision-making authority onto their nominee, they can:

- Retract it at any time, while they still have capacity to do so
- Limit the scope of the decision-making authority – saying it applies to some decisions and not others (it will not confer the power for decisions about life-sustaining treatment unless it explicitly says so); and
- Impose any conditions or restrictions, including provisions that more than one attorney is appointed and, if so, whether they can make decisions individually, or only jointly.

When an attorney does become the decision-maker for a medical treatment decision, they are still constrained by the legal framework of the MCA, i.e. they can only make a decision in the patient's best interests, and they are subject to all the duties of appropriate consultation to make a best interests decision as any other best interests decision-maker, including health or social care professionals. And so, though the legislation and court judgments talk of the LPA authorising the attorney to "give consent" to treatment, I really don't feel comfortable with that way of thinking about it.

"Consent" to me is all about my own decisions, and my ability to exercise autonomy fully and, at times, unwisely. An attorney can only make a best interests decision, and so I personally find it makes much more sense to speak of them as becoming the best interests decision-maker, not as someone giving "consent".

To be clear, an LPA does not entitle anyone to make decisions that are not in P's best interests, and if you think someone is trying to use the LPA in that way, you should challenge this.

If you are unsure whether there is an LPA, or about the validity or scope of it, or whether the attorney is acting in the patient's best interests, it is the role of the Office of the Public Guardian[11] to police this.

So if you have a patient before you and a best interests medical treatment decision to make, and someone presents themselves as holding a power of attorney, that is the start of a discussion, not the end of it. You will want to see the document itself to check that:

- it is an LPA applicable to health & welfare decisions (not an EPA or an LPA for property & affairs)
- it has a stamp to show it has been registered with the OPG (otherwise it is not valid)
- the decision in question is within the scope of the LPA granted, including whether it explicitly includes life-sustaining treatment, if that is the issue
- whether it is a sole or joint attorney and any restrictions on their decision-making.

And while there being a valid and applicable LPA essentially makes the attorney the best interests decision maker, the best interests decision-making process is still required to be collaborative and inclusive, just as it would be if there were no LPA. In my experience a lot of time and effort can be spent worrying about whether or not there is an LPA for health & welfare, or whether it is valid, and it doesn't really make a lot of difference in the end, for reasons I'll cover below. (The benefits of an LPA for property and finances, on the other hand, will be well known to anyone who has tried to sort out someone's finances without one).

11 https://www.gov.uk/government/organisations/office-of-the-public-guardian

Before that, though, let me get on my biggest hobby horse: the role of "next of kin" in best interests decision-making.

"Next of Kin"

To illustrate this point when I am giving training, I often put up a picture of "the Simpsons" family tree and give the assembled health or social care professionals a moment to contemplate: "who is Homer's 'next of kin'"?

Most people say "Marge" – his wife – fairly confidently. A few tentatively go for his father (Abraham), and there's an occasional "Bart". Some say "whoever he nominates". Others, rightly, will sense a trap. And increasingly, I'm pleased to say, some will give the correct answer, though there really is a long way to go.

In English and Welsh law, *there is no such thing as "next of kin"*.[12]

I'll say that again, as it comes as a surprise to most people, and this misconception is one of the biggest causes of difficulty and dispute in this context. There is no such thing as "next of kin". It is, in law, literally meaningless.

It feels like it works as a proxy for your nearest and dearest. Indeed, the Inheritance of Estates Act 1925 does set out in table form a hierarchy of family relationships who will inherit in case of intestacy (dying without a will). But it does not use the words, or define, "next of kin".

There is a role in the Mental Health Act 1983 of the defined "nearest relative" for the purposes of treatment of a mental disorder, and a similar idea in the Adults with Incapacity Act (Scotland) 2000. But there is no such thing as "next of kin". Once you are an adult, and no-one has

12 Although, in fairness, the Simpsons are *American*, and in the US there actually is a statutory definition of next of kin, unlike here.

parental responsibility for you from the age of 18, no-one gets authority to make decisions about you solely by virtue of their family relationship.

Which begs the question why the phrase is used so widely and repeatedly, including in all kinds of official and formal NHS documentation?!

The reality is that it is used, understandably, as shorthand for a different, entirely appropriate set of questions – "Who would you like us to call? Who do you want us to share information with? Who do you want involved in decisions about your care?" I like much better the growing practice of recording "ICE" (in case of emergency) contact details, but our habitual reference to "next of kin" is deeply engrained and may take generations to move on. The phrase is still being used in formal documents and guidance issued throughout the NHS.

But it is wholly wrong to think of anyone being "next of kin" and thereby acquiring some form of decision-making authority over an adult who lacks capacity for decisions for themselves. Actually it can be very damaging and harmful, and not only where decisions contrary to the patient's best interests are made, unquestioningly, at the behest of the "next of kin". I think it can also put an unfair and intolerable pressure onto the person who may identify themselves as "next of kin", if they feel that they therefore bear sole responsibility for a grave decision about a family member's medical treatment.

Instead, coming to a best interests decision for an adult who lacks capacity to make a medical treatment decision is a collaborative process, and it remains so even if there happens to be an LPA that appoints a family member (whether or not they might consider themselves "next of kin") as an attorney for health & welfare.

MCA s4 sets out how best interests decisions should be made, and s4(7) mandates that the best interests decision-maker:

> "must take into account, if it is practicable and appropriate to consult them, the views of—

> (a) anyone named by the person as someone to be consulted on the matter in question or on matters of that kind,
>
> (b) anyone engaged in caring for the person or interested in his welfare,
>
> (c) any donee of a lasting power of attorney granted by the person, and
>
> (d) any deputy appointed for the person by the court,
>
> as to what would be in the person's best interests and, in particular, as to the matters mentioned in subsection (6)".

Section 4(7) is massively important, and I'll pick a few key points out in turn.

In making a best interests decision, the decision maker **must** take into account the opinions of a list of specified groups of people, unless it is impracticable or inappropriate to do so.

It might be inappropriate to consult someone who would otherwise be on the list if, for example, the patient had said, or behaved in a way that showed, that they would not want a particular individual to be involved in such decisions. Bear in mind that asking for input into a medical treatment best interests decision involves telling someone a bit about the situation and options, necessarily sharing confidential information. This can be justified, in their best interests, where the patient lacks capacity to make decisions about sharing their information, as well as for the substantive medical treatment decision. But in some cases Bob may still be able to make his own decisions about sharing information (since it is a different and perhaps simpler decision than the medical treatment decision for which he lacks capacity), and decide that he wants his son to be involved in decisions, but no confidential information should be shared with his daughter. That would be his right.

Anyone with an LPA or any deputy (which is a very similar role to the LPA, but appointed by the court rather than the patient[13]) should be consulted, and so to my mind it doesn't really matter whether the attorney (or deputy) meets all the criteria to be the decision-maker or not, they are entitled to be involved in the decision-making anyway.

And anyone who might have an LPA, even if invalid / inapplicable, is very likely to be in the crucial catch all category – "those engaged in caring for P or interested in his welfare". Note that it does <u>not</u> say family and it does not, so help me, say "next of kin". It is deliberately wide, and it would equally include the neighbour who has known Bob for 40 years, or the guy who has a pint with him every day, as much as the estranged daughter. There's no "top trumps", so the duty to consult (as long as practicable) includes anyone who can help the decision-making. You need not (as you might if trying to identify the singular "next of kin") worry whether the son in Australia trumps the cousin who lives next door. In many cases it may be perfectly reasonable to rely on one family member to speak for the family as a whole, but don't forget that friends, carers and others might know Bob just as well as anyone else.

There might reasonably be an alarm bell if one family member seeks to control or withhold the flow of information to others, or to prevent them from being involved in the decision making.

And don't forget that the professionals involved are also "those engaged in caring for P or interested in his welfare" and so, in my view, there is an equal obligation on a family member (if they are the decision-maker by virtue of an LPA, for example), to consult with clinicians and carers, just as there is on clinicians to consult with family and others if they are the decision-maker.

---

13 I have not included deputies here – essentially the same role and restrictions as an LPA, but appointed by the court – as they are extremely rare for health and welfare decisions.

Knowing the individual is the key. You are not just asking someone what they think should be done for the best. The consultation duty in s4(7) is aimed "in particular as to the matters in subsection (6)", and that's all about Bob himself:

MCA s4(6) reads:

> [the best interests decision-maker] must consider, so far as is reasonably ascertainable—
>
> (a) the person's past and present wishes and feelings (and, in particular, any relevant written statement made by him when he had capacity[14]),
>
> (b) the beliefs and values that would be likely to influence his decision if he had capacity, and
>
> (c) the other factors that he would be likely to consider if he were able to do so.

I'll come back to the importance of P's own wishes and involving him in the decision-making. For now, note that this consultation duty is all about helping the best interests decision-maker make the right decision for Bob, as an individual. Not for a typical patient with condition X and treatment options Y and Z. Bob. So, when it comes to the consultation duty under s4(7), the questions you should ask are "tell me about Bob", "what is important to him", "what do you think Bob would want in this situation?" Or, "if Bob himself was in this best interests meeting, what would he say to us?" The people you should ask are those most likely to have useful answers to those questions.

This should generate a collaborative approach and tone, and if there is any sense of either family or clinicians being ridden roughshod over by

14 This would be where a so-called "living will" type document would come in, expressing wishes.

the other then something is going badly wrong. Any disputes, of course, can be referred to the Court of Protection.

Family's and others' views and best interests

We will come back to this when we tackle the issue of resolving disputes, in particular when cases need to go to court (see Chapter 7), and the imperative to avoid delay. But a really important recent case on these points also deals with the purpose of consulting others in the best interests decision-making process, so it requires to be dealt with here.

Such consultation is not – said Mr Justice Hayden – to find out what the family thinks is in Bob's best interests, but to help the best interests decision maker find out about Bob.

In JP, Hayden J had already given a judgment that it was in JP's best interests for life sustaining treatment to be withdrawn, having been in a persistent vegetative state for nine years[15]. Exasperated by the delay in having made the application, though, he gave another judgment in which he addressed the way in which the best interests decision making had happened in this case, and the reasons why this had taken so long[16]. He was critical of the passivity of the NHS bodies involved, in failing to proactively review not only JP's clinical care, but whether ongoing treatment continued to be in his best interests. When the public authorities finally addressed this, they established that there was a difference of opinion about whether it was in JP's best interests to continue life sustaining treatment: some family members wanted treatment to continue, apparently reflecting their own religious views, others were sure that JP would hate this situation and would want

15 South East London ICB v JP [2025] EWCOP 4 (T3) https://www.bailii.org/ew/cases/EWCOP/2025/4.html

16 South East London ICB v JP [EWCOP] 8 (T3) https://www.bailii.org/ew/cases/EWCOP/2025/8.html

treatment withdrawn. The judge said it was wrong for the NHS to have behaved as if obliged to try to resolve things to the satisfaction of the whole family, with the delay that this incurred. Mr Justice Hayden gave it both barrels:

> *"The views of family members, their own wishes, feelings, religious and cultural beliefs, are, in themselves, of little, if any, relevance. I emphasise that their views are being sought solely to illuminate the likely wishes and feelings of P. Their evidence is garnered to assert P's autonomy, not to subjugate it."*
>
> ...
>
> *"...the objective of the discussions with family members is* **not** *to ascertain their views and beliefs but to ascertain if what they have to say can illuminate P's wishes and beliefs. There has been some discussion as to the need to be sensitive to "the family's views". This referred to JP's sisters' and mother's strict religious beliefs. Of course, I would expect all concerned to be respectful and polite, and I have no doubt they were. However, delaying decision-making for JP in consequence of a heightened sensitivity to the religious views of some of his family would be to neglect him and to lose focus on the central question of what is in JP's best interests. The incapacitous individual, with no awareness of the outside world, is uniquely vulnerable and requires vigilantly to be protected".*

To put it another way: "there is no such thing as next of kin".

As I said above, I think this consultation with those who know Bob best is best expressed in terms of asking "tell me about Bob". But I don't know whether I would go quite so far, as Hayden J does here, as to say that their own view on his best interests is of zero value, and their only role is to help us identify Bob's own wishes and feelings, values and beliefs. After all, the legislation says that a best interests decision maker should consult those engaged in caring for P or interested in their welfare "*as to what would be in the person's best interests and, in particular, as to [his wishes and feelings, values and beliefs]*".

It will be interesting to see whether further case law rows back a bit from this high-water mark of disinterest in the family's own values and opinions in themselves. But it is certainly an important corrective to the cases in which we see real harm done to patients who have lost the ability to make the relevant decisions for themselves where clinicians find themselves under pressure to do things they do not think are appropriate, simply to respect (or placate?) a family's own demands, losing sight of the patient[17].

IMCA

In this process, there can be a particular role played by an Independent Mental Capacity Advocate (IMCA). An IMCA must be appointed where there is no appropriate non-professional to consult and a best interests decision must be made about serious medical treatment,[18] defined for this purpose as:

> *treatment which involves giving new treatment, stopping treatment that has already started or withholding treatment that could be offered in circumstances where:*
>
> *(a) if a single treatment is proposed there is a fine balance between the likely benefits and the burdens to the patient and the risks involved*
>
> *(b) a decision between a choice of treatments is finely balanced, or*

17 Again, we will see more of this in Chapter 7.

18 MCA s37

(c) *what is proposed is likely to have serious consequences for the patient*[19]

Demand for IMCAs can outstrip supply, and I am yet to see a case in which an IMCA's involvement has been other than hugely helpful, but their role should not be misunderstood. They are not appointed to be the decision-maker but more, in cases where we are short of those engaged in caring for P or interested in his welfare in a non-professional capacity, to help to get to the bottom of P's own wishes and feelings, values and beliefs, and to speak on his behalf to get these across and given due weight in the best interests decision-making.

MCA s5 and rule of thumb on the best interests decision-maker

At the end of the last chapter I mentioned the "general defence" of s5 MCA, that you won't get in trouble, for lack of consent at least, if you reasonably believe the patient lacks capacity for the relevant decision, and you reasonably think that you are acting in their best interests:

5 **Acts in connection with care or treatment**

(1) If a person ("D") does an act in connection with the care or treatment of another person ("P"), the act is one to which this section applies if—

(a) before doing the act, D takes reasonable steps to establish whether P lacks capacity in relation to the matter in question, and

(b) when doing the act, D reasonably believes—

19 The Mental Capacity Act 2005 (Independent Mental Capacity Advocates) (General) Regulations 2006 Regulation 4, http://www.legislation.gov.uk/uksi/2006/1832/pdfs/uksi_20061832_en.pdf

(i) that P lacks capacity in relation to the matter, and

(ii) that it will be in P's best interests for the act to be done.

(2) D does not incur any liability in relation to the act that he would not have incurred if P—

(a) had had capacity to consent in relation to the matter, and

(b) had consented to D's doing the act.

(3) Nothing in this section excludes a person's civil liability for loss or damage, or his criminal liability, resulting from his negligence in doing the act.

(4) Nothing in this section affects the operation of sections 24 to 26 (advance decisions to refuse treatment).

I think this also offers a good rule of thumb answer to the question, who is the best interests decision-maker? Unless an LPA is in place (or, exceptionally rarely, a court appointed deputy) for health & welfare, the decision-maker will typically be, I think, the person who would need to rely on s5.

So, for example, take a lower limb amputation. The surgeon would be facing prison for GBH, as anyone else would for just cutting someone's leg off, if it were not for the clinical indication, his professional qualifications, and the patient's consent. If the patient lacks capacity for that decision, it is the proper application of the MCA, including reliance on s5, that protects the surgeon (and his "accomplices"). It might be reasonable to see the surgeon as the best interests decision-maker.

Given the duties of consultation on the decision-maker, though, I am not convinced that it makes an enormous difference whether the decision-maker is a clinician with an obligation to consult the friends, family and others, or it is a family member (perhaps due to an LPA) with the same obligation to consult with other family and friends, as well as the clinicians, carers and others.

In either case, any substantial dispute must be referred to the Court of Protection, and any concerns about whether an attorney is acting in the patient's best interests should be referred to the Office of the Public Guardian.

What is important is the best interests decision making process, not the identity of the decision maker.

Best interests are ... and are not...

Moving on to how we define "best interests", I think in some ways it is easier to start by saying that best interests is:

- **Not** something that is not actually being offered
- **Not** (necessarily) whatever the "next of kin" or family want
- **Not** (necessarily) the least restrictive thing
- **Not** what P would have decided for himself (necessarily, though we are perhaps getting closer to this)
- **Not** (necessarily) the safest option

The first three of these are largely covered in the preceding chapters, so now I'll focus on the last two.

Best interests is not (necessarily) whatever P would have decided himself

MCA s4 sets out the what is sometimes called the "best interests checklist" of issues to consider, including (in s4(6)) the need to consider, as far as is reasonably ascertainable, the person's "past and present wishes and feelings", and "the beliefs and values that would be likely to influence his decision if he had capacity" and "the other factors that he would be likely to consider if he were able to do so".

But it stops short of something that would properly be called "substituted judgment", i.e. determining best interests according to exactly what P would have decided for himself, if he had capacity for this decision now.

When P has capacity he can make a decision for himself, however unwise, but in incapacity, the decision must be in P's best interests, giving appropriate weight to his wishes, values and beliefs, but is not necessarily simply what he would have decided for himself. As the courts trend towards putting ever more weight on P's wishes in making best interests decisions[20] this distinction may shrink in practice, but it is important in principle, because it means that P's wishes, however important, are not the only question.

That said, the further that we go away from what P wants (or wanted – see below), it is reasonable to look for a greater justification of this being in his best interests.

Best interests is not (necessarily) the safest option

Bob's best interests might well be to have the treatment that saves his life, or that gives him the best chance of the best medical outcome, but the

20 See for example Barnsley Hospital NHS Foundation Trust v MSP, at footnote 3 above, and discussed further below.

question needs more shading and colour than a reductive assessment of prognosis or QALYs.[21]

As we will see, the preservation of life at all costs is not necessarily in a patient's best interests, as interpreted by the courts at least. And a view of best interests must be taken at a more holistic level:

> *"The most that can be said, therefore, is that in considering the best interests of this particular patient at this particular time, decision-makers must look at his welfare in the widest sense, not just medical but social and psychological; they must consider the nature of the medical treatment in question, what it involves and its prospects of success; they must consider what the outcome of that treatment for the patient is likely to be; they must try and put themselves in the place of the individual patient and ask what his attitude to the treatment is or would be likely to be; and they must consult others who are looking after him or interested in his welfare, in particular for their view of what his attitude would be".*[22]

Those words are from the judgment of Lady Hale in *Aintree University Hospitals NHS Foundation Trust v James*, the first Supreme Court case to consider a medical treatment decision (withholding life-sustaining treatment) under the MCA.

In another context (a case under the inherent jurisdiction dealing with capacity for sexual relationships[23]) Munby J (later Lord Justice Munby)

---

21 Quality Adjusted Life Years, used by rationing bodies such as NICE to assess the value for money / clinical benefit of a particular intervention, using 1 as a full year of full health, and then reduced according to shorter time or diminished health.

22 [2013] UKSC 67, at paragraph 39. https://www.bailii.org/uk/cases/UKSC/2013/67.html

23 *Local Authority X v MM* [2007] EWHC 2003 (Fam). The quote is at paragraph 120. https://www.bailii.org/ew/cases/EWHC/Fam/2007/2003.html

coined one of the most familiar phrases on this point, at the end of a passage I'll set out in full:

> *"A great judge once said, "all life is an experiment," adding that "every year if not every day we have to wager our salvation upon some prophecy based upon imperfect knowledge"... The fact is that all life involves risk, and the young, the elderly and the vulnerable, are exposed to additional risks and to risks they are less well equipped than others to cope with. But just as wise parents resist the temptation to keep their children metaphorically wrapped up in cotton wool, so too we must avoid the temptation always to put the physical health and safety of the elderly and the vulnerable before everything else. Often it will be appropriate to do so, but not always. Physical health and safety can sometimes be bought at too high a price in happiness and emotional welfare. The emphasis must be on sensible risk appraisal, not striving to avoid all risk, whatever the price, but instead seeking a proper balance and being willing to tolerate manageable or acceptable risks as the price appropriately to be paid in order to achieve some other good – in particular to achieve the vital good of the elderly or vulnerable person's happiness. What good is it making someone safer if it merely makes them miserable?"*

A similar point has been made in judgments time and again. In a case about whether a 67 year-old lady must remain in residential care, or could return to her own home as she wished, Mr Justice Peter Jackson said:

> *"In the end, if M remains confined in a home she is entitled to ask "What for?" The only answer that could be provided at the moment is "To keep you alive as long as possible." In my view that is not a sufficient answer. The right to life and the state's obligation to protect it is not absolute and the court must surely have regard to the person's own assessment of her quality of life. In M's case there is little to be said for a solution that attempts, without any guarantee of success, to*

> *preserve for her a daily life without meaning or happiness and which she, with some justification, regards as insupportable".*[24]

As I have said, it is easy to understand the anxiety in public bodies, and in the dedicated individual professionals working in health and social care, to keep people safe, and secure the best outcome for them within the scope of their expertise. At times this can incentivise a tendency to find a lack of capacity as a means to intervene and / or, having done so, to lean towards the best interests decision that tends towards the safest outcome (the "protection imperative").

In the case of Peggy Ross,[25] Cardiff City Council rushed off to court on a Friday seeking an order to prevent an 82 year-old lady who was resident in one of their care homes from going on a cruise holiday, which was due to depart the following Monday. She had been admitted to the care home due to her dementia around 3 months earlier. The local authority assessed Mrs Ross to lack capacity to make a decision about going on the cruise, as she "lacked insight into her needs", and were concerned that it would not be safe for her to do so, because she was prone to wandering and might fall overboard.

The judge was critical of the assessment of capacity, saying that it was a comparatively simple decision for her to make, especially as she had been regularly going on cruise holidays with the same gentleman for the last 20 years. But, without time to really get into the evidence on this, he concluded that it was in her best interests to go on the holiday in any event, even if she did lack the capacity to make the decision for herself.

---

24 *Re M (best interests: deprivation of liberty)* [2013] EWCOP 3456. https://www.bailii.org/ew/cases/EWHC/COP/2013/3456.html

25 *Cardiff City Council v Peggy Ross* (2011) COP 28/10/11 12063905. http://www.mentalhealthlaw.co.uk/media/Cardiff_Council_v_Peggy_Ross_%282011%29_COP_28-10-11_12063905.pdf. The case attracted significant media coverage.

Not without some sympathy, I think, for the concerns of the professionals involved, he said:

> *"My strong impression is that her social worker and the staff at the home want to do the right thing for her but are focussed on her safety and are acutely aware of things that might go wrong. Perhaps the prime example of this was the concern that Mrs Ross might 'wander' (as she undoubtedly has in the past when living alone) on the ship and go over the side. It was suggested, not without some force in my view, that this smacked of saying that her best interests were best served by taking every precaution to avoid any possible danger without carrying out the balancing exercise of considering the benefit to Mrs Ross of what, sadly, may be her last opportunity to enjoy such a holiday with Mr Davies. This led, in my view, to trying to find reasons why Mrs Ross should not go on this holiday rather than finding reasons why she should".*

What use is it making someone safer if it only makes them miserable, indeed.

And while lack of capacity for a particular decision may diminish the exercise of your autonomy, it should not extinguish it.

Incapacitous autonomy

Even once capacity for a particular decision is lost, the MCA continues to respect the value of autonomy in many ways. Every practicable attempt should be made to support the attainment of capacity[26]. Any decision that can reasonably be deferred until capacity is recovered should be so.[27] And in making a best interests decision, P should not only be permitted but encouraged to participate as fully as possible[28] and appropriate weight

26 MCA s1(3).

27 MCA s4(3).

28 MCA s4(4).

must be given to P's past and present wishes and feelings and his beliefs and values.[29]

I have seen cases in which a note has been made: "if Bob has capacity, ask him what he wants". No! Ask him anyway! What he wants does not stop mattering, even if he does now lack capacity to make the decision for himself.

Mr Justice Peter Jackson put it more eloquently:[30]

> *"As the Act and the European Convention [of Human Rights] make clear, a conclusion that a person lacks decision-making capacity is not an 'off-switch' for his rights and freedoms. To state the obvious, the wishes and feelings, beliefs and values of people with a mental disability are as important to them as they are to anyone else, and may even be more important. It would therefore be wrong in principle to apply any automatic discount to their point of view".*

That case, *Wye Valley NHS Trust v B*, is a prime example of the court's approach to best interests decisions, the individuality of the patient and respect for their wishes, even in incapacity.

The facts were reminiscent of *Re C*, mentioned at the start of Chapter 4. In this case, Mr B was a 73 year-old with a long history of mental illness, diagnosed as paranoid schizophrenia, and poorly controlled type 2 diabetes, for which he had typically bounced between acute hospitals who struggled to deal with his mental health and mental health admissions which could not readily meet his physical health needs. For many years he had heard auditory hallucinations of the voices of angels directing his (non)compliance ("*If the Lord says it's no, it's no.*") and of the Virgin Mary, who was persuading him to become a Catholic (although, in a line

29 MCA s4(6).

30 Wye Valley NHS Trust v B [2015] EWCOP 60. https://www.bailii.org/ew/cases/EWCOP/2015/60.html

I love, he declined to join any organised religion because, he said, "*I'm not fussy*").

A chronic foot ulcer developed and became infected, for which he refused treatment other than allowing his dressings to be changed. When his bone was infected the treating trust applied to court. The medical evidence was that without an amputation his infection would be fatal within days, but with successful amputation he would be expected to live for another 3 years.

Mr Justice Jackson found that Mr B lacked the capacity for the decision about the treatment, and so had a best interests decision to make. The judge went to meet him, and recorded that Mr B told him ("with great seriousness"):

> *"I don't want an operation.*
>
> *I'm not afraid of dying, I know where I'm going. The angels have told me I am going to heaven. I have no regrets. It would be a better life than this.*
>
> *I don't want to go into a nursing home, [my partner] died there.*
>
> *I don't want my leg tampered with. I know the seriousness, I just want them to continue what they're doing.*
>
> *I don't want it. I'm not afraid of death. I don't want interference. Even if I'm going to die, I don't want the operation."*

The trust argued that little weight should be given to Mr B's wishes because he lacked capacity, which the judge accepted only to the extent that, of course, his wishes would have been entirely decisive if he had capacity. The judge declined to disregard the religious aspects of Mr B's beliefs, saying that they were

> *"...an inextricable part of the person that he is. In this situation, I do not find it helpful to see the person as if he were a person in good health*

who has been afflicted by illness. It is more real and more respectful to recognise him for who he is: a person with his own intrinsic beliefs and values. It is no more meaningful to think of Mr B without his illnesses and idiosyncratic beliefs than it is to speak of an unmusical Mozart.[31]"

The Judge concluded, poignantly and eloquently, in a passage I respectfully quote in full:

> 42 *"Having considered all of the evidence and the parties' submissions, I have reached the clear conclusion that an enforced amputation would not be in Mr B's best interests.*
>
> 43 *Mr B has had a hard life. Through no fault of his own, he has suffered in his mental health for half a century. He is a sociable man who has experienced repeated losses so that he has become isolated. He has no next of kin.*[32] *No one has ever visited him in hospital and no one ever will. Yet he is a proud man who sees no reason to prefer the views of others to his own. His religious beliefs are deeply meaningful to him and do not deserve to be described as delusions: they are his faith and they are an intrinsic part of who he is. I would not define Mr B by reference to his mental illness or his religious beliefs. Rather, his core quality is his "fierce independence", and it is this that is now, as he sees it, under attack.*
>
> 44 *Mr B is on any view in the later stages of his life. His fortitude in the face of death, however he has come by it, would be the*

31 But of course case law can often be found pointing the other way on the same issue, for example in *Manchester University NHS Foundation Trust v DE* [2019] EWCOP 19 at para 28. https://www.bailii.org/ew/cases/EWCOP/2019/19.html

32 Used, no doubt, in the lay sense, but this is the one line of this judgment I would, with the greatest respect, quibble with!

envy of many people in better mental health. He has gained the respect of those who are currently nursing him.

45 *I am quite sure that it would not be in Mr B's best interests to take away his little remaining independence and dignity in order to replace it with a future for which he understandably has no appetite and which could only be achieved after a traumatic and uncertain struggle that he and no one else would have to endure. There is a difference between fighting on someone's behalf and just fighting them. Enforcing treatment in this case would surely be the latter.*

46 *The application, which was rightly brought,*[33] *is accordingly dismissed".*

I find this a very powerful and moving account of the weight to be put on Mr B's autonomy notwithstanding his lack of capacity to make the decision for himself.

There are also some practicalities underneath this as well, of course. In reality, the prize here was another 3 years of life, which was attainable only with a good recovery and full co-operation with rehabilitation. With an unwilling and uncooperative patient, we may need to accept that the real benefits sought are often much smaller or less likely, or both, and this must be taken into account in a real-world view of the best interests of this patient, including how compliant he will be. If ever greater coercion is to be required to deliver treatment, where that's even feasible, of course that must be factored into whether that is still in P's best interests.

In the *Barnsley* case, mentioned above in the context of ADRT[34], a man in his thirties was refusing lifesaving treatment, and though he was

33 This is worth noting. Though he rejected the trust's arguments that the amputation was in B's best interests, the judge said it was absolutely the right thing to do to bring it to court for a decision.

34 See footnote 3 in this chapter.

assessed as lacking capacity to make that decision for himself, the court put a great deal of weight on his (incapacitous) wishes and autonomy. In the words of Hayden J:

> *"He has made a practical, utilitarian calculation that life in these circumstances is not what he wants. In a real sense this is not a case about choosing to die, it is about an adult's capacity to shape and control the end of his life.* ***<u>This is an important facet of personal autonomy which requires to be guarded every bit as jealously for the incapacitous as for the capacitous</u>****" (emphasis added).*

<u>P's wishes</u>

It is tempting to look at the recent trend of the case law, then, and conclude that the "best interests" test is in fact coming ever closer to a "substituted judgement" test where P's wishes are effectively decisive[35]. There are certainly a number of those cases, and of course it is in keeping with our general social and cultural movement towards putting ever greater value on autonomy. And, as I have said, the further we are going away from what someone wants, the greater the justification may be required, and – in very practical terms – the greater the coercion may be needed to make it happen, which can itself then shift the balance of best interests.

But there are still plenty of cases in which a medical treatment decision is made, in the face of P's indifference or opposition, to impose treatment, including being brought into hospital coercively if need be, in P's best interests[36].

---

35 Again, see the *Barnsley* case at footnote 3.

36 E.g. *NHS Foundation Trust v QZ* [2017] EWCOP 11. https://www.bailii.org/ew/cases/EWCOP/2017/11.html

For all the weight and prominence properly given to them in many recent judgments, there is no precedence accorded to P's wishes, and indeed no hierarchy at all, in the list of factors set out in MCA s4.[37]

And the concept of respecting P's own wishes can itself become a bit slippery. For instance, the Act refers to P's "past and present wishes" but gives no guidance how to balance or prioritise. When they are not in line, should more weight be given to Bob's views prior to the loss of capacity, or his views now? Is our respect for autonomy owed more to the Bob who would have said "yes" before his accident, or to the Bob who is saying "no" now? What about the elderly man, a lifelong ethical vegetarian who, post-stroke, now says that he wants a bacon sandwich? What about the young woman who had planned a termination of pregnancy, thwarted only by a car accident from which she is slowly recovering, who now, at the legal deadline for a termination, says she wants to keep the baby, though she's not yet regained the capacity to make that decision?

And if we reach a view that our priority is toward the views of the person before they lost capacity, how can we make any sense of that for someone with a lifelong learning disability, for example, rather than capacity having been had and lost e.g. by an acquired brain injury or dementia? Can we conjure up the person's views absent their learning disability, any more readily than we can imagine "an unmusical Mozart"?

Putting the appropriate weight on P's own wishes, feelings, values and beliefs can be easier said than done. But there is no excuse for not trying to do this, or for failing to get all the help we reasonably can from those who know P best.

A very recent example illustrates this well in a relatively rare case of a Trust's application to withdraw treatment being refused by a judge

37 Though in 2017 the Law Commission did propose a reform to MCA to that effect, https://s3-eu-west-2.amazonaws.com/lawcom-prod-storage-11jsxou24uy7q/uploads/2017/03/lc372_mental_capacity.pdf recommendation 40, at para 14.2 onwards

(clearly the clinicians must have told the court that they were willing to continue the treatment, though their own view was that it was not in his best interests, allowing themselves to be overruled by the court taking a view on best interests. The ongoing treatment must be an available option for this decision to be possible – see Chapter 2).

In this case,[38] decided on 14 May 2025, the question was about continuation of NG feeding for a 73 year-old man, described as a beloved family man and a devout Muslim.

A jointly instructed expert explained PK's current situation and treatment was burdensome to him:

> "*[Removal of the NG tube] in no way is a clinical act to hasten his death. It is about not prescribing a current treatment that has ceased to be of benefit.*"

He concludes that the NG tube trial has come to an end as it is futile in reversing any of PK's "*unrelenting and underlying conditions*".

The family opposed the withdrawal of this treatment, and said that it would be firmly against PK's own wishes – he felt strongly that "*only God decides when you die*". PK "*definitely smiled*" when his favourite football team (Arsenal) was mentioned.[39]

The Official Solicitor, representing PK, supported the family in opposing the Trust's application:

> "*He has awareness and interacts. She emphasises his past wishes that life be extended and that he receive all treatment. ...She identified the magnetic factor as PK's religious beliefs.*"

38 University College London Hospital NHS FT v PK [2025] EWCOP 17 (T3) – https://www.bailii.org/ew/cases/EWCOP/2025/17.html

39 I definitely smiled too, as it's my team as well.

The judge agreed.

Without evidence on PK's present wishes, much weight should be put on his past wishes. The weight to be put on those views should not be diluted because the patient did not (and could not!) anticipate the exact circumstances he would later be in.

PK's beliefs and values are deeply rooted in his family and his faith.

The judge concludes:

> *"I accept the clinical evidence there will, in all likelihood, be no improvement from the October 2024 stroke, but it does not follow from that, that his treatment is futile.*
>
> *I have not overlooked the fact that my conclusions depart from the evidence of the two experienced clinical witnesses. However, as is clear from the case law, whilst I must consider the expert and clinical evidence, the best interests decision is mine alone.* ***I depart from the expert because I place greater weight on PK's past and present wishes, feeling, beliefs and values than the expert does.*** *I do not find the treatment futile. Its burdens do not (yet) outweigh the benefits I have identified above.*
>
> *...many patients would rather quickly and quietly slip away from a life of artificial hydration and nutrition when bed bound, particularly in circumstances when they are both non verbal and subject to a nil by mouth regime. However, Aintree makes clear that the court's assessment of best interests is rooted in a best interests analysis from the perspective of the particular patient in their particular circumstances. I therefore conclude that it is in the best interests of this devout Muslim, family man, who is often conscious and in limited pain, and who enjoys his family, to continue to receive CANH through his NG tube". (emphasis added).*

The "best interests" test is not explicitly the same as a substituted judgment – ie what P would decide for himself if he could, and there are other broader factors to take into account. And it is important to remember that there is a prior question whether the thing that P did or would want is actually on offer from the clinicians (see Chapter 2 – eg the case of AVS). But subject to that, the courts do seem to be putting ever more weight on the question of P's own wishes and feelings, values and beliefs in their approach to best interests decision making, in delivering the "empowering ethos" of the MCA, and respecting the importance of autonomy.

The further we propose to go from what P would have wanted (or does want) for themselves, the greater the burden there is to justify it.

Deception / covert medication

One distinct issue worth picking out is the question of the use of deception to treat a patient, including to secure their conveyance into hospital, or to have particular treatment.

Bearing in mind the obligation to encourage P to participate in any best interests decision-making, the starting point is that it should be exceptional, and require distinct justification, for there to be deception of a patient, even if they lack capacity for the decision for themselves. It is also an obstacle to involving P fully in the court process as well, if it comes to that, if she is not to be given the chance to express her views to the Official Solicitor as her litigation friend and/or perhaps directly to the judge.

But there are cases where it is not in P's best interests to be told about the court process or the best interests decision-making, where it would be likely to increase non-compliance and therefore the degree of coercion, and associated distress, for example.

In *University Hospitals of Derby and Burton NHS Trust v J*[40], the plan was for a trusted GP to give a sedative to a young woman with a learning disability, in place of her routine medication she was expecting, to enable her to be brought into hospital for a proposed therapeutic hysterectomy, to reduce her unbearable pain and distress from menstruation. Recognising that the plan involved a degree of deception, Mr Justice Williams said:

> *"It is a fact of the proposed care plan that it will involve an element of deception of Anne. In NHS Trust v K and Ors [2012] EWCOP 2922; Re AB [2016] EWCOP 66; Re P [2018] EWCOP 10 and NHS Trust (1) and (2) v FG [2014] EWCOP 30 the court has confirmed that this is compliant with the individual's Article 8*[41] *rights provided the best interests exercise has been carried out. It seems to me that if it is in P's best interests for deception or misrepresentation to take place then the court would be obliged to authorise that. The question of the level of deception would no doubt feed into the evaluation of whether the best interests of P were met by the plan which involved that deception; the greater the deception the more it might potentially weigh against P's best interest and vice versa, but as a matter of principle it seems to me that deception cannot be a bar to authorisation of a procedure. To hold otherwise would be to supplant the best interests of P by some other principle, perhaps of public policy, that the court should not condone white lies".*

The best interests test remains paramount, though the degree of deception must be factored in and recognised as in itself a compromise

40 [2019] EWCOP 16. https://www.bailii.org/ew/cases/EWCOP/2019/16.html

41 Article 8 of the European Convention of Human Rights is the right to private and family life.

of P's autonomy, described by Mr Justice Hayden in another case as "a different and more subtle form of coercion".[42]

It is a separate, and higher, test whether something is in P's best interests even with deception, than whether it would be in P's best interests anyway. In the context of giving covert medication, the question is not just whether the particular drug is in P's best interests, but whether it is still in their best interests *even if it has to be administered covertly with the greater interference in the person's autonomy which that involves.*

There is, then, a perfectly rational basis for giving medication to someone who lacks capacity for the decision about it when they accept it, but not forcing it on them, or giving it covertly, when they refuse. However, if that is the thinking, it should be considered and recorded clearly as a piece of best interests decision-making, and not simply noted that "meds refused", as if implying that the patient was assessed as having capacity to refuse, and no alternative was possible.

In the case of *AG*[43] in 2016, District Judge Bellamy gave very useful general guidance on the use of covert medication, in the context of a challenge to a "standard authorisation" under the Deprivation of Liberty Safeguards:[44]

a) "Where there is a covert medication policy in place or indeed anything similar there must be full consultation with healthcare professionals and family.

b) The existence of such treatment must be clearly identified within the assessment and authorisation.

---

42 *Sherwood Forest Hospitals V H* [2020] EWCOP 5. https://www.bailii.org/ew/cases/EWCOP/2020/5.html

43 *AG v BMBC* [2016] EWCOP 37. https://www.bailii.org/ew/cases/EWCOP/2016/37.html

44 I'll explain about deprivation of liberty next.

c) If the standard authorisation is to be for a period of longer than six months there should be a clear provision for regular, possibly monthly, reviews of the care and support plan.

d) There should at regular intervals be review involving family and healthcare professionals, all the more so if the standard [Deprivation of Liberty Safeguards] authorisation is to be for the maximum twelve-month period.

e) Each case must be determined on its facts but I cannot see that it would be sensible for there to be an absolute policy that, in circumstances similar to this, standard authorisation should be limited to six months. It may be perfectly practical and proportionate provided there is a provision for reviews (or conditions attached) for the standard authorisation to be for the maximum period.

f) Where appointed an RPR [relevant person's representative for the DoLS process] should be fully involved in those discussions and review so that if appropriate an application for part 8 review can be made.

g) Any change of medication or treatment regime should also trigger a review where such medication is covertly administered.

h) Such matters can be achieved by placing appropriate conditions to which the standard authorisation is subject and would of course accord with chapter 8 of the Deprivation of Liberty Safeguards' code of practice".

In May 2024, these issues came before the Court of Appeal, in a case called Re A (Covert medication: Residence)[45], in which a local authority and the Official Solicitor appealed against earlier findings by Poole J that

45 [EWCA] Civ 572, https://www.judiciary.uk/judgments/re-a-covert-medication-residence/

covert medication should be stopped for A (a 25 year-old woman who lacks capacity to make decisions about her care, contact, residence and medical treatment), that she should be told about it, and that she should return to live with her mother. The Court of Appeal upheld Poole J's decision, commenting in passing on A's strong personality, as shown in her "very clear and colourful language". As an example, the judgment directly quotes her own solicitor's note of meeting A including this memorable exchange:

> *Solicitor: "Is there anything else you would like to tell the court?"*
>
> *A: "Just fucking cork it".*

Though the Court of Appeal declined to give any more general guidance on the issue of covert medication, it was clear that they agreed with Poole J that this was a complex issue, and a serious interference with A's autonomy. They also made some very helpful remarks about the role of the Court of Protection, and the proper aspirations of best interests decision making in challenging real-world scenarios:

> *"The statutory term "best interests" has an inherent optimism, but there are cases where every option is problematic and even the best outcome is troubling."*

Peter Jackson LJ (in the Court of Appeal by now) said that the court is entitled to make its own decision about A's best interests (among the actual, available options of course), and is not limited only to choosing among one of the arguments proposed by the parties.

In doing so, making a best interests decision calls for a sensible decision, "not the pursuit of perfection". Here, the aim was to "select the best practical outcome that was realistically available, even though all options were, to say the least, imperfect. It was beyond [the court's] powers to eliminate risk or make A's many problems go away".

Proportionality, restraint and deprivation of liberty?

This may, then, be a useful point to digress a little into deprivation of liberty, though typically this topic generates more heat than light.[46]

To my mind, it is best understood as all about *proportionality, appropriate scrutiny* and *due process.*

As I have said, MCA s5 protects clinicians who reasonably believe that a patient lacks capacity for a particular decision and who take a decision reasonably believing it to be in their best interests. But this only goes so far.

If what you intend to do amounts to restraint.[47] then you need more justification, given the greater degree of interference in the person's life, however well intentioned. So the law requires not just the s5 criteria, but in addition (s6) that the step is *necessary to prevent harm and is proportionate to the likelihood and seriousness of that harm*.

And as you go further down the continuum of degree of interference in someone's life, beyond restraint and into something that amounts to a "deprivation of their liberty" (DoL) you need a greater level of protection still. This is done in two ways: (1) a higher level of justification for the interference to be permitted, and (2) a more robust process of scrutiny to ensure that any such power to interfere is being exercised properly.

Pausing here, we should recognise that the continuum of increasing degrees of interference in someone's life is, well, continuous, and though it is necessary for the purpose of triggering a step change in the legal safeguards to have a line drawn between mere "restraint" and "DoL", this

46 See A Practical Guide to the Law of Deprivation of Liberty (2024), Ben Troke, Law Brief Publishing.

47 MCA s6 clarifies that you are restraining P if you "(a) use, or threaten to use, force to secure the doing of an act which P resists, or (b) restrict P's liberty of movement, whether or not P resists."

is inevitably a little arbitrary and subjective. It is best not to get too hung up on this, and to focus instead on the underlying, fundamental principles of the MCA, though it must be said that the current state of the legal framework and case law on DoL does us few favours.

In brief, the need for greater safeguards when an intervention amounts to a DoL derives from the individual's rights under Article 5 of the European Convention of Human Rights (the right to liberty). But it is not an unqualified right, and it can lawfully be interfered with if:

- The person is in one of the specific categories (for this context the relevant one is "persons of unsound mind"[48])
- The DoL is in accordance with a due process of law;[49] and
- The person has a right to challenge their DoL, to be speedily decided by a court[50].

So what amounts to a DoL and in particular how is it interpreted in the context of medical treatment?

The leading case on DoL is a Supreme Court judgment from March 2014 ("*Cheshire West*" [51]), in the context of long-term social care placements, which made clear that a DoL arises when:

1. the person lacks capacity to consent[52] to arrangements for their care and residence

48 ECHR Article 5(1)(e).

49 ECHR Article 5(1).

50 ECHR Article 5(4).

51 [2014] UKSC 19.

52 If the patient has capacity and consents, then no question of a DoL arises.

2 those arrangements are "imputable" to the state[53] (i.e. the state has some responsibility for them), and

3 they amount to the person being under "continuous supervision and control" and "not free to leave".[54]

An example might be someone with dementia being placed in a care home in their best interests ("free to leave" refers to being able to decide to go and live somewhere else, not to just go out to a day centre or a shop); or in a long-term inpatient rehabilitation scenario, especially if the discharge home is being delayed. If that is the case, even if the arrangement is perfectly appropriate and in the best interests of someone who cannot decide for themselves, and even if they are passively compliant not actively resisting, there must be a legal process to authorise this to meet the person's Article 5 rights. It is, simply, a matter of proportionality, appropriate scrutiny and due process.

Where a DoL arises in a hospital or care home, there is an administrative scheme available to fulfil the "due process of law" requirement – the

---

53 Any intervention being carried out by a public body such as the NHS or a local authority will certainly meet this element. In fact, the search for a case where the DoL is not imputable to the state has been pretty fruitless so far, given the state's role as regulator of health and social care provision and, ultimately, through the role of the court, even if not the provider or commissioning for a particular patient. See *SRK v Staffordshire County Council* [2016] EWCOP 27. http://www.bailii.org/ew/cases/EWCOP/2016/27.html

54 This part is described as the *Cheshire West* "acid test" which broadened our understanding of what a DoL is, and caught many thousands more people than had previously been recognised to be DoL. The Court of Appeal judgment saying that care that was appropriate for P was no DoL was overturned, and instead it was recognised that perfectly appropriate care can be a DoL, but it just needs due process and scrutiny to comply with Article 5 ECHR and protect P's rights.

Deprivation of Liberty Safeguards ("DoLS"[55]), together with a right of appeal to the Court of Protection.[56] If the proposed deprivation of liberty falls outside the scope of DoLS, for example because the deprivation will be in the patient's own home (DoLS only applies in hospitals and care homes), then it can only be authorised by the court.[57]

When DoLS was introduced the MCA was amended to reflect this, and s4A and 4B of the MCA now state that the MCA does not authorise anyone to be deprived of their liberty, unless under a DoLS authorisation, or by an order of the Court of Protection, or in an emergency to provide life sustaining treatment or a perform a vital act *while seeking a decision from the court.*

While this is not the place for a full account of this especially thorny topic, note that DoLS was due to be replaced entirely by a new statutory scheme (the Liberty Protection Safeguards – "LPS"). This is already on the statute book in outline,[58] and there has been a consultation on a draft Code of Practice to deal with this, as well as updating the MCA Code of Practice more generally. But at the time of writing we still await any indication of a date for implementation, which has already been set (and

---

55 Schedules A1 and 1A to the MCA 2005, added to the MCA, with effect from April 2009, by the Mental Health Act 2007. In a nutshell, care homes and hospitals can apply to the local authority for a DoLS "standard authorisation" which can, after appropriate assessments, authorise a DoL for a patient in their care for up to 12 months.

56 MCA s21A.

57 I am sorry this is confusing. It doesn't help that these court orders are often then, casually and misleadingly, referred to as "DoLS" orders – I suppose as the plural of DoL – but strictly DoL*S* is the Safeguards which apply to care homes and hospitals only, and a DoL elsewhere requiring court approval might better be described as a "DoL in the community", for example. See http://www.lawbriefpublishing.com/product/deprivationofliberty/

58 Mental Capacity (Amendment) Act 2019. http://www.legislation.gov.uk/ukpga/2019/18/enacted/data.htm

abandoned) as October 2020, and then April 2022.[59] At the time of writing there is no sign whether LPS will be brought into force at all, never mind when, and the chaos that is the legal system regulating deprivation of liberty will have to be navigated without this reform for the foreseeable future, since implementation is likely to take a number of years. For now, we have to deal with the problems in this area with the tools that we already have.

If implemented, LPS would make significant changes and in particular, as regards medical treatment, will amend MCA s4B dealing with provision of life-sustaining treatment or a vital act.[60] It appears to say that this would be authorised by the legislation itself, without needing to trouble the LPS scheme or the courts, but a lot of detail about how it would work in practice is awaited.

Helpfully though, for NHS bodies, in the meantime the trend of case law has recently been to regard medical treatment as not in itself being a deprivation of a person's liberty anyway, as long as it is physical healthcare treatment of the same kind that any patient would receive.[61] In *Ferreira*, the Court of Appeal held that a woman who had died in intensive care at King's College Hospital London was not being deprived of her liberty. The significance of this was that it would have meant – under the law as it was then, since changed – that the inquest into her death would have had to be held with a jury, as the family wanted. Lady Justice Arden held that provision of life-saving medical treatment does not warrant the same degree of scrutiny and protection of a patient's right to liberty as would a decision about longer term residence or care, and so

---

59 https://www.parliament.uk/business/publications/written-questions-answers-statements/written-statement/Commons/2020-07-16/HCWS377/

60 The amended legislation, not yet in force, is here https://www.legislation.gov.uk/ukpga/2005/9/section/4B/2019-05-16.

61 *Ferreira v Coroner of Inner South London* [2017] EWCA Civ 31. http://www.bailii.org/ew/cases/EWCA/Civ/2017/31.html

provision of such treatment need not engage Article 5 safeguards in the same way.

A few months later in *Briggs* in the Court of Appeal,[62] Lady justice King said

> *"In my view, Ferreira confirms what I myself would regard as an obvious point, namely that the question of deprivation of liberty does not arise where a person who lacks capacity is so unwell that they are at risk of dying if they were anywhere other than in hospital and therefore, by virtue of their physical condition, they are unable to leave the hospital. It may be the case however that as the treatment progresses and P's physical condition improves, his or her ongoing care becomes a deprivation of liberty and, at that stage, a standard authorisation [i.e. DoLS] or court order will be required if the continued retention of P on the ward is not to become unlawful".*

Back before the Supreme Court in 2019 in the case of *Re D* (mainly concerned with the possibility of consent being given by someone with parental responsibility to stop any restrictions on a child being considered a deprivation of their liberty, especially once the child is older than 16), Lady Arden (who had been in the Court of Appeal in *Ferreira*) explained the case like this:

> "… there will be cases where a person loses their liberty but the acid test in *Cheshire West*, as Lady Hale describes it, does not apply. That conclusion is shown by observing that D's case is about living arrangements. It is not about a child, or anyone else, needing life-saving emergency medical treatment. For the reasons which the Court of Appeal (McFarlane LJ, Sir Ross Cranston and myself) gave in *R (Ferreira) v Inner South London Senior Coroner* [2018] QB 487, the situation where a person is taken into (in that case) an intensive care unit for the purpose of life-saving treatment and

62 *Director of Legal Aid Casework & Ors v Briggs* [2017] EWCA Civ 1169, at para 106. http://www.bailii.org/ew/cases/EWCA/Civ/2017/1169.html

> is unable to give their consent to their consequent loss of liberty, does not result in a deprivation of liberty for article 5 purposes so long as the loss of liberty is due to the need to provide care for them on an urgent basis because of their serious medical condition, is necessary and unavoidable, and results from circumstances beyond the state's control."

The cases do still emphasise that if distinct, restrictive conditions above and beyond the treatment anyone would get are imposed to deliver physical healthcare, however essential, as a result of the patient's mental incapacity, then this can still be regarded as a deprivation of liberty that needs authorisation.[63]

Where we now draw the "*Ferreria* line" to identify how far the exception to the *Cheshire West* acid test reaches, and when a deprivation of liberty may still arise in an acute hospital is a difficult question, and more than we can tackle here. I commend to you the guidance published on this by the Law Society in 2024.[64] On balance, though, the issue of DoL in this context is likely to arise mostly in the context of treatment which in itself may well need authorisation by the court anyway. For example, if someone is to be brought into hospital using sedation or restraint against their wishes, for the purpose of investigations or treatment in their best interests when they cannot make the relevant decisions for themselves, then the whole care plan is likely to need to be considered by the court, which will include authorisation of any DoL that is involved.

If anything, the issue of deprivation of liberty arises more often now in the hospital setting for people who are not there to receive medical treatment at all. Tragically, all too often we see children and young

63 *NHS Trust v FG* [2014] EWCOP 30. http://www.bailii.org/ew/cases/EWCOP/2014/30.html

64 https://www.lawsociety.org.uk/topics/private-client/deprivation-of-liberty-safeguards-a-practical-guide see Chapter 5, on which – full disclosure – I was the lead author, in my role as a member of the Law Society's Mental Health and Disability Committee.

people brought into hospital when a care package breaks down, perhaps after some self-harm, or as a result of apparent mental health problems, and then having to be held there long past any need for inpatient medical treatment, sometimes with very high levels of restraint, and causing disruption to entire wards as a result of their behaviour, while the local authority with their care struggles to find a suitable placement for them. In such cases, we are often before a High Court judge asking for authorisation of a DoL for that child, on behalf of the hospital, where there is no argument that the *Ferreira* exception for life saving medical treatment applies, as there is no medical need to be in hospital at all.

As I said, and as you can see from the density of the footnotes in this bit, more heat than light is generated by the law around DoL just now. But by and large, do not allow concern about the issue of DoL to detract from provision of appropriate treatment, or distract the focus from the fundamentals of the MCA, which is where things have typically gone awry in such cases. Again, the focus should be first and foremost on provision of the appropriate treatment, and we would much rather explain ourselves to a judge than to a coroner, as this guidance for intensive care clinicians making decisions out of hours ("Midnight Law") sets out.[65]

Get the MCA stuff right, and the DoL issues will usually follow. And it seems likely that, if implemented, the LPS will continue the trend already seen in the case law to further reduce the emphasis on DoL as an issue in the context of acute provision of medical treatment.

65 https://ficm.ac.uk/new-midnight-law-on-deprivation-of-liberty-in-intensive-care – and, again, full disclosure: I was a joint author of this, in my role as a member of the Faculty of Intensive Care Medicine's Law and Ethics Policy Unit.

Life and death

For the sake of completeness, though the answer is self-evident by now, can it ever be in P's best interests for life sustaining treatment to be refused, withheld or withdrawn?

Yes, obviously (at least in law; ethics may be another, more individual, matter).

As a result of an amendment demanded by those concerned that the new legislation should not provide a back door to euthanasia, as they saw it, the MCA s4(5) says that "*Where the determination relates to life-sustaining treatment he must not, in considering whether the treatment is in the best interests of the person concerned, be motivated by a desire to bring about his death*"

Of course, a "desire to bring about death" is not what is in mind when the balance of an incapacitous patient's best interests is against life-sustaining treatment at all costs.

The landmark case here is Tony Bland,[66] the young Liverpool fan who was among the last of the 97 victims of the Hillsborough disaster on 15 April 1989 because he was sustained in a persistent vegetative state (PVS) for several years afterwards until the hospital successfully brought a case to court for authority to withdraw that treatment and allow him to die.[67]

In February 1993, the House of Lords allowed the application, life-sustaining treatment was removed, and Tony Bland died on 3 March

66 *Airedale NHS Trust v Bland* [1993] AC 789. http://www.bailii.org/uk/cases/UKHL/1993/17.html

67 For a powerful account of her own experience of a family going through this tragic process, I strongly recommend Cathy Retzenbrink's "The Last Act of Love".

1993, nearly 4 years after he went to an FA Cup semi-final in Sheffield and never came home.

This was the first time that the highest courts in England had dealt with a case of withdrawal of life-sustaining treatment from a patient in a PVS, and the judges wrestled with the question of how absolutely we should treat the principle of the sanctity of life. (See Chapter 7 on whether all such cases still need to go to court (they don't)).

As Lord Browne-Wilkinson said[68], the questions for us are questions of law, but "behind the questions of law lie moral, ethical, medical and practical issues of fundamental importance to society."

A crucial distinction was drawn between an act and an omission. Taking positive steps to end someone's life raises questions of criminal as well as civil liability.[69] But an omission is different. There can be no liability for a failure to provide treatment where there is no right to do so. The lawfulness of treatment depends on the patient's consent or, for a patient who lacks capacity to consent, the treatment being in the patient's best interests.

> *"… the correct answer to the present case depends upon the extent of the right to continue lawfully to invade the bodily integrity of Anthony Bland without his consent. If in the circumstances they have no right to continue artificial feeding, they cannot be in breach of any duty by ceasing to provide such feeding".*[70]

> *"the question is not whether it is in the best interests of the patient that he should die. The question is whether it is in the best interests of the*

68 At page 877.

69 Subject to potential changes to the law to allow assisted dying, which is going through parliament at the time of writing but – with a proposed timeline to implementation in 2029 if it does pass – can be covered in a Third Edition if need be!

70 Per Lord Browne-Wilkinson at p883.

> *patient that his life should be prolonged by the continuance of this form of treatment".*[71]

Setting aside the value of the sanctity of life in itself, the sad truth was that Tony Bland himself had no meaningful interests in his ongoing existence in a PVS. He had no consciousness and no prospect of recovery. Treatment was futile as it could not possibly achieve any benefit. Lord Goff said "it is the futility of the treatment which justifies its termination".[72]

If his best interests cannot justify ongoing treatment where, done without his consent, it would be unlawful, then there is no justification at all. Going further, it is not only lawful but mandatory for treatment to be withdrawn, as continuation would constitute an assault.

Given the sanctity of life, there is, of course, a strong presumption in favour of the preservation of life[73], but this does not displace the best interests test as the paramount consideration for a patient who cannot decide for themselves.

The MCA code of practice says:

> *5.31 All reasonable steps which are in the person's best interests should be taken to prolong their life. There will be a limited number of cases where treatment is futile, overly burdensome to the patient or where there is no prospect of recovery. In circumstances such as these, it may be that an assessment of best interests leads to the conclusion that it would be in the best interests of the patient to withdraw or withhold life-sustaining treatment, even if this may result in the person's death.*

---

71 Lord Goff (with whose judgment Lord Keith and Lord Lowry expressly agreed) at p 868.

72 At p869.

73 See for example *Re M* [2011] EWHC 2443 (Fam). https://www.bailii.org/ew/cases/EWHC/Fam/2011/2443.html

The decision-maker must make a decision based on the best interests of a person who lacks capacity. They must not be motivated by a desire to bring about the person's death for whatever reason, even if this is from a sense of compassion. Healthcare and social care staff should also refer to relevant professional guidance when making decisions regarding life-sustaining treatment.

5.32 As with all decisions, before deciding to withdraw or withhold life-sustaining treatment, the decision-maker must consider the range of treatment options available to work out what would be in the person's best interests. All the factors in the best interests checklist should be considered, and in particular, the decision-maker should consider any statements that the person has previously made about their wishes and feelings about life-sustaining treatment.

5.33 Importantly, section 4(5)[74] *cannot be interpreted to mean that doctors are under an obligation to provide, or to continue to provide, life-sustaining treatment where that treatment is not in the best interests of the person, even where the person's death is foreseen. Doctors must apply the best interests checklist and use their professional skills to decide whether life-sustaining treatment is in the person's best interests. If the doctor's assessment is disputed, and there is no other way of resolving the dispute, ultimately the Court of Protection may be asked to decide what is in the person's best interests."*

The court has at times gone further and agreed it would be in the best interests of a patient in a minimally conscious state[75] (MCS, as opposed to a PVS, though to a layman such as myself the distinction can seem a little blurry) to discontinue attempts to maintain CANH[76]. And a

74 The provision mentioned above that a best interests decision must not be motivated by a desire to bring about death.

75 *United Lincolnshire Hospitals NHS Trust v N* [2014] EWCOP 16. https://www.bailii.org/ew/cases/EWCOP/2014/16.html

76 Clinically assisted nutrition and hydration.

prolonged disorder of consciousness ("PDOC", a blanket term including PVS and MCS) is not a prerequisite for withholding or withdrawal of life-sustaining treatment to be in a patient's best interests.

A little over 20 years on from *Bland*, in 2013 the issue of end of life medical treatment returned to the highest court in England, in its new guise as the Supreme Court, in the first case about the MCA it had considered: *Aintree University Hospitals NHS Foundation Trust v James.*[77]

David James was 68 years old when he was admitted to hospital in May 2012 for a problem with his stoma,[78] which had been fitted when he survived colon cancer more than a decade earlier. The stoma was quickly fixed, but he acquired an infection which led to serious complications and Mr James ended up in Intensive Care, dependent on artificial ventilation and CANH through a tube directly into his stomach. As described by Lady Hale, he:

> *"… suffered from gross muscle wasting, owing to his prolonged period of near immobility, so could not sit or stand for himself. He also suffered from contractures, similar to very severe cramps, causing grimacing, raised pulse, breathing and blood pressure, indicating distress and pain. He had suffered a stroke, with severe neurological damage. He was completely dependent on artificial ventilation and required regular tube suction. His kidney function was extremely fragile, with a maximum function of 20% or so, although he had not so far required renal therapy. It was almost inevitable that he would face further infections leading to lowered blood pressure and the prospect of further multiorgan failure. Daily care tasks could cause*

77 [2013] UKSC 67. https://www.supremecourt.uk/cases/docs/uksc-2013-0134-judgment.pdf

78 A surgical connection between the bowel and the surface of the stomach to allow bowel contents to empty into an external bag.

> *discomfort, pain and suffering. Overall, his prospects of leaving the critical care unit, let alone the hospital, were extremely low".*[79]

On the other hand, of course, Mr James was more than a collection of complaints and symptoms. A talented guitarist, he had spent more than 50 years in the music business. He had recently celebrated his golden wedding anniversary, and had three children, three grandchildren and many friends, who regularly visited him in hospital. Though diagnosed formally as in a minimally conscious state, the "minimally" could be misleading, the first instance judge had said, and his level of consciousness might better be described as "very limited".

While it was not in dispute that he lacked capacity for decisions about his medical treatment, still it appeared that

> *"... he recognised and was pleased to see his wife and his son when they visited; kissed his wife when she leaned into him; looked at her when she moved round the bed; mouthed what appeared to be words in answer to his wife, Ms Baker and nursing staff; turned the pages of a newspaper, smiling while he did so, although it was not clear to the doctor whether he was actually reading any of the articles or looking at the pictures; put on and took off his glasses while doing so; and appeared to enjoy watching videos on his son's phone".*[80]

The trust applied to court for a declaration that it would be in Mr James' best interests that certain interventions (including CPR) should not be given if he deteriorated further (i.e. a "ceiling of care"), though there was no suggestion that the ongoing treatment already in place such as CANH and ventilation would be withdrawn. The clinicians felt that there was no prospect of success for such treatment, if needed, and it would cause Mr James harm to even try it.

---

79 Paragraph 3.

80 Paragraph 5.

The family opposed this. They argued that he had recovered from infections before, that he still enjoyed seeing family and friends and so had some quality of life worth maintaining, and that he would want to fight on, as he had against his cancer.

On 6 December 2012, Mr Justice Peter Jackson refused the trust's application in the first instance, saying that not enough weight was being given to the "non-medical" factors around his current quality of life. The trust appealed, and though the Court of Appeal heard the case only 15 days later, in that time there was new evidence that Mr James' condition had deteriorated significantly, and it was now difficult even to maintain his ventilation. The Court of Appeal allowed the appeal and granted the declarations sought, saying that treatment would be futile unless it had "*...a real prospect of curing or at least palliating the life-threatening disease or illness from which the patient is suffering*".[81]

Mr James had a cardiac arrest and sadly died in the early hours of 31 December 2012. Despite this, the Supreme Court agreed to hear an appeal on the matters of principle because of the importance of the issues raised, and in particular the crucial question of how "futility" ought to be interpreted in this context.

If you only read one case on medical treatment decisions, this Supreme Court judgment is it[82]; the leading judgment was given by Lady Hale, and it sets out a clear summary of the legal framework and key cases.

Of course, it is possible that treatment might be not "futile" but still not be in a patient's best interests, but Lady Hale felt that the Court of Appeal had set the bar too high for the test of "futility".

81 Sir Alan Ward in the Court of Appeal [2013] EWCA Civ 65 at para 35 https://www.bailii.org/ew/cases/EWCA/Civ/2013/65.html

82 [2013] UKSC 67 – https://supremecourt.uk/cases/uksc-2013-0134

She endorsed the approach of Peter Jackson J at the first instance hearing that futile means "*ineffective or of no benefit to the patient*".[83] It is asking too much to say that treatment is pointless unless it can return a patient to "good health" or "avert the looming prospect of death":

> *"A treatment may bring some benefit to the patient even though it has no effect upon the underlying disease or disability".*[84]

Considering whether a patient has a prospect of recovery, 'recovery' meant the resumption of a quality of life which was *worthwhile for that individual patient*, and:

> *"it is not for others to say that a life which the patient would regard as worthwhile is not worth living".*[85]

The emphasis, plainly, is on the familiar theme of treating the patient as an individual and respecting their autonomy accordingly.

Futility v not in best interests

Futility is an important concept, as it can take options off the table that a patient or their family might want, but it can be a slippery one and easily muddled with ideas about best interests.

To sum up: I tend to think of "futile" as meaning there's *no benefit*, and so no balance or calculation to be done, and no indication for treatment. This is likely to be the clinicians' decision, albeit subject to consultation and if need be challenge (see *Tracey,* in the context of DNACPR, as set out in Chapter 2).

83 At para 40.

84 At para 43.

85 At para 44.

In contrast, something not in best interests is where there is ***no net benefit,*** i.e. there is *some* benefit but it is outweighed by the disadvantages (for this patient as an individual). This is a balancing exercise, and for a patient unable to make their own decision needs a proper process under the MCA, involving others appropriately, and deferring if need be to the Court of Protection's better view on best interests.

As a good acid test, if a clinician would provide the treatment to a patient with capacity, deferring to the patient's own judgement of the price they are willing to pay for the benefit in question, however limited it is likely to be, then they cannot say the treatment is "futile". Any refusal to provide that treatment to a patient who lacks capacity to make that decision for themselves is a best interests decision and should follow a rigorous process to comply with the MCA.

To tease out the difference here, it can be useful to ask a clinician: "if a judge said that [treatment] is in the patient's best interests, would you be willing to do it?". If the answer is "no" it is vital to be clear about this at the outset, to ensure that it is understood by the patient / family and by the court that it is not an option that is "on the table".

You'll appreciate from the discussion of DNACPR decisions, for example, in Chapter 2 that this is an important distinction and is fudged at our peril.

Treating adults as adults

All this, though, has been in the context of adults and we will get on to the situation for children, including some very high-profile disputes, in the next chapter. One final thought, though, before we do.

In the leading case on deprivation of liberty, *Cheshire West*, which I mentioned earlier, a 39 year-old man with cerebral palsy and Down's Syndrome which caused "significant physical and learning disabilities" was accommodated by the local authority in a placement to meet his needs. He lacked capacity to consent to the arrangements, and if it was a deprivation of his liberty it needed court approval, as it was outside the scope of the Deprivation of Liberty Safeguards (as it was not a registered care home). Among the other features of his presentation requiring a very high level of care was his pica (i.e eating things which should not be eaten) and his incontinence, which combined to have him frequently putting his incontinence pads into his mouth. When this happened, the carers would use physical restraint as need be and a "finger sweep" to remove the material from his mouth. Better yet, to prevent this, the carers then adopted a new approach, involving P "wearing an all in one body suit sewn up at the front, to prevent his hands touching his groin area, the only access being via a zip at the back".[86] These were among the features which led Mr Justice Baker, in the first instance hearing to decide that P was deprived of his liberty, albeit that it was proportionate and, he declared, lawful having had the scrutiny of the court.

The reason that I mention this here is that in the Court of Appeal, reversing Baker J's decision, Lord Justice Munby held that it was no deprivation of liberty because P was getting the care that was relatively normal for people with his condition and needs. In particular, he was dismissive of concerns that the "body suit" was anything like a straight-jacket, but instead was "more akin to a child's baby-grow". Likewise, as regards the "finger sweep" of the mouth:

> *"This is obviously intrusive, as Baker J says, but again it has to be looked at in context. It is little different from what any properly attentive parent would do if a young child was chewing or about to swallow something unpleasant or potentially harmful. The only*

86 From the Court of Protection first instance judgment of Mr Justice Baker [2011] EWCOP 1330 at para 10. http://www.bailii.org/ew/cases/EWCOP/2011/1330.html

> *difference is that with an adult like P two people are needed to do what one could manage alone if dealing with a smaller child.*"[87]

This language was ignored by the Supreme Court in overturning the Court of Appeal and restoring Baker J's initial finding that P was deprived of his liberty in that situation, albeit that it was lawful subject to the appropriate scrutiny and authorisation by the court.

But for me the Court of Appeal's language feels significant; infantilising adults who lack capacity; saying that for a 39 year-old man who cannot make some decisions about his care the appropriate point of reference is the way a parent treats a toddler.

The Supreme Court judgment[88] in that case ultimately showed us that it is not right to treat disabled adults as if they were children.

I can imagine, though, that the habits and attitudes that may come to a parent caring for a child with profound care needs for their whole life do not change readily at some arbitrary age, whatever the law provides. So it was, for example in one of the more acrimonious cases in the Court of Protection case law; An ICB v G.[89]

This extraordinary case was described by the judge as "lawfare" between the family and the NHS bodies involved. It should have been centred on the welfare of G, a 29 year-old woman with a profound, degenerative neurological condition. Instead, the proceedings became "a theatre of conflict" and involved extreme and florid allegations made by the family about the care being provided (as "abusive", "negligent" and "torture").

---

87 *Cheshire West* in the Court of Appeal [2011] EWCA Civ 1257 at para 114. http://www.bailii.org/ew/cases/EWCA/Civ/2011/1257.html

88 [2014] UKSC 19. https://www.supremecourt.uk/cases/docs/uksc-2012-0068-judgment.pdf

89 [2024] EWCOP 13. https://www.bailii.org/ew/cases/EWCOP/2024/13.html – see also Chapter 7.

In turn, the ICB had concerns about the family allegedly tampering with equipment (which were upheld by the judge), as well as being abusive to the staff.

This all meant long running, and vastly costly litigation, including a fact-finding hearing in the Court of Protection running over 21 days of court time, and involving 8 barristers including 4 King's Counsel.

The (predictably lengthy) judgment covers some really useful ground, including the family's use of covert recordings, and the need for professionals to be more assertive in challenging the role of the family where decisions were being made counter to G's best interests (see chapter 7).

Most relevant, for these purposes, Hayden J was clear that adults with disabilities should not be infantalised by the courts, and nor by their parents. In making best interests decisions, the judge noted that the family's engagement with G is "in content and tone, that of an adult interacting with either a very small child or a baby… I can understand why G might always be seen as their little girl", but he noted that the staff at her care provider "treat her as a woman in her late 20s".

In the next chapter, we will look at actual children, and how the law around their decision-making (usually) comes over time to treat them as adults.

Key points

- Capacity Part A (**A**ble to make a decision?) must always come before Capacity Part B (**B**est interests, and who decides?)

- A valid Advance Decision to Refuse Treatment (ADRT) can be a binding refusal of treatment in advance; it cannot demand treatment. But setting out your wishes and feelings, values and beliefs is helpful to make sure that these are properly taken into account in any best interests decision.

- Even if not strictly binding, an ADRT might well give enough information about the patient's wishes to make it clear what best interests decision ought to be made.

- If you want to, you can appoint someone to be the best interests decision maker for you, but whoever it is (LPA or the treating clinicians) they are bound by the duties of the MCA, to make a decision in your best interests, in a collaborative and inclusive way, and in particular involving "those engaged in caring for you or interested in your welfare" (not limited to "next of kin"; in law there's no such thing). Doing this properly is more important than the identity of the decision-maker.

- Best interests is about you as an individual. It goes far beyond the narrow best clinical outcome, and includes social and emotional needs, and is not necessarily the path that is safest ("what use is it making someone safer if it only makes them miserable?"). Nor must life be preserved at all costs.

- The Court of Protection can provide the reassurance of an order, and can resolve any dispute.

CHAPTER 6

CHILDREN AND PARENTS

- 16–17 year-olds
- Under 16 – *Gillick* competence
- Parental responsibility
- Case studies and lessons:
    - *Charlotte Wyatt*
    - *Ashya King*
    - *Charlie Gard*
    - *Alfie Evans*
    - *Archie Battersbee*
- The role and approach of the court
- Saying no and changing your mind
- Adult children

In law, as in life, dealing with children can be complex and difficult.

To begin at the beginning, an unborn child has no rights,[1] and termination of pregnancy for reasons of serious fetal abnormality can be performed right up until birth.[2]

So – If an unborn baby is at high risk of being born with HIV (or another infection), but the mother has repeatedly refused testing – should a court order now that the baby should be tested (and treated) as soon as it is born?

This was the dilemma for Mr Justice McKendrick in an urgent application brought on 25 March 2025,[3] when the mother was 38 weeks pregnant.

There was some evidence that her risk of having a blood borne virus (such as HIV, Hepatitis B or syphilis) was much higher than usual, but she had consistently refused testing.

The child had a real risk of being born with such an infection, which could only effectively be helped with treatment that starts within hours of birth. The blood test proposed was simple, and the mother had given "no good reason for the tests not to take place".

The judge said that he had no doubt that "the balance of the rights would come down in favour of the child" and "I am clear this innocuous blood test is essential to the baby when born".

---

1 *Paton v British Pregnancy Advisory Service Trustees* [1979] 1 QB 276. There can, of course, be a claim by the child, after birth, for harm it has negligently suffered in utero.

2 Abortion Act 1967 s1(1)(d). Otherwise the limit is usually 24 weeks.

3 Manchester University NHS Foundation Trust v PP [2025] EWHC 783 (Fam) https://caselaw.nationalarchives.gov.uk/ewhc/fam/2025/783

However (and it is a *big* but)... an unborn baby has no legal identity until it is born. "It is part of the mother's body and does not have independent rights".

The judge held that he could not sidestep this by treating this decision in the same way as the anticipatory declarations that we sometimes see in the Court of Protection ("there is not a read across from a capacitous P to a foetus").

He reaches – "with some regret" – the conclusion that there is no power for the court to make a decision about this until the baby is born.

The foetus having no rights means that there are no rights now to balance against the mother's Article 8 rights to private life.

There are practical concerns as well as principled – the unborn child cannot be a party to these proceedings, is not represented (through a guardian, as a child would be), and could not appeal a decision that would affect it.

The judge ordered that the proceedings should be brought back to him immediately the child was born, and in fact a postscript (dated 27 March 2025) says that he heard the case again within an hour of the birth, and ordered that the blood tests (and, presumably, and treatment indicated) should be given to the baby.

After birth, however, the child has a legal identity and ordinarily gains maturity and legally recognised decision-making ability over time (under the case of *Gillick*, below) while the powers of those with parental responsibility "dwindle". But in most respects[4] the MCA treats them as

4 Exceptions, for example, are that you cannot make an ADRT or appoint an LPA under the MCA until you are 18.

adults from the age of 16,[5] while the Children Act 1989 treats them as children until they are 18,[6] which can cause confusion.

Mental Health Act treatment

Though our focus here is on treatment for physical health, it is worth noting in passing that there is no minimum age limit to the Mental Health Act, if the coercive powers for treatment of a mental disorder are required.

"The Inbetweeners" – age 16–17

The Family Law Reform Act 1969 s8 provided that:

> *"The consent of a minor [i.e. under 18 years] who has attained the age of sixteen years to any surgical, medical or dental treatment which, in the absence of consent, would be a trespass to his person, shall be as effective as it would be if he were of full age; and where a minor has by virtue of this section given an effective consent to any treatment it shall not be necessary to obtain any consent for it from his parent or guardian".*

But it is hard to see what this adds any more now we have the MCA 2005, which presumptively provides 16 year-olds with the autonomy to make their own decision on any issue, and not just to "consent" to these narrow categories of treatment. (There may be, by the way, a difference between the approach the law takes when a 16 year-old *consents* to their proposed treatment, and when she refuses; arguably in the same way as

5 And, strictly, the MCA does also have jurisdiction under 16 if there is a property and finances decision to be made for a child under 16 who is thought to lack capacity to make the decision for themselves and likely to continue to do so past the age of 18 – MCA s18(3).

6 Children Act 1989 s105.

the law might find an adult to have capacity to consent to treatment but lacking capacity to refuse it – see chapter 4).

Under the MCA a person has an absolute right to refuse medical treatment, even if it is life saving and an unwise decision, if they have capacity to do so. But if the person is 16 or 17, then they still fall potentially within the jurisdiction of the Children Act 1989, typically opening the door for two other decision-making bodies: the parent/s,[7] and the court.[8]

So despite the progress, if that's how you see it, that the MCA essentially treats anyone over 16 as an adult, the Children Act 1989 still treats 16-17 year-olds as children, and there can be some confusion where both bits of legislation apply at the same time to those in that age group.

But let's start with the question when those under 16 may also be able to make the decision about their treatment for themselves.

Under 16s – *Gillick* Competence

As a father of two young girls (eight and eleven years old at the time of writing this second edition), I do feel a little for Mrs Victoria Gillick, who had 5 daughters all under the age of 16. In 1984 she brought a challenge against Department of Health guidance that it was a matter for the individual doctor whether he was willing to prescribe contraception for girls under 16 without parental consent. Mrs Gillick's firm view was that it was wrong that her daughters could, in principle, be given contraception medication without her knowledge, that it undermined parental authority, and that it encouraged underage sex.

7 Strictly, those with parental responsibility – see below.

8 The family division of the High Court.

Should parents effectively have a right to veto any treatment for children under 16? The case went all the way to the House of Lords,[9] and ultimately Mrs Gillick lost.

Rather than looking through the lens of parental responsibility, the focus in the judgments was on the child's ability to consent. The answer is not a blanket assertion of parental authority, but an assessment in any individual situation of whether the child him or herself has enough understanding to make the particular decision in question. Plainly, the more significant the decision, the higher the level of understanding is required:

> *"as a matter of law the parental right to determine whether or not their minor child below the age of sixteen will have medical treatment terminates if and when the child achieves sufficient understanding and intelligence to understand fully what is proposed".*
>
> *"…it is not enough that she should understand the nature of the advice which is being given: she must also have a sufficient maturity to understand what is involved".[10] (emphasis added)*

So, even under 16 years of age, a child who can tick those boxes can consent to medical treatment, i.e. they are "*Gillick* competent".

Note a few things:

1 The emphasis here is on the child's ability to *consent*, regardless of parental views. It does not address what happens if the (competent) child refuses any treatment or whether that can be overridden.

2 The first quote above in particular captures the relationship between the child's growing "*Gillick* competence" and the

9 [1986] AC 112.

10 Per Lord Scarman.

declining scope of parental responsibility, which is sometimes described as a "dwindling right".

3 Each of the five judges in the Lords put the test in slightly different terms, but there's a common emphasis on sufficient understanding, intelligence and maturity.

4 This was around 20 years before the Mental Capacity Act and *Gillick* was not framed in exactly the same terminology of ability to understand, retain and use or weigh the relevant information to make a decision and communicate it. But in practical terms I am not sure that there is much material difference as between the MCA test for capacity for a 16 year-old and a reasonable assessment of a 15 year-old's Gillick competence. The reference to maturity might distinguish them in theory, but if a child is too immature to make the relevant decision, wouldn't you probably say that they cannot understand, retain or use or weigh the relevant information? That said, take care not to refer to a child under 16 as "having *capacity*", as opposed to *Gillick competence*, as it could ring an alarm bell about whether you are applying the correct legal framework.

So Mrs Gillick lost her case, with the courts refusing to uphold a blanket right of parents to determine or veto the medical treatment of their children under 16, regardless of the child's ability to make the relevant decisions for themselves.

A related question about confidentiality often arises: it may be little gain in practice for a child to be enabled to make a decision about treatment for themselves if the doctor tells their parents about it in any case.

The starting point is that each patient is owed a duty of confidentiality, and a child who is competent to make a decision about treatment can usually expect that confidentiality to be respected. But there is an exception explicitly for children:

> *"However, where a competent young person or child is refusing treatment for a life threatening condition, the duty of care would require confidentiality to be breached to the extent of informing those with parental responsibility for the child who might then be able to provide the necessary consent to the treatment"*[11]

As it says, this is about giving a safety net, in the case of a child's refusal of life or death treatment, as a chance for the parents either to exercise parental responsibility, to take the case to court or, more likely, to press the doctors to do so.

Bell v Tavistock

One of the great controversies in medical law over the last few years has been the provision of care or treatment for children and young people in the context of gender dysphoria. This is not the place to grapple with the ethical or clinical issues around this, which are definitively addressed in the Cass Report, published in April 2024.[12] The strictly legal issues are complex enough.

In particular, is a child or young person (treated in the Report as being under 16 and under 18 respectively) ever able to give lawful consent to decisions about services for gender dysphoria, given the implications of this? Should a child be able to make a decision about taking medication that "blocks" the onset of puberty, to allow them "time to think" about their gender identity, perhaps, at an age when they are still so young as to be pre-pubescent?

---

11 Department of Health Code on Confidentiality, 2003, p31. https://assets.publishing.service.gov.uk/government/uploads/system/uploads/attachment_data/file/200146/Confidentiality_-_NHS_Code_of_Practice.pdf

12 https://webarchive.nationalarchives.gov.uk/ukgwa/20250310143933/https://cass.independent-review.uk/home/publications/final-report/

In 2020, the High Court wrestled with this in a case in which concerns were about the adequacy of the consent procedures for hormone treatment (described as "experimental").[13] The case was heard as a Judicial Review, which focuses on the lawfulness of a particular decision or practice.

The High Court found that the processes at the gender identity services were lawful, setting out the information that it felt the patient should know in order to make this decision. Because of the scope of this, however, the court controversially went on to conclude that it would be "doubtful" that 14/15 year-olds would have such competence, and "highly unlikely" that children aged 13 or under have competence.

This part of the High Court decision was criticised by the Court of Appeal,[14] which decried the use of age-based guidelines for competence, given that the very basis of *Gillick* is that the stage at which a child can demonstrate competence in relation to a decision about a particular medical intervention is individual.

In any case, the government acted to restrict the use of puberty blocking drugs in patients under 18 in May 2024, in light of the findings of the Cass Report.

Who has parental responsibility?

In most cases it is easy enough to see who has parental responsibility (PR) in law,[15] though it can be a little fiddly in places. In broad terms:

---

13 Bell v Tavistock ([2020] EWHC 3274 (Admin)

14 [2021] EWCA (Civ) 1363

15 Children Act 1989 s2.

- A mother has parental responsibility by virtue of having given birth to the child.

- A father will have PR only if he's married to the mother at the time of the birth[16], or if he is named as the father on the birth certificate.[17] In England, there is also an option for an unmarried father to get a parental responsibility agreement with the mother, or a parental responsibility order from the court.

- And you can also have PR as:

    - A person with a residence order.

    - A local authority with an interim or final care order.

    - A guardian appointed under a will, when the parents die.

    - Same sex civil partners will both have PR if they were civil partners at the time of the assisted reproduction (e.g. IVF or donor insemination).

    - For same sex non civil partners, the second parent can get PR by becoming civil partners, or an agreement or application to court.

    - A person appointed by the court.

---

16 In England and Wales. In Scotland, being married at the time of conception, or marrying anytime afterwards confers PR. In Northern Ireland, the father has PR if married to the mother at the time of the birth, but if he marries her later he only acquires PR if he lives in Northern Ireland at the time of the marriage.

17 This came into force at different times around the UK, but those dates are all more than 18 years ago now, so this is academic.

So even though it is usually fairly clear, it is not daft to ask "who has PR for this child?" just to be sure.

In some cases, the rules can work unexpectedly. Where a surrogacy arrangement is in place for a child to be born and given to new parents, using donated gametes so the child is no genetic relation to the surrogate mother, nonetheless the surrogate mother will have PR for the child at birth. And so will *the surrogate's husband at the time of the birth,* even if he was totally uninvolved in the surrogacy. The intended parents must apply to court to acquire the PR for the child and remove PR from the surrogate mother and her husband.

A surrogacy contractual agreement may provide that the decision-making about the child should pass to the intended parents on birth. But if urgent medical treatment decisions are necessary soon after birth, discussions between the treating clinicians and the parents need to allow for the fact that the intended parents do not yet have PR, and those with PR, the surrogate and her husband, are both unrelated to the child!

What does PR mean?

The Children Act 1989 s3 defines parental responsibility as:

> *"all the rights, duties, powers, responsibilities and authority which by law a parent of a child has in relation to the child and his property".*

Which seems little more than circular, to be honest.

For these purposes, someone with PR can make decisions about medical treatment or care on behalf of their child, at least until the child attains the ability to make those decisions for themselves, whether as under 16 *Gillick* competent, or under the presumption of capacity from the age of 16 years under the Family Law Reform Act 1969 and the MCA.

Someone with PR cannot give it away to someone else, at least without the court ordering this, but can arrange for some or all of it to be met by someone acting on their behalf[18].

More relevant, perhaps, the fact that no one with PR is available to give consent to an urgent treatment decision for a child should not hinder appropriate care being given, of course. Anxiety about who should sign the consent forms is not a good reason to delay or deny appropriate treatment, for instance where the parents are uncontactable and it is a grandparent, who does not have PR, in attendance to a child in hospital. You can rely on this:

> *"A person who—*
>
> *(a) does not have parental responsibility for a particular child; but*
>
> *(b) has care of the child, may (subject to the provisions of this Act) do what is reasonable in all the circumstances of the case for the purpose of safeguarding or promoting the child's welfare".*[19]

Treating clinicians are certainly covered by this to do what is reasonable to provide appropriate care for a child, though it is best understood in interim terms where possible, to give a chance for those with PR to be involved before longer term decisions are taken, where the urgency allows.

Crucially, PR is not a blank cheque, and the emphasis is properly on *responsibility* rather than parental rights. Its purpose is to protect and nurture the child, and its exercise is always constrained by the primacy of the child's welfare. Its scope will decline as the child matures, in the ordinary course of events, and it may well conflict with others as usually more than one person will have PR. Typically, everyday decisions do not require consultation and unanimity, but very significant decisions are

18 Children Act 1989 s2(9).

19 Children Act 1989 s3(5).

best taken by everyone with PR together. Certainly, it is not appropriate for a substantial medical treatment decision to be made for a child in reliance of consent from one parent, if it is known that the other parent opposes this.

Where a child clearly lacks *Gillick* competence and the treating clinicians and those with parental responsibility all agree about what is best, there is very rarely any need for anything further[20].

There is plenty of professional guidance and it will be important that it is properly considered and followed, for example the Royal College of Paediatrics and Child Health: "Making Decisions to Limit Treatment in Life-limiting and Life- threatening Conditions in Children: A Framework for Practice", most recently updated in March 2015.[21]

Quoting from the Executive Summary:

> *The RCPCH believes that there are three sets of circumstances when treatment limitation can be considered because it is no longer in the child's best interests to continue, because treatments cannot provide overall benefit:*
>
> ***1 – When life is limited in quantity***
>
> *If treatment is unable or unlikely to prolong life significantly it may not be in the child's best interests to provide it. These comprise:*

---

20 Perhaps an exception might be a "saviour sibling scenario" where an organ or bone marrow might be taken from a child too young to consent for the benefit of a sibling, which would require the court's prior approval and sufficient evidence that this is truly in the best interests of the donor child as well as the recipient, see *Re Y (mental patient: bone marrow donation)* [1997] Fam 10.

21 https://adc.bmj.com/content/100/Suppl_2/s1

A. *Brain stem death, as determined by agreed professional criteria appropriately applied*

B. *Imminent death, where physiological deterioration is occurring irrespective of treatment*

C. *Inevitable death, where death is not immediately imminent but will follow and where prolongation of life by LST confers no overall benefit.*

2 – When life is limited in quality

This includes situations where treatment may be able to prolong life significantly but will not alleviate the burdens associated with illness or treatment itself. These comprise:

A. *Burdens of treatments, where the treatments themselves produce sufficient pain and suffering so as to outweigh any potential or actual benefits*

B. *Burdens of the child's underlying condition. Here the severity and impact of the child's underlying condition is in itself sufficient to produce such pain and distress as to overcome any potential or actual benefits in sustaining life*

C. *Lack of ability to benefit; the severity of the child's condition is such that it is difficult or impossible for them to derive benefit from continued life.*

3 – Informed competent refusal of treatment

Adults, who have the capacity to make their own decisions, have the right to refuse LST and to have that refusal respected. So an older child with extensive experience of illness may repeatedly and competently consent to the withdrawal or withholding of LST. In these circumstances and where the child is supported by his or her parents and by the clinical team there is no ethical obligation to provide LST.

> *In situations other than those described, or where there is uncertainty about the nature of the child's condition or its likely outcome, treatment should be continued until greater certainty is possible. The degree of certainty should be proportionate to the gravity of the decision to be taken. Adequate time must be allowed to collect evidence and this may entail obtaining second opinions from clinicians with appropriate skills, knowledge and expertise of the child's condition.*

As we will see in chapter 7, the remarkable thing about such difficult decisions is how often they are made collaboratively between clinicians and families, without conflict or court applications. In any case of uncertainty or dispute, however, the court can resolve this.

Just as with the treatment of adults, the very development of our knowledge, expertise and clinical capacity has brought challenges – now that we can do so much more than a few years ago, should we? Perhaps this is nowhere more acute than at the start of life, with children now surviving at birth with far greater levels of disability and healthcare need than would once have ever been thought possible, and with profoundly disabled children now commonly living well into adolescence and adulthood in a way that once would have been exceptional. We should recognise the agony of whether to do something is a by-product of the medical and technological advances that allow us to save and sustain life beyond anything imaginable not long ago. The social, legal and ethical issues can sometimes lag well behind the technical developments.

The dilemmas this might bring shouldn't obscure this success, which should be celebrated, but that does not lessen those dilemmas. I will pick out just five very high-profile cases for the lessons we can learn.

In Chapter 2 I mentioned the 1995 case of Jaymee Bowen (the health authority's refusal to fund increasingly implausible but expensive attempts to treat a 10 year-old girl's leukaemia) in the context of allocation of resource decisions. Sometimes these cases do revolve around an argument that something should be made available or funded that is not routinely done (see Ashya King, below). But the earliest case that really struck the public consciousness that I can remember, Charlotte Wyatt, was an argument about whether or not it would be in her best interests to provide treatment that was readily available.

Charlotte Wyatt

Charlotte was expected to die. She was born three months prematurely in October 2003, weighing 1lb, and suffering from serious damage to her brain, lung and kidneys. Years later I saw a presentation by one of the lawyers who dealt with the court case about her treatment, and he made the point about her fragility unbearably graphic by holding up a pen, which he said was the size that she was at birth.

The treating doctors at Portsmouth Hospitals NHS Trust felt that if she stopped breathing it would not be in her best interests to try to revive her, given the grim quality of life, dominated by pain, that she faced even if they could succeed.

Her parents, Darren and Debbie, disagreed. She ought to be given every chance, they said, and so the court had to decide whether it would be lawful not to resuscitate her.

Over the following few months, the case played out in the courts and in the media. The doctors argued that attempts at resuscitation would be pointless and possibly inhumane, as it could only prolong her suffering, and there was no way to improve her life or for her to survive beyond infancy.

A High Court Judge agreed with the doctors, and this was later upheld by the Court of Appeal in August 2005. In fact, Charlotte then seemed to improve significantly, and the judge withdrew any declarations. By February 2006, however, she deteriorated badly, and the same judge restored the order that it would be lawful not to resuscitate her, if the clinicians did not wish to do so, at the time she collapsed.

That was that for the proceedings, but the last information available publicly (in 2017[22], in the context of coverage of the Charlie Gard case) was that Charlotte in fact remained alive and well, albeit inevitably still profoundly disabled.

I would highlight three things from this case:

1 When the judge made the order that the trust were allowed to not resuscitate, it was *permissive* not *mandatory*. In other words, the judge did not say that they *must* not resuscitate her, but that if they chose not to then it would be lawful. The coalface decision remains with the clinician at the frontline, who could follow their clinical judgement when the need arose with the reassurance that the court has considered and confirmed that it would be lawful not to resuscitate, if that's what they decide. And this was about "ceilings of care" – situations in which specific escalation of treatment would not be right – not about withdrawing treatment that she was already getting.

2 We all look to clinicians for certainty and want to see confidence. No one wants a doctor wracked by indecision or self-doubt[23], and no doubt her parents pushed for a clear opinion, just as I would. The fact that Charlotte survived to her teens, at least, does not mean that her chances were ever good. But I suspect that the certainty with which doctors asserted that she had no chance at

22 https://inews.co.uk/news/health/charlie-gard-case-charlotte-wyatt-high-court-522541

23 That said, see "Anything for my Child" by Stephanie Nimmo for the powerful story of a mother's experience of medical treatment decisions for her daughter with a life limiting condition, and the was in which trust was built by the clinicians' honesty about what they knew about the condition and what they did not.

all was matched by the family's certainty that she was a fighter, which was only reinforced as she defied the worst predictions.[24]

3 Finally, the colossal impact on the whole family. I find two healthy young daughters more than a handful. I cannot imagine the strain of caring for a child with such profound disabilities, or of compounding this by a battle through the legal system about her welfare or her very survival. Darren and Debbie had three other children as well. It adds another layer of tragedy to read later that the strain led to the marriage breaking down, and that when Charlotte, against the odds, was well enough to be discharged home from hospital, at the age of 3, it was to a foster family placement.

Ashya King

The Ashya King case was more about access to unusual treatment.

Ashya was only 5 years old when he was treated for a serious form of brain cancer, a medulloblastoma, which was removed by surgery. The question was over follow-up treatment as his parents wanted him to have proton therapy, rather than conventional radiotherapy and chemotherapy. At that time, proton therapy was not routinely available on the NHS in England and Wales. Exceptionally, it could be funded by the NHS for treatment abroad, but not for this particular condition.

24 See NR (A Child: Ceilings of Treatment after Survival of Withdrawal of Life Sustaining Treatment) [2024] EWHC 2400, in which Poole J had to deal with a situation where a child had survived for months and indeed improved after the court had approved the withdrawal of life sustaining treatment in the expectation that the child would die within a short period, quoting Sir William Osler saying that "medicine is a science of uncertainty and an art of probability."

On 28 August 2014 Ashya's parents took him out of hospital without telling the doctors, and boarded a ferry to France, prompting an international manhunt. At the time of his removal, Ashya was still being fed by an NG tube[25] due to his difficulty swallowing, and the immediate concern was that his parents had no training in managing this and no supplies of appropriate feed. His parents were arrested on 30 August 2014 in Malaga, Spain and imprisoned for 24 hours, while Ashya was taken to a local hospital for urgent treatment.

On 5 September 2014 the High Court ruled that, since funding for the treatment was in fact now available (the judge referred to a combination of the parents' assets, "substantial donations" from the general public in response to the publicity around the case, and a donation from a social fund administered by the parents' lawyer in Spain), he could go for proton therapy in Prague, and a private flight was arranged for him.

The outcome was contentious, with an NHS report finding that denying Ashya the regular chemotherapy had reduced his chances of long-term survival by 30%. His parents disputed this, and reported in 2015 that he was free of cancer, which was confirmed by MRI scans back in Southampton in 2018.[26]

It was an extreme example of a breakdown in trust and the communication between family and clinicians, bringing huge practical challenges in the glare of global media, but the legal framework about the treatment itself was not especially contentious. The treating hospital trust had never said that it would stand in the way of proton therapy if it were available and could be funded. And once it got to court, with that

25 Naso-gastric tube i.e. a tube inserted through the nose, all the way to the stomach, to provide nutrition.

26 https://www.telegraph.co.uk/news/2018/03/03/ashya-king-cleared-cancer-three-years-parents-abducted-hospital/

treatment option now available, the judge was happy to allow it, as being in Ashya's best interests.

He said:

> *"...it is a fundamental principle of family law in this jurisdiction that responsibility for making decisions about a child rest with his parents. In most cases, the parents are the best people to make decisions about a child and the State – whether it be the court, or any other public authority – has no business interfering with the exercise of parental responsibility unless the child is suffering or is likely to suffer significant harm as a result of the care given to the child not being what it would be reasonable to expect a parent to give".*[27]

We would hear these words again in later cases, pleaded by parents in support of their arguments against clinicians over medical treatment decisions, as in one case which really raised the bar for media interest.

Charlie Gard

Charlie was born on 4 August 2016, with a rare genetic disorder called MDDS[28] which usually causes death in infancy due to progressive brain damage and muscle failure, including the muscles used to breathe. There was no established treatment.

In October 2016, Charlie was transferred to Great Ormond Street Hospital (GOSH) in London, where he was supported on a ventilator. An experimental treatment (nucleoside therapy) being developed in New York was considered, but by January 2017, after seizures caused further brain damage, the hospital's view was that ending life support and

---

27 *Portsmouth City Council v King* [2014] EWHC 2964, per Baker J at para 31. https://www.judiciary.uk/wp-content/uploads/2014/09/judgment-ashya-king-08092014.pdf

28 Mitochondrial DNA Depletion Syndrome.

provision of palliative care was appropriate, rather than prolonging his suffering. Charlie's parents strongly opposed this and campaigned to raise funds to pay for the nucleoside therapy privately.

At a High Court hearing on 11 April 2017,[29] Mr Justice Francis made declarations supporting the GOSH position. His parents fought this, but the guardian acting on behalf of Charlie supported the withdrawal of treatment. The evidence of the doctor in New York gave little hope for successful treatment, and it appeared likely that Charlie suffered pain, albeit without being able to express this.

The parents appealed, among other things relying on the passage quoted above from the *King* case saying that where a treatment option existed it should be left to the parents to decide about it.

Extraordinarily, over the next 12 weeks the case went through the English Court of Appeal (25 May 2017), the Supreme Court (twice, on 8 June 2017, and again on 19 June 2017), and the European Court of Human Rights (on 27 June 2017). At each stage the parents were unsuccessful in overturning those initial declarations.

But then GOSH brought it back to Mr Justice Francis in the High Court for a fresh hearing, listed on 13 July 2017, as the parents said that new evidence was available, specifically that the New York doctor's opinion had become more positive about the prospects of successful treatment, and that another major hospital (in Rome) was now willing to accept him there as well.

Over the next few days, however, the parents recognised that it was too late for a meaningful chance for Charlie to survive, and accepted the plan for palliative care and the withdrawal of ventilation.

---

29 *Great Ormond Street Hospital v Yates and Gard* [2017] EWHC 972 https://www.bailii.org/ew/cases/EWHC/Fam/2017/972.html

Unfortunately, the fragile truce then broke down over the practical arrangements for Charlie's final few days, and the judge again had to resolve a dispute over this, in court on 26 July 2017.

On 27 July 2017, Charlie was discharged to a hospice, and his mother announced at 6.30pm the following day that he had died minutes after ventilation had been withdrawn, with morphine to relieve any pain. He was just a few days short of his first birthday.

This account can only be superficial and based on what is publicly available in the various judgments, but it barely scratches the surface of the story or the extent to which it captured and dominated the media and social media at the time.

The very public interventions of the US President and the Pope were unprecedented. Charlie's case was used in the US as an argument against a "socialised" system like the NHS. And in the UK, "Charlie's Army" campaigned strongly for his right to life, while staff at GOSH received thousands of abusive messages, as well as death threats and harassment.

The strain it must have put on the parents, wider family and friends, and on the treating clinicians and other staff at GOSH are beyond imagining.

But, again, in legal terms the principles were clear and well established. The child's welfare was paramount. The court rejected the parents' argument that it should simply be up to them (a "zone of exclusive parental control") unless it would cause their child *substantial* harm, which would effectively have imposed a harm threshold before the court's jurisdiction applies[30]. It was always likely to be unappealing (to a judge) to argue that a parent can harm a child *up to a point* by their decisions, and there's nothing that a judge can do about it. Instead, the court

30 Note that under the Children Act 1989 there is a harm threshold test in the context of care proceedings for a child to be removed from a family by a local authority, but that is a very different context than making a decision what medical treatment is best for a child.

reasserted that it is ultimately in the court's power to resolve any dispute and the only question is what is in the *child's* best interests. Parental *responsibility* is about *responsibility* not *rights*.

Again, three things:

1 The role of the media and social media was unprecedented. Increasingly, the issues around use of the communications, removal of social media material, and fully supporting staff appropriately in the face of harassment will be an essential part of the management and the legal advice required in these cases. The clinicians and NHS trust are bound, of course, to respect the patient's confidentiality not to share information about his condition or treatment, which makes it difficult to correct or challenge any material, however inaccurate or unfair, posted or broadcast by others.

2 The speed with which the case went through the layers of appeal was extraordinary. But for those few months, treatment was being continued on an interim basis, even after the treating clinicians (and a judge) had come to a clear view that it was doing Charlie more harm than good to do so. When the parents were in the Supreme Court arguing for a stay of the proceedings to allow time for more evidence, Lady Hale said "By granting a stay, even of short duration, we would in some sense be complicit in directing a course of action which is contrary to Charlie's best interests."[31] It is appropriate and proper to seek consensus and if need be to litigate, including rights of appeal, but don't lose sight of the fact that continuing to provide treatment in the interim may be harmful and undue delay may only perpetuate this.

3 Finally, an email came out in court between the clinicians describing the parents as the "spanner in the works" for the

31 https://www.supremecourt.uk/cases/docs/charlie-gard-190617.pdf

treatment decision. Though the judge did not make a big deal of it, I do not envy the author when that was read out and obviously this would not have done much to restore any trust or relationship. Remember that the medical records and all relevant correspondence, including emails, will be "disclosable"[32] i.e. will have to be shared with the other parties in any court proceedings. Never write anything you're not comfortable hearing read out in court or seeing on the front page of the papers.

Alfie Evans

We might have thought the *Charlie Gard* case was utterly exceptional, but just a few months later, it began to look like the start of a trend, with the case of Alfie Evans dominating the media in the early part of 2018.

It is quite wrong to simply bracket together Charlie Gard and Alfie Evans, two different little boys, with different families and stories, as well as different medical conditions. The temptation to do so comes from the parallels in terms of the litigation and especially the media coverage, so soon afterwards, and in raising similar questions of legal principle.

Everything had seemed OK when Alfie Evans was born, on 9 May 2016. Concerns grew after a few months, and by November 2016 he was in the care of Alder Hey, the leading specialist children's hospital in the North West. At just over 7 months old, in mid-December, Alfie was desperately unwell and dependent on artificial ventilation. A year later (during which the Charlie Gard case unfolded as above), on 19 December 2017, lawyers acting for Alder Hey Hospital issued proceedings asking the High Court to declare it would be lawful for ongoing ventilation to be withdrawn.

---

32 There may be an exception for legal advice and for documents produced for the purpose of litigation, which can be protected by legal or litigation privilege.

The parents disputed both the gravity of his condition, saying that he was more responsive than the clinicians recognised, and the conclusion that treatment should be withdrawn, arguing that the hospital was giving up on him. They were fortified by Alfie overcoming an infection in January 2018, reinforcing their view that his prospects were better than the doctors were giving credit for.

Though an exact diagnosis was elusive, the expert evidence was that Alfie sadly had a progressive, ultimately fatal neurodegenerative condition and that his brain was "entirely beyond recovery". While high quality ongoing intensive care support could sustain him in his "semi-vegetative state" for a long time, he would not be able to breathe for himself for long if the ventilator were removed. The picture was grim. He would never make any developmental progress (hearing, vision, social, emotional, fine or gross motor, or meaningful response to stimuli). He may still have had some awareness of pain, but it was unlikely that he could experience any comfort from the voices and touch of his parents. There were no treatment options.

But, as the judge described it, the family were "unable to relinquish hope". The same hospital in Rome as had offered Charlie Gard a place again said they would accept Alfie and would offer ongoing care, as did another in Munich. The family argued that this should be taken up. They presented evidence about the potential for Alfie's transfer and care there. The judge criticised some of that evidence for falling short of the required professional standards, and deplored the behaviour of one doctor called by the family, who posed as a friend of the family to visit Alfie at Alder Hey, hiding his professional credentials and the purpose of his visit.

On the substance of the case, quoting from the Court of Appeal judgment in *Charlie Gard*, Mr Justice Hayden said:

> *"...the sole principle is that the best interests of the child must prevail and that must apply even to cases where parents, for the best of motives, hold on to some alternative view."*[33]

The judge reviewed the medical evidence and found that ongoing treatment for Alfie was futile. He noted that the guardian appointed to represent Alfie supported the trust's application.

The risk of transfer elsewhere might, he said, be worth it if there were any prospect of treatment, but there was none. No-one would want Alfie to die in transit, and the journey itself would be burdensome, even if it were possible. On 20 February 2018, Hayden J granted the trust's application[34].

The parents appealed but were unsuccessful in the Court of Appeal on 6 March 2018[35], which upheld Hayden J's judgment in full, and permission to appeal further was then refused by the Supreme Court (20 March 2018) and the European Court of Human Rights (28 March 2018).

However fiendishly difficult to apply in practice, the legal principles about a child's medical treatment are simple: the only question is the child's best interests.

That said, the case was still back in court before Mr Justice Hayden just a few days later, on 11 April 2018[36], as the family and clinicians had not

---

33 *Yates and Gard v Great Ormond Street Hospital NHS Foundation Trust* [2017] EWCA Civ 410 per Macfarlane LJ.

34 [2018] EWHC 308 (Fam). https://www.judiciary.uk/wp-content/uploads/2018/02/alder-hey-v-evans.pdf

35 [2018] EWCA Civ 550. https://www.bailii.org/ew/cases/EWCA/Civ/2018/550.html

36 [2018] EWHC 818 (Fam). https://www.bailii.org/ew/cases/EWHC/Fam/2018/818.html

been able to agree a plan or date for the withdrawal of ventilation. At that hearing the judge gave very short shrift to a new argument on behalf of the parents that it was a deprivation of his liberty[37] to stop Alfie being discharged from Alder Hey to their care, so that they could arrange to take him elsewhere. Counsel for Alfie noted that 7 weeks had passed since it was determined to be in his best interests that treatment be withdrawn. The family did not object to the detail of the plan so much as to the plan itself and, with nothing else on the table, the judge endorsed it and encouraged the family to understand and accept this.

Sadly, reconciliation was not what followed. When further attempts to appeal to the Supreme Court (20 April 2018[38]) and European Court of Human Rights (23 April 2018[39]) were unsuccessful, a group of around 200 protestors described as "Alfie's Army" tried to enter Alder Hey hospital, and were blocked by the police.[40]

Life support was withdrawn on 23 April 2018, and on the evening of the same day the High Court[41] again refused another application for permission to fly Alfie to Italy, the Italian ambassador having offered him citizenship. There was no basis to concede priority to Italian law, and Alfie had no connection to that country. The only prospect on offer in Rome was an alternative palliative care regime. The Court of Appeal, sitting even later that evening, again agreed.

In publishing a judgment on 24 April 2018, Hayden J noted that the support and advice sometimes given to the family had not always aligned

---

37 See Chapter 5 – and A Practical Guide to the Law of Deprivation of Liberty, Law Brief Publishing.

38 https://www.supremecourt.uk/news/permission-to-appeal-application-in-the-matter-of-alfie-evans.html

39 https://www.echr.coe.int/Documents/Decision_Evans_v_UK.pdf

40 https://www.bbc.co.uk/news/uk-england-merseyside-43867132

41 [2018] EWHC 953 (Fam). https://www.bailii.org/ew/cases/EWHC/Fam/2018/953.html

with their true interests, citing a statement that had been prepared on their behalf with a view to pursuing a private prosecution against certain medical staff for murder, which had been thrown out by another court.

Alfie's death was announced by his father at 2.30am on 28 April 2018.

It is hard to know what to say. It has felt pretty harrowing just to write a fairly superficial account of the events. I cannot begin to imagine the all-consuming strain of living through it for the family, the clinicians and NHS managers or – even – the lawyers involved, not to mention the experience for a child him or herself at the centre of all this, with every step covered by the media, and contested in social media. And these are cases where actually it was never in dispute that the child himself could not make the treatment decision and the only question to answer was what was in his best interests. If only in that superficial way, these are not complex cases, in law. But nothing could be further from the truth at the emotional, human level where these cases really resonate.

And something is going badly wrong when advice about the Protection from Harassment Act 1997, or protection from defamation or abuse on social media for the sake of the treating clinicians, becomes a core focus, alongside the Children Act 1989. (The implications of this for whether clinicians should be named or anonymised in such proceedings is tackled in Chapter 7, with the benefit of a very recent Supreme Court judgment).

Further cases

I worried, watching these two cases unfold, that a genie was out of the bottle and, fed by toxic social media, the stakes and expectations had been raised for anyone who loved their child enough to "fight" for them. Litigation as a means of showing your love and faith in your child. All the more so when, given an awful prognosis with undue certainty, they beat the odds, defy the worst predictions, and show they are 'a fighter', 'resilient', 'courageous' and 'a warrior'.[42] (It is not entirely unknown for there to be a dispute where the clinicians want to continue treatment for a child when the parents want it stopped, though this is much more unusual[43]).

Perhaps, though, not all is lost. In the years since the *Alfie Evans* case there has not (at the time of writing) been a case quite like it. I know some hospital trusts, especially those dedicated to the specialist treatment of the most sick children, are investing very heavily in training for clinicians focussed on communications and relationships with families, and in formal or informal mediation of any disputes at the earliest possible stage, to avoid litigation. We can only hope, for the sake of all involved, that cases like these remain exceptional.

That is not to say that there have been no further difficult or high-profile cases, among them those involving Tafida Raqeeb[44] (2019), Alta Fixsler[45]

---

42 In the words of Hayden J, about Alfie Evans, in the final judgment, given on 24 April 2018.

43 Re B [1981] 1 WLR 1421 is one well known example – the parents of a young child refused consent to surgery that clinicians wanted to do to remove an intestinal blockage because they thought that the child, who had Down's Syndrome, would enjoy no quality of life in any case. The High Court initially made the child a ward of court, and then upheld a decision by clinicians to defer to the family position, before the Court of Appeal held that the surgery should be given, as being in the child's best interests. More recently, Re C (a child) (re life saving medical treatment) [2025] EWHC 413 (fam) approved a liver transplant for a 14 month-old child with hepatic cancer, against the wishes of her parents, a case in which – full disclosure – my colleagues and I acted for the hospital trusts involved. https://www.bailii.org/ew/cases/EWHC/Fam/2025/413.html

44 [2019] EWHC 2530 (Fam) – https://www.bailii.org/ew/cases/EWHC/Fam/2019/2530.html

45 [2021] EWHC 2664 (Fam) – https://www.bailii.org/ew/cases/EWHC/Fam/2021/2664.html

(2021), Archie Battersbee[46] (2022), and Indi Gregory[47] (2023), though – as with Charlie and Alfie – it would be quite wrong simply to lump them together as just the same.

Tafida Raqeeb was five years old, and was being raised in her parent's Muslim faith, when she suffered a large bleed in her brain earlier that year, causing extensive and irreversible brain damage. Mr Justice McDonald heard the application by Barts Health NHS Foundation Trust for approval of withdrawal of her life sustaining treatment. Her parents wanted her to be transferred to a hospital in Italy for treatment. The judge refused the trust's application,[48] finding that:

> *"Tafida is not in pain and medically stable; where the burden of the treatment required to keep her in a minimally conscious state is low; where there is a responsible body of medical opinion that considers that she can and should be maintained on life support with a view to placing her in a position where she can be cared for at home on ventilation by a loving and dedicated family in the same manner in which a number of children in a similar situation to Tafida are treated in this jurisdiction; where there is a fully detailed and funded care plan to this end; where Tafida can be safely transported to Italy with little or no impact on her welfare; where in this context the continuation of life-sustaining treatment is consistent with the religious and cultural tenets by which Tafida was being raised; where, in the foregoing context, transfer for treatment to Italy is the choice of her parents in the exercise of their parental responsibility and having regard to the sanctity of Tafida's life being of the highest importance, I am satisfied,*

46 Over three judgments, concluding with [2022] EWHC 2098 (Fam) – https://www.bailii.org/ew/cases/EWHC/Fam/2022/2098.html

47 Three judgments, culminating in [2023] EWHC 2798 (Fam) – https://www.bailii.org/ew/cases/EWHC/Fam/2023/2798.html

48 And later, separately, made an order that the trust should pay 80% of the family's legal costs for one part of the proceedings – [2019] EWHC 3322 (Fam) – https://www.bailii.org/ew/cases/EWHC/Fam/2019/3322.html

on a fine balance, that it is in Tafida's best interests for life sustaining treatment to continue."

In contrast, in May 2021 the same judge reached the opposite conclusion in the case of Alta Fixsler, a 2 year-old girl who had been born prematurely with catastrophic brain damage. Her parents were Chassidic practicing Jews and Israeli citizens, and opposed the application by Manchester University NHS FT to withdraw her life sustaining treatment. They asked instead for her to be transferred to Israel, if not for ongoing treatment then at least for withdrawal of treatment to happen there so that she could live her last days, and be buried there, in accordance with her parents' faith.

I say *her parents'* faith, rather than her own, as McDonald J rejected the suggestion that the court should assume that Alta herself had, or would have, their beliefs, where her brain injury was such that she had no understanding at all of their religion (in contrast to Tafida who had lived five years, brought up as a Muslim). Crucially, McDonald J also found that Alta consistently demonstrated pain as a result of her condition and her care, and that this was a "very heavy counter-weight" to the presumption of preserving life. In the absence of any detailed plan for the proposed transfer to Israel, the court could not approve this, and there was compelling medical evidence that any such transfer would cause her pain, only for the sake of the "adult concerns" about the rituals of her parents' religion, for no benefit to herself.

The Court of Appeal upheld this decision in July 2021,[49] considering in some detail – and dismissing – the parents' arguments that the judge has overstated the evidence about Alta's experience of pain, and had not given enough weight to the importance of the family's religious beliefs. Sadly, another High Court judgment by McDonald J was needed in October 2021 to determine that the withdrawal of treatment should take place in

---

49 [2021] EWCA Civ 1018 – Fixsler & Anor v Manchester University NHS Foundation Trust & Anor [2021] EWCA Civ 1018 (09 July 2021)

hospital or a hospice, rather than at home as the family wished, where this was not clinically viable.

Indi Gregory had mitochondrial disease, an incurable condition which prevented cells in her body producing energy. She was less than a year-old when the High Court heard her case three times between October and November 2023, as well as the Court of Appeal twice refusing permission to appeal, and the European Court of Human Rights declining to hear the case. Mr Justice Peel approved the treating trust's plan for palliative care, with the "burdens of invasive treatment outweighing the benefits", and the parents, "understandably" not recognising the pain she was suffering. In his second decision, the judge refused an application by the parents to thwart that decision by allowing Indi to be transferred to a hospital in Rome. The third decision, as with Fixsler, dealt with the location of the withdrawal of treatment, and held that this should be done in accordance with the clinically led care plan, not in the family home, as the parents sought.

Of these, though, it was perhaps Archie Battersbee's case that came closest to the media fervour seen in those earlier cases, and in turn it raised some new issues.

Archie Battersbee

Archie Battersbee died on 6 August 2022, a 12 year-old boy from Essex who loved martial arts and gymnastics.

Over the previous four months, after he was found unconscious with a ligature round his neck at his home on 7 April 2022, decisions about his medical treatment, and indeed whether or not he was still alive or already dead, played out through the courts and the media in a way not seen in this country since the Charlie Gard and Alfie Evans cases in 2017/18.

Over those months, Archie's case went through the High Court (four times), the Court of Appeal (three times) the Supreme Court and the

European Court of Human Rights, as well as being referred to the United Nations Committee on the Rights of Persons With Disabilities (UN CRPD).

Legally the case was simple: ultimately (if Archie was not already brain stem dead, and it was best to proceed on the basis that he was not), it was held not to be in his best interests for life sustaining treatment to continue, and he died after his ventilation was withdrawn by his treating clinicians. In every other way, of course, it was anything but.

The only unusual thing about the case, legally, was that it started not as a best interests decision, but as an attempt to establish whether Archie had already died. His heart was beating, and blood was pumping, but this was entirely sustained by the medical machinery. It was thought that his brain may have already irreversibly lost the ability to do this for himself, and so that he might meet the criteria developed to recognise 'brain stem death' (see the Coda, following this chapter).

On 13 May 2022, the High Court (Mrs Justice Arbuthnot) allowed testing for brain stem death to go ahead, against the family's wishes. However, it could not be performed because Archie did not react to a peripheral nerve stimulation test which was a precursor to the brain stem test. The Guardian therefore made an application that Archie undergo a further MRI scan, which was granted (on 27 May 2022). The scan took place and showed global shrinkage of Archie's brain, and, having considering the evidence, Arbuthnot J declared (on 13 June 2022) that Archie had, on the balance of probabilities, died on 31 May 2022, shortly after the MRI scans were taken.

Arbuthnot J granted the parents' permission to appeal on the single ground that she should have applied the criminal standard of proof (ie beyond all reasonable doubt) rather than the civil standard of proof (ie balance of probabilities) when declaring death. The Court of Appeal allowed the parents to add 5 additional grounds of appeal. Even though Arbuthnot J went on to say that if she was wrong about Archie being dead, then it was in his best interests to withdraw treatment, her decision that he was already dead tainted that finding, and the Court of Appeal directed that this be considered afresh purely as a best interests decision.

Once the case went back to court on that basis, Mr Justice Hayden held that it was not in Archie's best interests for life sustaining treatment to be continued:

> *"Where, as here, the treatment is futile, it compromises Archie's dignity, deprives him of his autonomy, and becomes wholly inimical to his welfare. It serves only to protract his death, whilst being unable to prolong his life".*

As we have repeatedly seen, the law is not complex – in any decision to be made about a child, the child's welfare is paramount. Applying the law in practice is the problem, especially when there is, in good faith, a profound disagreement over where the child's best interests lie.

In those cases, just saying that 'the child's best interests' is the test does little more than reframe the question, rather than offer an answer. I am yet to see a case in which either clinicians or family think that their own position is not in the child's best interests.

But that reframing does usefully show that the question is not simply: what do the parents want? but neither is it simply: what do the clinicians want?

There should be alarm bells in any case where it feels that either clinicians are riding roughshod over a family, or vice versa. Both perspectives must inform a decision, and though care must be taken not to lose sight of a child's best interests in the search for such a consensus, in the vast majority of cases a respectful compromise is possible.

Of course, that will not always be possible – and where not, these disputes inevitably play out in the most fraught and emotional circumstances, and all too often against a background of broken relationships and distrust. And in those cases, it is right that the court resolves that dispute.

We can only know of the Battersbee family experience that which was reported in the press, ie that they felt stripped of their rights, as parents, to make decisions about their child.

It would help, perhaps, if the legal framework were better understood. It is rightly presumed that parents know their child best, and so know what is best for their child. As Baker J said in the Ashya King case, the court will not lightly interfere with this.

But no judge has yet bought the argument that the Gard, Evans and Battersbee families have tried to build on this: ie that there is 'a zone of exclusive parental control' where it is none of the court's business what the parents decide.

It is not, ultimately, about parental **rights**. Parental **responsibility** brings a duty to do what is in the child's best interests, not a power to determine beyond challenge that something **is** in the child's best interests because the parents say so.

The **rights** at the centre of such cases are the **child's** – to have a decision made which is in their best interests. For an insight into the complexity of the answer to the face value simplicity of the question "what is in the child's best interests?", and the experience of a family going through the agonised decision making around a much-loved child with a life limiting illness, I strongly recommend reading Steph Nimmo's recent, powerful book "Anything for my child"[50].

Funding and reform

Sadly, the unavailability of legal aid (at the time) to help the family get independent and expert legal advice meant that the Battersbee family, like the families of Charlie Gard and Alfie Evans before them, were

50 Jessica Kingsley publishers, 2023, https://uk.jkp.com/products/anything-for-my-child

dependent on the Christian Legal Centre for advice and support, bringing their particular perspective and agenda into the dispute alongside their resources.

One development since the first edition of this book is undoubtedly a positive thing. Since August 2023, the rules for legal aid have changed so that families in litigation about withdrawal or withholding of life sustaining treatment for a child under 18 are automatically entitled to non-means tested legal aid[51]. As well as ensuring that families get the specialist legal support and advice that they need in these most fraught situations, we might also hope that it means that families are not driven towards those who might have their own agendas to pursue in the midst of these tragedies.

Such funding reforms were just one element of the changes proposed by 'Charlie's Law' (The Children's Medical Treatment (Dispute Resolution) Bill, introduced on 18 March 2020), advocated by the family of Charlie Gard, and introduced as a private member's bill in the last parliament by Labour MP Bambos Charalambous MP on 18 March 2020.

In summary, the bill also asserted parental **rights** in medical treatment decisions for their children by:

- requiring that the views of parents must be 'listened to and taken into account'; and
- that the court must defer to a parent's decision about a moving a child elsewhere for treatment unless the proposed provider is 'not a reputable institution', or it will bring 'a disproportionate risk of

51 The Criminal and Civil Legal Aid (Amendment) Regulations 2023 No. 745

substantial harm' to the child (ie introducing a zone of exclusive parental control, or a threshold before the court can intervene).

- And, in cases of dispute, the Bill required mandatory:
    - mediation; and
    - referral to a clinical ethics committee.

Mediation is already used effectively in a number of cases, and a discussion at an ethics committee should be standard practice, though it is not usually expected to be a forum with responsibility for making decisions, still less for resolving disputes (see Chapter 7).

But Charlie's Law never passed.

More recently, Baroness Findlay proposed an amendment to the Health and Care Act 2022 which would have introduced a duty to ensure that the parents 'are listened to and taken into account' in any dispute about palliative care for a child but would have explicitly not have affected 'the principle of the best interests of the child'.

That amendment fell away as well, but we did get – in s177 of the Health and Care Act 2022 – an obligation on the Secretary of State to arrange for 'a review into the causes of disputes between (on the one hand) persons with parental responsibility for a critically ill child and (on the other) persons responsible for the provision of care or medical treatment for the child as part of the health service in England'.

That review was delivered by the Nuffield Council on Bioethics in September 2023[52]. It is worth reading in full if you have an interest in this area, informed by extensive consultation with families as well as with

52 NCOB-Disagreements-Critical-Care-Indepdent-Review-FINAL.pdf

clinicians, and their voices ring through the report. Entirely in keeping with the stories we have just heard, the report noted:

Key causes of disagreements, and aggravators of existing ones, include communication issues, mismatched expectations and a lack of information available to parents.

In particular, diagnostic and prognostic uncertainty about a child's clinical condition was not always communicated well, with healthcare professionals sometimes lacking confidence in communicating uncertainty. Where uncertainty was communicated honestly, however, this was seen to have a positive impact on relationships and the building of trust between parents and healthcare professionals.

Healthcare professional experience more distress and moral injury [and] also struggle with feelings of powerlessness emanating from their inability to respond to inaccuracies in the media, or on social media, as a result of the professional duty to maintain patient confidentiality.

"The 'best interests' test has had its merits debated in academic literature, with some proposing an amended or alternative test, but there is insufficient evidence at present to support a change to the law".

In total, 16 recommendations are made – focussed around provision of information to parents and support / training to clinicians – but I am not aware of any steps towards implementation.

Context

As the Nuffield Council on Bioethics Report confirmed, the law (which is simply that a decision must be made in the child's best interests) is not really the problem, so much as the challenges about relationships, communication, trust, and managing expectations in unimaginably fraught and emotional situations.

For context, such litigation is not commonplace in all other jurisdictions: As of 2020[53], there had never been a reported case of a medical treatment dispute over a child in Scotland, and only a handful in Ireland. (In Ireland, the parents are presumed to know best for their child, but only if they are married – arguably giving the child greater protection in an unmarried family, where their best interests still hold sway rather than deference to marital family). In Spain, conversely, deference to clinicians is such that their decisions are almost never challenged by families. In France, parents have some leeway so that decisions for their children are only challenged if parental refusal to agree to clinicians' proposals is 'unreasonable obstinacy'.

The English experience of fairly frequent and hotly contested litigation seems to be rooted in a combination in our culture of prominence of individuality and rights (in particular of the child), of not deferring unquestioningly to either medical authority or to parental authority, and of a well-established legal mechanism to bring cases.

Harrowing though such litigation is, I suspect that many people would not wish to change much of that.

The role and approach of the court

When the court is required, its role in these cases is very similar to the Court of Protection. It may have to determine whether a child can make the relevant decision for herself and, if the child cannot make her own decision, the court will determine the best interests of the child.

53 Medical Decision Making on Behalf of Young Children: A Comparative Perspective, ed Imogen Goold (2020)

The courts seem to be settling into consistently describing the approach here as involving five "intellectual milestones":[54]

1) "*The judge must decide what is in the child's best interests.*

2) *In making that decision, the child's welfare is the paramount consideration. The term "best interests" encompasses all welfare issues.*

3) *The judge must look at the question from the child's assumed point of view.*

4) *There is a strong presumption in favour of the course of action which prolongs life, but that presumption is not irrebuttable.*

5) *The judge must conduct a balancing exercise in which all the relevant welfare factors are weighed."*

Strictly, the court for tackling this is the family division of the High Court, and it may be exercising the inherent jurisdiction of the court to make orders and declarations, or the statutory powers in accordance with the Children Act 1989, which puts front and centre that in determining any question "the child's welfare shall be the court's paramount consideration".[55]

In practice though, you may well be in front of the same judge as in the Court of Protection, in the same courtroom, in the same building, and increasingly the child's "welfare" and "best interests" are used more or less interchangeably. The comments in Chapter 7 about going to court,

54 Drawn from the Court of Appeal judgment in the *Charlotte Wyatt* case, above, and see para 78 of *Fixsler* [2021] EWCA Civ 1018, and for a recent example *Great Ormond Street Hospital v MG*, 24 April 2025 [2025] EWHC 1042 (Fam) – https://www.bailii.org/ew/cases/EWHC/Fam/2025/1042.html

55 Children Act 1989 s1(1).

if you have to, in the context of the Court of Protection are largely just as applicable to the family court.

In 2014, Ian McEwan published "the Children Act", a novel about a High Court judge dealing with a case of a Jehovah's Witness child refusing blood transfusions for treatment of his leukaemia. It was made into a film starring Emma Thompson in 2017. I won't spoil the ending. But as the child in the story was only a few months shy of his 18th birthday, it was a little odd (for a lawyer, rather than for a clean narrative, perhaps) that there was not a peep about the Mental Capacity Act!

The messy reality is a patchwork of different legal frameworks:

- Say we have a 1 year-old child and a medical treatment decision to be made, for example for treatment of a brain tumour. The child will not be *Gillick* competent. Someone with parental responsibility can consent / refuse. But if there is a dispute the court can decide, and would expect professionals to refer the case to court if there was concern about the exercise of PR.

- Now take the same decision for a 15 year-old. If she is *Gillick* competent – i.e. she understands the situation and options, and has the maturity to make the decision, then she can consent (and, arguably, refuse). But someone with PR can also consent. Again, the court can resolve any dispute.

- Perhaps just days later, the same child is now 16 years old. Now she is presumed to have capacity to be able to make the decision for herself under the MCA, unless shown otherwise (and in fact would have been presumed as able to consent under the Family Law Reform Act 1969). But the parents' PR continues until 18 so in theory they also have decision-making responsibility (though you'd expect it to defer to a child at that stage). And, again, the court can resolve any dispute.

- For another child of 16 or 17 years, if they lack capacity to make the decision per the MCA, then a best interests decision must be made for them, involving of course family and others "engaged in caring for her or interested in her welfare", as explained in Chapter 5. But at the same time, the parents' PR also continues to age 18. And the court (whether the Court of Protection or the family division of the High Court) can make a decision.

The Court of Appeal in 1992[56] described a theory of needing a "flak jacket" for the doctors to protect their decision from being unlawful, and it was possible for this to be provided by the parents' PR, or the child's own consent if capable of giving it, or the court.

In practice, though, I am not sure it would be advisable to simply rely on the consent of a parent with PR to authorise forcing treatment coercively onto a 17 year-old who has capacity to refuse, or even onto a 15 year-old who is uncontentiously *Gillick* competent to refuse it. If this was ever OK, I think those times have changed, and it would always be advisable to seek the authority of the court.

The MCA Code of Practice (para 12.14) says:

> *"Difficult issues can arise if a young person [ie 16/17 years old] who has legal and mental capacity and refuses consent – especially if someone with PR wishes to give consent on the young person's behalf. The family division of the High Court can hear cases where there is disagreement".*

The only constant is the power of the court to have the final say, confirmed recently in Re X (no 2)[57]. This case involved a 15 year-old girl who had sickle cell disease, as a result of which clinicians felt that she

56 *Re W* [1992] All ER 627.

57 [2021] EWHC 65 (fam) – https://www.bailii.org/ew/cases/EWHC/Fam/2021/65.html

needed blood transfusions from time to time. Given her and her parents' objection, the Trust applied to court for authority on an urgent basis each time a transfusion was needed, and then applied for wider ranging permission to use transfusion if indicated until X turned 18 years of age, to avoid repeated urgent applications. Though Sir James Munby declined to give the clinicians such a blank cheque, saying that it might tend too much to promote medical paternalism and that such decisions should be made by the court on the facts at the time, he reaffirmed clearly that the court retains the ability to override the refusal of medical treatment until 18 years of age, regardless of whether a child is *Gillick* competent or capacitous.

Again, in Re E & F,[58] the Court of Appeal upheld declarations authorising blood transfusion for two young people aged 16 and 17, and commented on the classic Re W case (above) that:

> *"Re W does not establish a presumption in favour of the mature adolescent's decision, but instead affirms welfare as the overriding principle. It speaks for the young person's decision to be upheld where possible but also speaks of those rare circumstances where the gravity of the consequences and the imperative to preserve life may require the court to intervene"*

So the court can override even a competent or capacitous refusal of treatment by anyone under 18 years, but whether it should do so in the case of a child assessed as *Gillick* competent, or having capacity under the MCA, is another matter.

One good example was in *Re P,*[59] which was dealt with out of hours "in the middle of the night" on 13/14 May 2014 by Mr Justice Baker as the

58 [2021] EWCA Civ 1888 https://www.bailii.org/ew/cases/EWCA/Civ/2021/1888.html

59 [2014] EWHC 1650 (Fam), https://www.familylawweek.co.uk/site.aspx?i=ed129874

duty High Court judge on call. A 17½ year-old girl had been admitted earlier that afternoon after an overdose of paracetamol. She was refusing all treatment. She had a history of self-harm, and previous detention under the MHA, but at this time was not detained, and the opinion of the on-call psychiatrist was that although she suffered from a personality disorder, she had capacity to make her own decision about treatment. P's mother attended and gave her consent to the treatment, but the hospital was reluctant to force this on P in the circumstances. Without treatment within 8 hours of the overdose, there was a risk of fatal liver damage. The treatment required was a drug infusion (parvolex) which had to run over a 21-hour period, and so sedation / restraint over that period might be necessary to complete the treatment in the face of non-compliance.

The trust's lawyers contacted the out of hours judge and a telephone hearing was urgently arranged. By the time Mr Justice Baker heard the case, P had accepted the first dose, but clinicians worried that she might still refuse to allow it to continue over the necessary period.

On the evidence available, he could not say that she lacked capacity to make the decision for herself, allowing a best interests decision under the MCA, but nonetheless the court would authorise treatment to be forced on her if need be. The judge recognised that this is not to be done lightly, but while P's wishes and feelings were important they were not decisive in this situation.

Of course, if she had been a few months older, the court would have had no jurisdiction at all over an adult patient with capacity.

There is an obvious double standard here. If P in that case had been consenting to the parvolex, her decision was unimpeachable. Looking back to the wording of the Family Law Reform Act 1969 that a 16 year-old would be presumed able to "consent" to treatment, it can feel as if they can make their own decision, as long as it is to agree with the doctors. This purported respect for the autonomy of the near-adult child could feel pretty hollow; you can choose any colour you want, as long as it is the one the doctors want.

The argument we saw in Chapter 4 on the MCA for possibly finding capacity to *consent* but lack of capacity to *refuse* treatment may apply more convincingly, perhaps, where it is possible that the consequences of refusing vital treatment may be harder to understand fully for a young mind than the consequences of consenting.

Personally, though, I am fairly comfortable with accepting that the courts (like the rest of us) have a paternalistic streak and tend to err on the side of preserving life for children, at least until they are 18.

This remains the case whatever the reasons for the refusal, so typically a child of Jehovah's Witness parents will not be allowed by the court to refuse blood products on religious grounds, where an adult with capacity would be allowed to make their own decision, however unwisely.[60]

The ever-growing influence of autonomy though might also be softening these borders a little, especially as a child gets closer to adulthood. In April 2024, Mr Justice Cobb heard a case involving J,[61] a Jehovah's Witness of 17 years 7 months, who would be 18 in September that year. He was due to have urological surgery for kidney problems, but there was a risk that blood products might be needed, which J refused. The Trust applied to court, and Cobb J reflected on the two key factors to be

---

60 While we mention Jehovah's Witnesses, I'll note here that in my experience contacting the local Hospital Liaison Committee of the Jehovah's Witnesses can be very helpful. In some cases the parents' position has been that they do not implacably oppose a trust's request for a court order permitting treatment for their child, but that they did not feel able in good conscience to give consent for the treatment themselves – ie they do not oppose the treatment being given but want it to have been the court's decision. I have known NHS Trust clients with strong views on the need to incur the legal costs of making a court application in that situation.

61 Re J (Older child, Jehovah's Witness) [2024] EWHC 1034 (fam) https://www.bailii.org/ew/cases/EWHC/Fam/2024/1034.html

balanced in such cases: preservation of life, and personal autonomy, and concluded:

> *"J is only a matter of weeks away from being an adult as a matter of law. He has limited – but nonetheless evolving – experience of mature decision-making; he has first-hand experience of the death of someone of whom he was fond. He already shows many attributes of adulthood. I found him to be an impressive young man with clear thoughts and expression. I am satisfied that he knows his own mind, and is aware of the risks to which he is exposing himself in declining blood products in the unlikely event that they would be needed in this operation. J's clear and unequivocal decision in this regard, and his reasoning, are rooted in his faith; I respect his well-recognised right under Article 9 of the ECHR to manifest and observe his religion. The Applicants recognise that J's beliefs about blood products are "long held and considered". I accept that if I were to accede to this application and blood products were therefore administered intra-operatively or post-operatively, this would be likely to affect J's sense of self-determination, his fidelity to the tenets of his religion, and the quality of his life going forward. I am satisfied that while blood products may save his life, their administration against his wishes would lead to him experiencing a much reduced quality and enjoyment of that saved life, and he would be 'tormented' by having other blood in his veins.*
>
> *Having weighed all of the matters outlined above, I have concluded that in this case it is in J's best interests for his own decision to refuse the administration of blood or blood products in surgery to prevail, and I propose therefore to refuse the application for the court's authorisation to administer blood products in the event of emergency in the upcoming operation."*

Saying no, and changing your mind

There has been one other high profile counter-example, where a much younger child has been allowed to refuse life-saving medical treatment.

In 2008, Herefordshire Primary Care Trust started court proceedings when a 13 year-old girl named Hannah Jones refused to agree to a heart transplant. She would need a transplant to survive as she had a hole in the heart, but said that she felt that the procedure was too risky, and she preferred to enjoy her remaining days with her family and friends. Her parents supported her decision. Proceedings were started, but after a discussion with a child protection officer, according to the press coverage, her views were relayed to the legal teams at court who decided to abandon the case[62]. As a result, there is no reported judgment, and we can only speculate what happened, but it appears that she was assessed as *Gillick* competent and the public bodies involved decided to respect her refusal. It is not clear what a judge would have done if the case had been pursued.

Press coverage shows that she later changed her mind and accepted the transplant when she was 14, after her condition deteriorated, and went on to university. She said:

> *"At the time it was right for me to do it. I wasn't going to be pushed into making that decision.*
>
> *"I was exhausted by the drugs and the pressure I was under and I don't regret my decision. It was right for me to challenge the doctors at the time.*
>
> *"I changed my mind when I was 14 when I started to think of the things I wanted to do with my life and just thought I have to have a transplant in order to do them.*
>
> *"If I had chosen to have a transplant earlier then I might not be in the position I am in now. I regret nothing about the decisions I made."*[63]

---

62 http://news.bbc.co.uk/1/mobile/england/hereford/worcs/7721231.stm

63 https://www.walesonline.co.uk/news/health/schoolgirl-who-won-right-die-13398058

We must not forget that capacity, or *Gillick* competence, not only means the autonomy to make your own decision, however unwise, but also means *the ability to change your mind*. Treatment options must appropriately stay open, and be offered again, perhaps, from time to time, though taking care to stay the right side of the line of not just harassing people until they take your advice. It is not enough for the NHS to offer treatment, and then simply walk away if refused, as we saw in Chapter 4.[64]

My adult, still my child

I said at the beginning that a child will "ordinarily" develop her own maturity, expanding the scope of her (*Gillick*) competence and autonomy to make her own decisions, while the scope of parental responsibility "*dwindles*" in reflection. But that won't be the case for every child or every parent.

Whether as a result of a disability from birth or a misfortune in childhood, there are children who will not acquire the competence to make a decision for themselves about serious medical treatment and for whom, sadly, many such decisions may need to be made.

In these cases, the parents will often have been providing ongoing levels of care and devotion to their child, towards and into adulthood, which may be inconceivable to others. Parents may often have been routinely making every decision, from the most trivial to the most significant, for the whole of the child's life. And they can be wholly unprepared for the fact that, at 16, the MCA becomes the principal decision-making framework, with no necessary priority for the parents' views, other than including them as someone to be consulted under s4(7)(b) (see Chapter

64 In Chapter 4 because of the possibility that the patient may not have capacity to make that decision (as covered in the Mencap report referred to); here, because people with capacity or *Gillick* competence to make their own decision can always change their minds.

5). And indeed at 18, parental responsibility ceases in law, even if the child's dependence on their parents, in fact, does not.

If the legal framework is not well explained and understood in advance, then these changes might only come to light at the worst of times, when a contentious or critical decision about medical treatment needs to be made, perhaps when the child is already well over 18 years old.

A children's and young person's hospice once asked me to support a workshop together with a group of parents to explain, essentially, that from the age of 16 onwards the parents no longer had sole decision-making responsibility for their child, even if their son or daughter would only ever have the cognitive function of a very much younger child. That must feel an insult, at best, without regard for the years of sacrifice and dedication they had given.

It was without doubt one of the most intimidating bits of training I've ever had to give, and it was no easy session, but I learned an enormous amount, and the consensus from the families was that they wished this had been discussed with them sooner. As a result, using the phrase that was coined by that group, we worked together to develop a website of resources titled "my adult still my child", with a jargon buster and explanation of the legal framework and some FAQs.[65] I hope that it remains useful.

A common understanding of the legal framework can only help. Together with good communication, relationships and trust, this seems likely to give the best chance of avoiding disputes. But the issues are such that disputes area inevitable sometimes, and in the next chapter we will move on to how best to address and resolve these, including going to court if need be.

65 https://myadultstillmychild.co.uk/

Key points

- Growing autonomy of the child must be given appropriate weight, but it co-exists within a patchwork of overlapping authority also held by those with parental responsibility and the court.

- Where a child cannot make a medical treatment decision, the only question is the welfare or the best interests of the child, which (as for adults) must be interpreted widely, and is not just limited to medical factors.

- The starting point is that parents can be expected to be the best judge of their child's welfare or best interests, and their views should not lightly be overridden by clinicians or by the court, but doctors cannot be ordered to provide treatment which they are unwilling to do for a child any more than for an adult.

- It is not always in the interests of the child for life to be preserved at any cost.

- Wherever possible, the clinicians and the family ought to try to resolve any disputes, though informal means such as mediation, before going to the court only as a last resort. Good communication is critical.

Cases about children can reach a fever pitch of press and social media attention which are not typically seen in other cases, and which bring their own very real challenges. It is important that the family, and the clinicians, get good advice and real support throughout.

CHAPTER 6½

CODA: DEFINING AND DISPUTING DEATH

It is important to know when someone has died, for all sorts of legal, practical and emotional reasons. We need to know when it is appropriate to stop providing treatment, when preparations can be made for post-mortem, for organ donation, or for burial / cremation. When we grieve and for cultural and ritual reasons. And when – for legal purposes – a person no longer owns property or rights, which may now pass to someone else.

Given the fundamental issue, it is astonishing that there is inconsistency in the way this is addressed in legal systems around the world. In the New Jersey Declaration of Death Act 1991, for example, death cannot be declared on the basis of neurological criteria when there is reason to believe that "such a declaration would violate the personal religious beliefs of the individual". So two patients might be in neighbouring beds in New Jersey, in identical conditions, and one would be dead and the other would not, *based on their own beliefs.*

In the UK, there is no statutory definition of death, but until relatively recently defining death was never really very controversial. You could generally tell whether someone was dead or not. Death meant that the heart had stopped beating, the person had stopped breathing (the cliché of leaning over the body with a mirror to check for respiration), and was cold.

With the development of ventilators by Danish doctors in the 1950s to deal with a polio epidemic, it became possible to maintain respiration and circulation mechanically, long after the body lost the ability to do this for itself. In some cases, of course, this was a bridge to recovery, but in some cases there is no such hope.

The spectre arose of warehouses full of unconscious people sustained by machines, if the sanctity of life meant that everything should be done to maintain human life at all costs.

Conversely, after the first heart transplant was performed in 1967, by Dr Christiaan Barnard, the development of organ transplantation technology allowed this apparent horror to become a vital resource, and an increased opportunity to save lives[1].

The Ad Hoc Committee of the Harvard Medical School to Examine the Definition of Brain Death reported in 1968. The opening paragraph of their report asserted that irreversible coma should become the new criterion for death because of the great burden on those patients, families and on resources, and with a view to organ donation.

At the time of writing, there were a little over 8,000 people on the UK organ transplant waiting list, with around 1,400 deceased patient organ donors in the year 2024/25. Around half of them were donors after brain death, as opposed to circulatory criteria (see below).

We struggle to think of as dead someone who is still warm, and pink and (apparently) breathing – because machines are doing all this for them.

In 1993, Trisha Marshall had been dead, under Californian law, for some 3 ½ months when her son was born, having had her bodily functions sustained by mechanical ventilation to complete her pregnancy. That support was then withdrawn, and the press coverage used the headline: "Brain dead woman gives birth, then dies".[2]

1 Statistics about organ donation – NHS Organ Donation

2 San Francisco Chronicle, 4 August 1993.

Tony Bland's case, at around the same time (see Chapter 4), was heard on the basis that he was not already dead. He was in a persistent vegetative state, but still had some residual brain stem function, though the parts of the brain that provide consciousness had been lost. As Lord Hoffman put it: "His body is alive, but he has no life in the sense that even the most pitifully handicapped but conscious human being has a life". A best interests decision was made that the treatment keeping him alive should be stopped. But the Lords recognised him as being alive because his brain stem had not been destroyed, in contrast to what the court described as "the ventilated corpse":

> *"In some cases it is now apparently possible , with the use of a ventilator, to sustain a beating heart even thought the brainstem, and therefore the patient, is dead".*

As we have just seen in Archie Battersbee's case, the argument initially was whether he had already died, and the family's objection to the hospital testing to establish this.

Definition of death

Having recognised the concept of "brain stem death" since the *Bland* case in 1993, and in the absence of any statutory definition of death, the courts have always accepted the professional guidance on this as determinative.

In a decision in 2023, the Court of Appeal acknowledged the "*widely accepted consensus in this country for almost 50 years that brain stem death, correctly diagnosed, is the proper indicator of death in the legal sense. The contrary is not reasonably arguable at any level of court*".[3]

So the law has always simply adopted the professional guidance, as set out in The Academy of Medical Royal Colleges' document "A Code of

3 In *Casey* – see below.

practice for the diagnosis and confirmation of death[4]", which was recently updated with effect from 1 January 2025.[5]

There is only one definition of death:

- The permanent loss of the capacity for consciousness; and
- Permanent loss of the capacity to breathe.

But there are three different ways to establish it:

- Circulatory criteria,
- Somatic criteria, or
- Neurological criteria.

The circulatory criteria will be familiar – that the person has stopped breathing and the heart has stopped beating. This applies to around 1,600 people a day, and can usually be confirmed by a healthcare professional who is competent in using a stethoscope.

The somatic criteria were only alluded to in the previous (2008) version of the Code, but are now more explicit. Somatic criteria are appropriate where death follows overwhelming physical trauma (for example, when there is decapitation, massive cranial and cerebral destruction, incineration, or half the body is blown away); or when death is suspected

4 https://www.aomrc.org.uk/wp-content/uploads/2025/01/Code_of_Practice_Diagnosis_of_Death_010125.pdf

5 Full disclosure – in my role as a member of the Faculty of Intensive Care Medicine's Law and Ethics Policy Unit, I was invited to join the working group on this updated Code, which included clinicians, lawyers, ethicists and others.

to have occurred a considerable time ago (for example there is rigor mortis, decomposition etc).

Deaths by neurological criteria are the rarest in reality, only being used for around 4 people per day, nationwide, but are nonetheless likely to be the most controversial and contested.

Note that when it comes to infants under two months of age, the AoMRC Code previously deferred to a separate guideline published by the Royal College of Paediatrics and Child Health in 2015, but in the 2025 version the RCPCH guidance is brought into the main Code document as Appendix 2, and provides guidance for all children up to the age of 18, excluding only pre-term babies under 37 weeks' gestation.

Diagnosing death

The Code sets out in great detail the clinical tests to be undertaken to establish death by neurological criteria – ie that a patient may have died due to a devastating brain injury, despite the fact that their circulation and other bodily functions are being maintained by machinery.

"Death by neurological criteria" is the preferred terminology, though you will still hear people (and the courts) refer to "brain stem death".

The neurological tests must be done twice, with a consistent finding of absence of brainstem function. Historically, the time of death was considered to be the time when the first set of tests were done, with the second just providing confirmation. But that caused confusion, and was out of line with the approach in other countries. One of the significant changes in the 2025 Code was to bring this into line with international practice and to take the time of the second set of tests at the time of death.

There are some cases in which the circumstances mean that the neurological tests cannot be used safely, as was found to be the case with

Archie Battersbee (see chapter 6), as there had been some damage to his neck that made it difficult to rely on the test results.

If the clinical situation allows it, though, the legal question is whether the family were allowed to block the tests that the hospital wished to perform, or whether they can dispute the outcome of those tests. I am told that in practice these disputes are not uncommon in intensive care medicine, but that they almost always resolve themselves through "tincture of time".

Disputing death

Nonetheless, the courts have had to deal with a number of cases on these issues.

Re M[6] involved a child named Midrar, who suffered a devastating hypoxic brain injury at birth. Andy Casey[7], by contrast, was a young man who was catastrophically injured after being punched in the head on a night out. In each case, death by neurological criteria has been tested and established, and the family disputed the outcome. In *Casey*, the Court of Protection had made an urgent decision out of hours that such neurological testing could go ahead against the family's wishes.

In both cases, applications were made to the Court of Appeal by the family, and the Court of Appeal refused permission to appeal in both cases. This means that they do not really address the full arguments, instead finding that each family had no real prospect of success, so the judgments may carry slightly less weight perhaps than substantive Court of Appeal decisions, though in both cases the refusal is explained in unusually long and detailed judgments.

In Midrar's case, the family argued that the brain stem tests could not be relied on by the trust because they had been carried out without the

6 Re M (declaration of death of a child) [2020] EWCA Civ 164.

7 St George's University Hospital v Casey [2023] EWCA Civ 1092.

family's written permission. At first instance Mrs Justice Lieven held that "I do not think that there is any requirement for written consent from the parents", but went on to find anyway that the family did consent to the tests, or at least that they were told about them and did not object. The Court of Appeal agreed that the family had in fact consented to the tests.

As such, this does not definitively resolve the question whether the consent of the family is necessary for the tests to be done or relied on. But it is certainly no support for any argument by a family that their consent is necessary, given that Lieven J thought otherwise, and the Court of Appeal did not take the chance to disagree.

Note that this was in the situation of a tiny baby and the role of those with parental responsibility, so it is reasonable to think that the argument that a (so-called) "next of kin" (see Chapter 5) has any right to veto neurological testing of an adult is even weaker.

Where testing has established death by neurological criteria, then the court expects that treatment should be withdrawn promptly, within say 24-48 hours at most, subject to any further steps needed to resolve any dispute. In Midrar's case, the court was concerned that the case concluded 4 months after he was diagnosed as dead, and though the court recognised that the trust was trying everything to get agreement with the family and said "*confirmation of a diagnosis of death is unlikely to be pressingly urgent*", there should only be a "short but reasonable time for the parents to assemble a legal team".

Aside from the issues of the dignity of the deceased, it is clear that there is real moral injury to the staff asked to continue caring for "*a ventilated corpse*" if there is undue delay.

In any dispute, it is important that this is approached in the right way. As the court said in Midrar's case:

> "*In contrast to issues concerning the medical treatment of the living, whether they be children or adults who lack capacity, where the best interests of the individual will determine the outcome, where a person is dead, the question of best interests is, tragically, no longer relevant*".

So in an application to court about a dispute over carrying out the tests, before death by neurological criteria is established, the argument would be about the patient's own best interests, with the patient joined as a party to the proceedings and represented by lawyers, likely to be the Official Solicitor (see Chapter 7).

But after diagnosis of death by neurological criteria, the patient would not be joined as a party to proceedings, and would not be represented.

In any case, the burden of proof would be on the applicant (ie the hospital trust), and the standard of proof is the balance of probabilities (ie more likely than not). In *Casey*, the Court of Appeal rejected the argument that proof "beyond reasonable doubt" (ie the criminal standard) was needed to establish death, though they did agree that the evidence should be considered with "anxious scrutiny" (which Peter Jackson LJ described as "*not so much a principle of law as a statement of the obvious*").

The language used is important as well.

In a 2019 case[8], Francis J ended his decision about AB, a 14 year-old boy, by declaring that he was satisfied that brain stem death had been established and so "*it is lawful and in AB's best interests for treatment to be withdrawn*".

The Court of Appeal in *Midrar* criticised this wording, noting again that "*once death has ben established then the concept of best interests no longer has*

8 Oxford University Hospitals NHS Trust v AB [2019] EWHC 3516 (Fam) – https://www.bailii.org/ew/cases/EWHC/Fam/2019/3516.html

any legal relevance". The Court of Appeal preferred the formulation used by Hayden J in another case[9] in which he concluded that

> *"Whilst expressing profound respect for the father's views, the time has now come to permit the ventilator to be turned off and to allow Child A, who died on 10th February [ie at the time of the neurological testing], dignity in death".*

Stopping treatment to allow "dignity in death", rather than addressing it in terms of "best interests", is the better way to put it when death by neurological criteria has been established, and time of death will be the time of the (second) testing, not the court's decision.

The order made should be in the form that:

> *"P died at [time] on [date], irreversible cessation of brain stem functions having been conclusively established"*

Note that though the AoMRC guidance covers the whole of the UK, and the case law has been almost exclusively in the English Courts, there is no reason to think that the courts in other jurisdictions in the UK would take a different approach.

At the time of writing there has been only one non-English case, a decision in Northern Ireland in 2022[10] in which the AoMRC Code (then in the 2008 version) is explicitly adopted, and the approach is entirely in line with the English case law.

---

9 In Re A (A Child) [2015] EWHC 443 (Fam) – https://www.bailii.org/ew/cases/EWHC/Fam/2015/443.html

10 A Health and Social Care Trust v RL [2022] NIFam 17 – https://www.judiciaryni.uk/files/judiciaryni/decisions/A%20Health%20and%20Social%20Care%20Trust%20and%20RL%20and%20The%20Parents%20of%20RL.pdf

One interesting thing in that Northern Irish case is the explicit judicial criticism of a medical "expert" who, without being a neurologist or intensive care specialist, and having views that were "controversial when set against current mainstream medical opinion", had been giving "totally unrealistic and false hope" to the parents of RL.

The difficulty in accepting the loss of hope while a loved one is apparently pink and warm is something that the updated AoMRC Code appreciates, noting that there are reflex movements that can be deceptive, but are not indicative of life. In *Casey*, McDonald J commented that "*cruelly, the flattering voice of hope convinces those that love Mr Casey that these are signs that he is not dead*". Poignantly, Mirdrar gained weight while the artificial support continued after his death.

It is no surprise that there are disputes in such fraught and emotional situations. It is a surprise, perhaps, that there are not more.

It is open to the treating clinicians, of course, to offer further or ancillary testing where this is clinically appropriate or where, perhaps, this might help to reassure the family. This might include seeking a second clinical opinion, repeating the neurological tests, or getting scans such as MRI or CTs. There could be a referral to the trust's ethics committee, or even instruction of an independent expert opinion. But none of that is mandated by the Code, and of course ultimately it is the role of the court to resolve any disputes, and such attempts – in good faith – to address a family's concerns can inadvertently amount to undue delay overall.

As with all decisions and disputes in this context, communication and trust are key. An important improvement in the 2025 Code from its predecessor is a new, lengthy section dealing with the principles of communication with families.

Where there is a dispute, though, the Code advises that "Legal advice should be sought urgently if agreement cannot be reached in a reasonable amount of time and at most within a few days" (para 6.69).

The most recent example is in the case of the Mother of G.[11] In this case, G was a 26 year-old woman who had ingested 1.5 to 2 litres of engine coolant. She was diagnosed as having died by neurological criteria on Wednesday 15 May 2024, and the results were discussed with her family over the following day. Her mother's view was that G needed more time and might recover.

The trust made an application to court on Friday 17 May 2024, and it was heard by Mr Justice Peel on Friday 24 May. He held that "declarations of death by reason of brain stem testing are usually urgent in the sense that it is unreasonable to wait any length of time for determination of such sensitive matters". He made his decision that day, and handed down his written judgment at 1030am on Monday 27 May 2024:

> *"The position of the family, in particular G's mother, is understandable but sadly futile".*
>
> *"... The brain stem tests were carried out in accordance with the Code of Practice and there is nothing to suggest that any further inquiry would reach a different conclusion. To allow more time in the hope of a miracle has no clinical justification. The family's wish to retain a vestige of hope is beyond reproach, but it has no clinical or other foundation.*
>
> *In my judgment, the evidence is overwhelming. I am satisfied that the Trust has established its case that G died at 13.30 on 15 May 2024. I shall so declare, and I shall further authorise withdrawal of mechanical ventilation and medical support. However, in my judgment such withdrawal shall not take place before 4pm on Monday*

11 University Hospitals of Bristol and Weston NHS FT v The Mother of G [2024] EWHC 1288 (Fam) https://www.bailii.org/ew/cases/EWHC/Fam/2024/1288.html

27 May 2024, which give the family a little more time to process this tragic event."

Key points

- Death is the permanent loss of the capacity for consciousness and the permanent loss of the capacity to breathe, though it can be established by circulatory, somatic or neurological criteria.

- Though establishing death by neurological criteria is the rarest, it is the most contentious, and at times there may be disputes about carrying out the neurological testing, or about the implications of their findings.

- The court can resolve any dispute, but it is wrong to frame things in terms of "best interests" for a patient who has already died, and better to think about the dignity of the deceased.

- As elsewhere in this book, communication is key, and undue delay in addressing and resolving any dispute is to be avoided.

CHAPTER 7

CONFLICT RESOLUTION AND COURT

- Lawyers
- Complaints
- Mediation
- Ethics committees
- Court of Protection – when should a case go to court?
- Who should make the application?
- Delay and timing
- Process and timescale
- Legal costs
- Official Solicitor / CAFCASS and costs
- Technology
- Anonymity, media and social media
- Practicalities:
    - Applying to court

- Medical records
- Drafting a witness statement
- Giving evidence

We have already covered lots of things we can do to make conflict less likely – good communication, managing expectations, and involving the patient / family and others appropriately, while being clear about which decisions are whose to make.

But sometimes, we will still end up in dispute, and there needs to be an appropriate way to resolve this.

Given the scope of this book, I'll mostly focus on the Court of Protection (medical treatment decisions for children in the High Court family division raise similar issues), though I hope that some of the practical points below may still be useful in other contexts.[1]

As I'll explain below, some cases must go to court whether or not there is any dispute, and for these the best thing is to get them to court as quickly as possible. For other cases, the starting point is that where there is a dispute, court ought to be a last resort, and any dispute should first be raised informally with the NHS body (or local authority or private sector provider) involved, and attempts made to resolve any issues by other means, such as the complaints process or Alternative Dispute Resolution, for example. Undue delay must be avoided in any case.

1 For example, litigation for clinical negligence; judicial review challenges to decisions of NHS bodies; mental health tribunals (now, strictly, the first-tier tribunal (mental health)) to challenge use of the Mental Health Act; coroners' inquests where required after a death; or disciplinary proceedings under the General Medical Council or Nursing and Midwifery Council etc.

Lawyers

Whether or not litigation is imminent, it may be helpful to get legal advice as appropriate, but we ought to accept that there are times when involving lawyers does not always improve things! One of my NHS trust clients used to say that "sometimes lawyers are bridges, and sometimes they're walls". There can be advantages to sorting things out without getting lawyers involved. Once one side gets legal advice, the other side often feels obliged to "lawyer up", as a matter of "equality of arms". Meetings attended by lawyers on each side can be more adversarial than they would have been otherwise (just see how easily here I've slipped straight into talking about the competing "sides"), not to mention the costs involved.

If a meeting or a process can go ahead without the benefit of independent legal representation then, sometimes, so much the better. That said, there are times when it is much better to get advice early on, and significant delay, damage and costs are incurred unnecessarily by not doing so. The trick, of course, is to know with some confidence which is which.

For this reason, most firms of solicitors acting for large NHS clients will typically offer an agreed amount of initial advice for free, to help to test the water whether something more substantive is appropriate without the client worrying about a clock starting immediately the phone is answered, and a bill arriving shortly afterwards. It is important to us that clients feel able to pick up the phone to run something past us, and that we reduce any barriers to them doing this, though invariably the client's in-house legal or governance team will act appropriately as gatekeepers to that resource.

Complaints process

As I mentioned in Chapter 1, with effect from April 2009[2] the old regulations for dealing with complaints against the NHS[3] were replaced and rolled together with the previous system for dealing with complaints about adult social care.[4]

The current regulations impose an obligation on each NHS body or local authority to have an appropriate mechanism for dealing with complaints supportively, efficiently and properly. A complaint may be made on behalf of a patient where appropriate (e.g. for a patient who has died, or lacks capacity to make decisions about any complaint, or for a child). No formal process is required where the complaint is resolved to the complainant's satisfaction within one working day, or where it is only made orally. Any complaint must be made within one year from the date of the thing complained about (or from when the complainant found out about it), and a substantive response must be given within 6 months, or an explanation given why not.

Throughout, the Patient Advice and Liaison Service (PALS) is available to help support patients and their families.[5]

If a complainant is dissatisfied with the completed complaints process or outcome, the next recourse is to the Parliamentary and Health Service Ombudsman (PHSO[6]). On investigation, the Ombudsman can make recommendations for the NHS body to put things right, which can

2 The Local Authority Social Services and National Health Service Complaints (England) Regulations 2009.

3 The National Health Service (Complaints) Regulations 2004.

4 Local Authority Social Services Complaints (England) Regulations 2006.

5 https://www.nhs.uk/common-health-questions/nhs-services-and-treatments/what-is-pals-patient-advice-and-liaison-service/

6 https://www.ombudsman.org.uk/

include explanations and apologies, as well as (usually fairly modest) financial remedy in some circumstances.

Mediation

Some things must go to court – we'll get to those – but even then, time permitting,[7] there can be real value in first trying some other ways to resolve or at least narrow a dispute.

Alternative Dispute Resolution (ADR) comes in many forms, but in this context perhaps the most familiar is mediation. This involves an impartial person (a mediator) being appointed by both parties to help them to reach an agreement for themselves that will resolve the dispute. It is flexible and confidential, and the role of the mediator is not to solve the problem for them or impose a solution, but to facilitate the discussions between the parties. It is very different from litigation in which a judge, though still impartial, will resolve the dispute by imposing a decision after a very formal process. Mediation is likely to be quicker and cheaper than litigation, and it can look beyond the narrow dispute itself and focus as well on restoring the relationship and trust between the parties, the breakdown in which is almost always at the root of the conflict.

In the clinical negligence context, the flexibility of the process allows the parties to come to agreement about remedies (such as an apology, assurances about changes in practice etc) which are potentially more meaningful and are beyond the court's power: in these proceedings the court can only award financial compensation (remember that the money was their primary motivation for only 6% of claimants, on their own account, as we saw in Chapter 2). In a report[8] on 12 February 2020 on

7 This always needs to be balanced against the strong comments from the court about the harm caused by delay in bringing proceedings – see below.

8 https://resolution.nhs.uk/wp-content/uploads/2020/02/NHS-Resolution-Mediation-in-healthcare-claims-an-evaluation.pdf

the use of mediation published by NHS Resolution, the indemnifier for clinical negligence claims against the NHS, Julienne Vernon, head of dispute resolution and quality, wrote:

> *"Mediation puts the patient/claimant at the heart of the claim, focussing on concerns which are very often not "all about the money", and would not be possible to address in any other dispute resolution setting such as a meeting with just the lawyers. Mediation is proven to be an effective forum for claims resolution with 74% of cases mediated under NHS Resolution's claims mediation service settling on the day of mediation or within 28 days of the mediation date".*

Given what we saw earlier about the motivations for litigation and its relative scarcity, perhaps we ought to rethink some of the perceptions of a "compensation culture" and be open minded about trying alternative approaches that might be more flexible and better suited to what people are really trying to achieve.

In the medical treatment dispute context, the judges in both *Charlie Gard* and *Alfie Evans* cases were vocal on the potential value of mediation. But we should recognise its limits. There are times when only a court order will do, and care should be taken that mediation is not used as a delaying tactic. In disputes about best interests it can be really helpful to get the warring family members, or the family and the clinicians, in the same room and (ideally) onto the same page, but the fact that consensus breaks out about what is in granny's best interests does not make it so. As we have seen, the Mental Capacity Act sets out an objective test for this, which takes due account of the views of family and clinicians but is not solely determined by them. Care must be taken not to assume that finding common ground, or an approach that placates a family, means that this would be lawful. This could be, for instance, a decision at the behest of the family to continue treatment of a child against the better judgement of the clinicians, but for a period of time which they can live with. This is a compromise not only between the parties, but also potentially compromising the child's best interests, which is the proper test. We will see below, in the context of the case law around when an application to court must be made (and how quickly), that "compromise" can be problematic when we are dealing with the question of best interests.

Even if a judicial decision is still required, though, it can substantially shorten any subsequent litigation or hearing, and reduce legal costs, if some time is spent getting as much consensus as possible first. And in many situations, successful ADR may be able to avoid going to court altogether.

The current MCA code of practice (2007) specifically endorses the use of mediation, saying (at para 15.9):

> *"Any case that can be settled through negotiation is likely to benefit from mediation. It is most suitable when people are not communicating well or not understanding each other's point of view. It can improve relationships and stop future disputes, so it is a good option when it is in the person's interests for people to have a good relationship in the future".*

It may be that unfamiliarity is a real barrier to using mediation more, but (speaking as a qualified mediator, I admit!) I firmly believe that it can have real value in the health and social care context in particular, where the ongoing relationships between the parties can be so important.

Ethics Committee

I hesitate to mention this here, as it is not exactly a mechanism for resolution of disputes, but I think that there is an important role for medical ethics committees, which I have not mentioned elsewhere. I have been lucky enough to be a member of the ethics of clinical practice committees of several very large NHS acute hospital trusts. I appreciate that they will work slightly differently in each place. The ones I have attended are a mix of clinicians and laymen, including people from the trust and members of the public. They are not decision-making groups, in that it did not fall within its remit to offer a solution, still less to determine a dispute. They are available to clinicians as a sounding board, to seek support, and a safe environment to reflect on lessons and different perspectives on a challenging case, which they could present to the ethics committee for discussion. Invariably, as a diverse group, perspectives were articulated and ideas expressed which would never have occurred to me individually, and perhaps had not occurred to the treating clinicians, and they always went away with food for thought, whether the case was ongoing or something in the past to reflect on.

I would very highly recommend the establishment and use of an ethics committee where possible, and it is a wonderful experience to have been part of and learnt from such wise, thoughtful, and compassionate colleagues.

That said, in some cases the role of the ethics committee has been controversial and criticised, in particular around the extent to which the patient's family is allowed to be involved in the discussion. For instance, in *Great Ormond Street v MX*[9], the court had an application by the Trust for approval of a palliative care plan for a 9 year-old, against the wishes of the parents who wanted all possible treatment. The child's case had been considered at the Trust's ethics committee, and the judge was very critical of the fact that this discussion had taken place without the parents being in attendance:

> *"I consider that a lack of involvement by patients and/or their families is itself an issue of medical ethics and I am most surprised that there is not guidance in place to ensure their involvement and/or participation. While it is a matter of common sense and good practice for medical professionals and members of a multidisciplinary treating team to have discussions sans the patient or their relatives to enable an uninhibited and frank exchange of professional views and information without the*

9 [2020] EWHC 1958 (Fam) – https://www.bailii.org/ew/cases/EWHC/Fam/2020/1958.html

need for the empathic, sensitive and supportive language used when speaking to patients and/or their families, the absence of any prior consultation or participation, cannot be good practice and should generally be unacceptable. Even at hastily assembled meetings there should be notice taken of the views of the patient and/or close relatives which could take the form of some written notes or letter submitted on their behalf. There should be guidance on patient/family participation and a clear protocol of how and when they are informed as to the arrangements being put in place for an Ethics Committee to meet along with being informed as to the outcome.

As observed by X's guardian in situations such as X's, where the quality of life of a disabled child with complex medical needs is a central issue, the involvement of parents in the clinical ethics committee process is essential. The Guardian may have been reassured, as I was to a degree, to be informed that the Applicant generally takes the approach of involving parents, but the fact that in this case, which was then the subject of proceedings in the Family Division and where there already were (and remained) issues between the parents and the hospital there was no involvement of the parents, or of their views being placed by the committee for consideration during their deliberations, is a matter of some concern. I remain uncertain as to why it was not felt possible to involve the parents with the Ethics Committee in this case, particularly as matters progressed and the urgency and nature of the decisions in issue changed, so that there was time for further advice and opinion from the clinical ethics committee to be obtained. The fact that outcome of the meeting was discussed with the parent's later that day and after the meeting does not cure the deficiencies set out above and had the effect of both raising their anxiety and contributing to their feelings of alienation and exclusion."

In *Manchester University NHS FT v Verden*[10] (a case which involved the question whether a 17 year-old boy with renal failure should be made

[10] [2022] EWCOP 9 – https://www.bailii.org/ew/cases/EWCOP/2022/9.html

eligible for a kidney transplant, despite concerns about his likely compliance with treatment due to his learning disability, autism and ADHD), Mrs Justice Arbuthnot suggested that it would be better to have an ethics committee meeting in two parts, one with and one without the family in attendance, rather than to exclude them altogether.

Clearly it would be difficult to explain why the family should not be involved fully in any process that makes decisions about the child's care; and so (especially if the committee does not have the family in attendance, or at least have their views represented in some way) it is important to explain that the ethics committee is <u>not</u> in any way such a decision-making body.

<u>Court of Protection – when should a case go to court?</u>

With or without prior attempts at mediation or other ADR, there are some cases that have to go to court. The question of when an application is needed is not always easy, and has been one of the livelier areas of case law in the last few years, since the first edition of this book.

The Court of Protection has jurisdiction to resolve any disputes about the MCA, for example whether a person has capacity for a specific decision, what option is in their best interests, and about the validity or application of any LPA. The court can appoint a deputy to make decisions, much like an LPA, but this is extremely rare for health and welfare. Specifically, the court can make a declaration that giving or withholding proposed medical treatment would be lawful, as being in the patient's best interests, despite them lacking the capacity to consent to it.

The MCA code of practice (para 15.35) notes that "the court is not always the right place to settle problems involving people who lack capacity. Other forms of settling disagreements may be more appropriate and less distressing".

Based on previous case law, the MCA code of practice set out (para 8.18) that

> *"Cases involving any of the following decisions should therefore be brought before a court:*
>
> - *decisions about the proposed withholding or withdrawal of artificial nutrition and hydration (ANH) from patients in a permanent vegetative state (PVS)*
> - *cases involving organ or bone marrow donation by a person who lacks capacity to consent*
> - *cases involving the proposed non-therapeutic sterilisation of a person who lacks capacity to consent to this (e.g. for contraceptive purposes) and*
> - *all other cases where there is a doubt or dispute about whether a particular treatment will be in a person's best interests".*

A Practice Direction (9E) to the Court of Protection Rules 2007 expanded on this, but was abolished and not replaced in the updated Rules in 2017[11].

The code of practice is, of course, only guidance, albeit it should be followed unless there is good reason not to, and in fact the code has also been overtaken in places by the case law. The sad case of Hillsborough victim Tony Bland[12], discussed in Chapter 5, was the first case in which the withdrawal of clinically assisted nutrition and hydration (CANH) was authorised for a person in permanent vegetative state. It held that withdrawal of CANH cases should always be brought to court 'at least

11 The current 2017 PD9E deals with statutory wills.

12 Airedale NHS Trust -v- Bland [1993] AC 789.

for the time being and until a body of experience and practice has been built up which might obviate the need for application in every case'.

In *Re Y*,[13] 25 years later, in July 2018, the Supreme Court confirmed that such a body of experience had now developed. If professional guidance has been properly followed, and there is no dispute between the family and clinicians, then it would not be necessary to bring each case to court before CANH could be withdrawn. Since then the comprehensive and helpful BMA guidance on the issue[14] (which was in preparation at the time of the *Re Y* judgment) has been produced. Of course, any *dispute* over withdrawal of CANH ought to still go to court, but it is no longer true that such a decision cannot be taken at all without a judge's blessing.

The current MCA code of practice (2007) was produced after *Bland*, of course, but before the *Re Y* judgment, which has changed the landscape fundamentally.

We also have some more general guidance from Lady Hale in the Supreme Court:

> *"section 5 of the 2005 Act gives a general authority, to act in relation to the care or treatment of P, to those caring for him who reasonably believe both that P lacks capacity in relation to the matter and that it will be in P's best interests for the act to be done. This will usually suffice, unless the decision is so serious that the court itself has said it must be taken to court. But if there is a dispute (or if what is to be done amounts to a deprivation of liberty for which no authorisation under the Deprivation of Liberty Safeguards in Schedule A1 to the 2005 Act)*

13 *An NHS Trust v Y* [2018] UKSC 22. http://www.bailii.org/uk/cases/UKSC/2018/22.html

14 https://www.bma.org.uk/media/1161/bma-clinically-assisted-nutrition-hydration-canh-full-guidance.pdf

> *then it may be necessary to bring the case to court...*"[15] (emphasis added)

So when is a decision "so serious" that the court itself must make it? Most recently, we have guidance on applications about medical treatment issued by Mr Justice Hayden, Vice President of the Court of Protection, on 17 January 2020,[16] which he described as being on an interim basis pending the issue of the updated MCA code of practice. The key points are that:

- Not every medical treatment case needs to go to the Court of Protection. Reliance on MCA s5 (see Chapter 5) ought to be the starting point, even for "serious" treatment, if professional guidance and the code of practice are followed, and there is consensus about capacity and best interests. It is the *contentiousness* of the decision rather than the *seriousness* of the treatment itself that is the trigger.

- However, s5 may not be enough to rely on, and consideration must be given to an application to court, if (for example)

    - the decision is very finely balanced;

    - there is difference of medical opinion;

    - best interests is in dispute; or

    - there is a potential conflict of interest for those making the decision.

---

15 *MN v A CCG* [2017] UKSC 22 http://www.bailii.org/uk/cases/UKSC/2017/22.html

16 https://www.bailii.org/ew/cases/EWCOP/2020/2.html

- And in any of those circumstances, an application *must* be made if the decision relates to life-sustaining treatment.

- An application is "highly probable" in cases of a serious proposed interference with the patient's human rights, for example:[17]

    - where a medical procedure or treatment is for the primary purpose of sterilisation;

    - where a medical procedure is proposed for a person who lacks capacity to consent to it, where the procedure is for the purpose of a donation of an organ, bone marrow, stem cells, tissue or bodily fluid to another person;

    - a procedure for the covert insertion of a contraceptive device or other means of contraception;

    - where it is proposed that an experimental or innovative treatment to be carried out; or

    - a case involving a significant ethical question in an untested or controversial area of medicine.

- Separately, an application "may also be required where the proposed procedure or treatment is to be carried out using a degree of force to restrain the person concerned and the restraint may go beyond the parameters set out in sections 5 and 6 Mental Capacity Act 2005. In such a case, the restraint will amount to a deprivation of the person's liberty and ... The authority of the court will be required to make this deprivation of liberty lawful." (see Chapter 5 on DoL)

---

17 Much of which echoes the code of practice and the old PD9E.

To make some of the more generic bits of this more tangible, I'd usually expect an application to court wherever:

- P is opposed to treatment and, in particular, where more than transient force will be required to carry it out;
- P will need to be brought to hospital against their wishes, using deception or coercion such as physical restraint or chemical sedation in the community;
- there is a disagreement about best interests that cannot be resolved;
- for whatever reason, the clinicians themselves are reluctant to proceed with the treatment (or non-treatment) without the authority of a court order (the "gut" test, if you like).

One significant case on this was a decision in January 2024 by Hayden J about EUP, a lady in her late 80s.[18] Sadly, she was in a very poor condition and near the end of her life. After repeated attempts to place a nasogastric tube to allow her to be fed, it was felt that there was no longer any clinically viable way to provide her with nutrition. Her family were insistent that nutrition and hydration should be provided to her, but of course were in no position to say how this should be done. The treating trust initially recognised this to be a dispute that should go to court and said that it would make an application, but then changed its position – presumably having taken legal advice that took a strict reading of the case law in which it was made clear that if there is no treatment on offer, then there is no best interests decision to make, and no decision (or jurisdiction) for the Court of Protection.

18 [2024] EWCOP 3 – https://www.bailii.org/ew/cases/EWCOP/2024/3.html

Proceedings were brought by the family instead (on which more below), and Hayden J gave short shrift to the niceties of the argument that this was not a matter for the court –

> *"...on 16th January 2024, the Trust confirmed to the family that they had been advised by their lawyers that it was not necessary for them to issue an application. The likely reasoning behind this is that the Trust considered that there was no ethical route to provide nutrition to EUP. The family disagreed and saw this as passivity, with profound consequences. They perceived an important decision having been taken, even though the decision was to take no action. They considered that the Court ought to be able to review that decision making process and identify its own evaluation of where EUP's best interests lay. I agree with the family. A decision not to provide nutrition is every bit as serious as a decision to withdraw nutrition.* ***Where there is conflict, these cases must be resolved by the court.****" (emphasis added)*

In substance, inevitably, the judge could not find that it was in EUP's best interests for artificial nutrition to be given when there was no clinical evidence that this was possible and so no treatment option "on the table". But nonetheless, bringing the dispute to the court meant that there was some scrutiny of the wider care plan (see below). I think that this does blur, a little, the crucial distinction I sought to make earlier in the book between (1) clinical decisions about the available options and (2) best interests decisions among those options, with step 2 being the bit where there is the duty of collaborative decision making discussed in chapter 5, and – if need be – the jurisdiction of the Court of Protection.

Certainly, this cuts away the idea that no application needs to be made if there is no treatment option, though it might be more proper in such cases to bring the case not to the Court of Protection (as if it were a best interests decision, when in reality it is not), but to the High Court under its inherent jurisdiction to effectively bring scrutiny to the decision not to offer treatment, though such niceties are best left to the lawyers and court to grapple with, and in reality the distinction is blurred, with the same judges hearing the case anyway, albeit with different hats on.[19]

And, of course, all this goes likewise for cases involving children, which will have to come to the High Court in any event as the Court of Protection's jurisdiction does not start until the age of 16.

On the other hand, there are always counter examples. In the "does what it says on the tin" judgment of "*AA (withdrawal of life sustaining treatment: No best interests decision)*"[20] Henke J heard about a 33 year-old man who had suffered a profound and irreversible brain injury as a result of a cardiac arrest after surgery, with 28 minutes of CPR required before circulation was restored. He was judged to be on the border of a minimally conscious minus / vegetative state, and no clinician or medical expert considered that there was any hope of improvement. Clinicians proposed palliative care only to minimise his pain and discomfort, and discontinuation of the artificial nutrition and hydration that was keeping him alive. His parents disputed this, arguing that there was hope for him to improve. An application to court was made by the ICB commissioning his care.

The evidence before Henke J was that the palliative care plan (PCP) was the only option that the treating clinicians were prepared to offer, and there was no alternative: "*The Applicant would be more comfortable proceeding with the benefit of a court order but if they did not get one, they would proceed in accordance with their clinical judgment and implement the PCP.*" The Official Solicitor, representing AA, complained that this rendered her role "impotent", and the judge had some sympathy with

---

19 Serious medical treatment cases for adults tend to be heard by High Court judges sitting in the Court of Protection, so they have the power of both jurisdictions anyway.

20 [2024] EWCOP 39 (T3) – https://www.bailii.org/ew/cases/EWCOP/2024/39.html

this, commenting that there might have been more than one option on the table had the case been brought to court sooner.

As such, the judge found that

> *"The clinical view is that there is only one option, and the clinicians will only treat AA in accordance with that option. This case is stark. There is only one available option before this court. The reality is that this court has no choice to make. Accordingly, I have concluded that there is no best interest decision to make here, and I do not do so".*

Going on to consider whether a declaration should be made instead under the inherent jurisdiction that the proposed plan would be lawful, again the judge declined to do so:

> *"Clinicians are not legally obliged to seek a declaration from a court as to the lawfulness of any proposed treatment – see Re Y [2018] UKSC 46 at paragraphs 29-33. Professor Turner-Stokes gave evidence that regardless of whether or not I granted the declaration, the clinicians would continue to treat AA in accordance with their clinical judgment and implement the PCP. That begs the question: why is the declaration being sought when whether or not I grant it does not affect the outcome for AA? It appears to me that the declaration is really being sought to protect the clinicians and medical staff now and in the future from potential legal action given AA's parents fundamental disagreement with the PCP. I have considered whether I should grant the declaration sought in such circumstances. If I thought that on the ground that the declaration would make any difference to the outcome for AA then I may have been persuaded to make it. But the reality here is that the declaration will not alter anything. The clinicians will continue to treat in accordance with their clinical judgment whether or not I make the declaration. AA's parents' views, whether reasonable or not, are deeply held. In my view, granting the declaration sought will not change his parents' views nor actually how they are likely to behave to staff implementing the plan. It is purposeless".*

Note – again – that there is no criticism of the application being made, and indeed that the court would have preferred that it had been done sooner, when there would have been an opportunity for the Official Solicitor to instruct independent expert evidence at an earlier stage, when other treatment options, or at least variations of the PCP that may have been more in line with AA's wishes, might have been possible.

However, she continued:

> *"I understand why it was not pursued. Given the stance of the Applicants it would have been futile to do so unless the expert was prepared to take clinical responsibility to implement any alternative plan. The stark reality of his case is that AA is too fragile to be moved to another hospital and that those at the [trust] are clear that the only treatment plan clinically viable for AA and which they are prepared to implement is the PCP. The court has no choice and I have asked myself whether in circumstances such as these, when the court has no choice at all, it should rubber stamp the decision of others. I have decided that I should not. In coming to that decision, I should emphasize that I have the greatest respect for the clinicians in this case and the difficult decisions that they have had to take and will have to take until AA's death. They do so in accordance with their Hippocratic oath and to the highest of professional standards. I do not criticise them or the judgment they have made. However, the reality of this case is that the treatment decision in this case is purely a clinical decision not the court's decision. The court's approval is not required to implement it. The court is not needed to sanction the plan and the court has no further role to play in what treatment AA does or does not receive."*

I don't know if the EUP case above (which was around 6 months earlier) was cited in court, but Henke J does not refer to it in her judgment, and it would have been helpful to hear her thoughts on that, given her different approach. (Sometimes, honestly, the hearing you get will depend entirely on the judge who hears it).

Equally, the court has recently considered whether an application must always be made about withdrawal of life sustaining treatment from a patient in a prolonged disorder of consciousness if they are "unbefriended" – ie that there was no one other than paid professionals who was available to consult about the P's wishes and feelings, values and beliefs. As above, we know that this means the involvement of an IMCA in the decision making, but the question for the court in An ICB v XR[21] was whether this situation means that the decision should always be reviewed by the court.

Mrs Justice Theis said that there should be no speculation or assumptions about XR's beliefs without supporting evidence. But she refused the suggestion made by the Official Solicitor that this situation should always be brought to court for a best interests decision. The absence of evidence from friends and family about the patient's wishes does not in itself make it the kind of "finely balanced decision" that ought to be made by a judge. The court noted that the 2020 Royal College of Physicians PDOC guidance on this was under review at the time.

However, foreshadowing issues we will get to in more detail shortly, the judge was very critical of the delay in thinking about best interests of continuing treatment after XR's injuries and condition was plain.

As I have said, though, not every case needs to go to court, even if the consequences of the decision are grave, but misunderstanding this is likely to cause trouble, especially where it brings delay.

For example, *Cardiff Vale University Health Board v NN*[22] concerned a 32 year-old woman who was detained under the Mental Health Act with a long history of schizophrenia and substance abuse, who was found to

21 [2024] EWCOP 66 (T3) – https://www.bailii.org/ew/cases/EWCOP/2024/66.html

22 [2024] EWCOP 61 (T3) – https://www.bailii.org/ew/cases/EWCOP/2024/61.html

be pregnant. She was assessed to lack capacity to make her own decision about continuing or termination of her pregnancy, but she said that she wanted a termination, and the treating NHS trusts were willing to provide this for her on a best interests basis, while it would accord with her wishes.

There was no question of forcing the medical termination of pregnancy on her if she refused this, but there was a concern about what would happen if she changed her mind once this had been started and refused the medication required to complete the process. The trusts were concerned that there might then need to be an intervention, on a best interests basis, that amounted to a deprivation of liberty that ought to be authorised by the court.

The problem here was that although NN had first said that she wanted a termination when she was only 8 weeks pregnant, the time taken to make an application to court meant that by the time the court heard the case the pregnancy had progressed to 21 weeks and 4 days. When the termination of pregnancy went ahead then, having been approved by the court, the baby was born alive, which was traumatic for all involved, and NN's experience was described as "absolutely barbaric".

We will come back to the crucial issue of timing and delay below, but for now note that in approving the proposed plan the court made it clear that there had been no real need to bring the case to court at all:

> *"In this case, the minutes of various professionals meetings held in June and July 2024 suggest that there was a mistaken belief that any best interests decision about termination of pregnancy for a person without capacity required court authorisation. If there is a professional consensus about the treatment proposed, no intention to impose treatment on P against her wishes, and no disagreement from those concerned with P's welfare such as close family members, the provisions of s.5 and s.6 MCA 2005 permit medical best interests decisions to be taken without court involvement, having followed the requirements of*

the MCA and any associated professional guidance: An NHS Trust v Y [2018] UKSC 46."

Victoria Butler-Cole KC, sitting as a High Court judge, went on to say that fanciful concerns about the possibility of a deprivation of liberty arising should not drive speculative applications. She referred to a judgment by Lieven J in which the court had refused to make an anticipatory declaration about the best interests of a woman detained under the MHA where there was a "small risk" that she might lose capacity at the time decisions would need to be made about delivery of her baby, noting that in an emergency clinicians can rely on the doctrine of necessity and, perhaps, MCA s4B to authorise any deprivation of liberty (see chapter 5 above). She quotes Lieven J's comment that "there needs to be some caution about turning what are in truth medical decisions into legal ones".

Fine – but:

- The real problem in this case was not that the application should never have been made, but that there was delay in making the application, which caused real harm to the patient involved, as it caused delay in giving treatment that was plainly time critical. I am not aware of any case in which an application about medical treatment made in good faith and **made in good time** has been criticised as having been unnecessary.

- The idea that you can just rely on the common law principle of necessity in the event of a crisis should not be taken as licence to fail to consider the care plan, anticipate problems and seek prior approval of the court where this is appropriate, and where disputes or difficulties are entirely foreseeable and should have been foreseen. You can expect to be criticised if you try to rely on crisis or urgency that is of your own making for lack of forward planning.

With the ongoing delay in producing an update to the MCA Code of Practice, we might wonder if there will be any further, more formal guidance from the court, especially as there have been a number of judgments (in particular from Hayden J himself) in which the decision making about application to court, and the timing of doing this, have been strongly criticised.

In the meantime, it is wise to take advice as need be on a case-by-case basis, of course, but whatever you do, get on with it! Timing is everything, as we will see.

Who should make the application?

MCA code of practice Para 8.8 says: "For cases about serious or major decisions concerning medical treatment ... the NHS trust or other organisation responsible for the patient's care will usually make the application..."

This is reinforced in Mr Justice Hayden's guidance, mentioned above: "In cases involving issues as to medical treatment, the organisation which is, or will be, responsible for commissioning or providing clinical or caring services to P should normally (although not always) be the applicant".[23]

If an application ought to be made, it is usually not good enough for a public body to leave the onus on an objecting family member individually to do so, and a failure by a public body to make the application appropriately can be punished by an award of costs against it.[24]

Hayden J himself made this clear in the *EUP* case mentioned above, being critical of the Trust for leaving it to the family to make the

23 At para 17.

24 *LB Hillingdon v Neary* [2011] EWHC 1377.

application, and for – as he saw it – not following the guidance that he had issued on the need to bring cases to court:

> *"Had the Trust followed [the guidance], and at an earlier stage, it would have greatly alleviated the stress to the family. … Neither can I imagine that the lawyers advising this Trust were unfamiliar with the guidance. It has been widely promulgated, see also [2020] EWCOP 2. Where there is conflict in these serious medical treatment cases, it is in everybody's best interests, but most importantly P's, to bring an application to court.* ***That will be most efficiently achieved where it is driven by the Trust's application****. There are many and obvious reasons why it is also to the Trust's advantage to have their treatment plans, in cases such as this, scrutinised by the court." (emphasis added).*[25]

Typically, the applicant will be the healthcare provider that proposes to give (or withhold) the particular treatment in dispute, and this is usually fairly clear when it is about acute inpatient NHS care. The situation can be more complex where it involves care outside hospital. In cases during the pandemic involving disputes about Covid vaccination – for example for a young adult with a learning disability who lacks capacity for the decision about vaccination, which is clinically thought to be in their best interests, but is opposed by their family – applications were typically made by the relevant NHS clinical commissioning group[26] or the local authority.[27] I cannot think of a reported case in which an application has

25 GUP v EUP [2024] EWCOP 3 at paragraph 50.

26 The local commissioning organisations for NHS services at the time, see Chapter 2, replaced since July 2022 by Integrated Care Boards.

27 For example in Re E (the local authority) [2021] EWCOP 7 – https://www.bailii.org/ew/cases/EWCOP/2021/7.html, or in CR (the CCG) [2021] EWCOP 19 – https://www.bailii.org/ew/cases/EWCOP/2021/19.html

been made by a GP practice (or a dentist), with primary care usually looking to the relevant CCG / ICB for support with this.

There is a question whether more still should be expected of commissioners and ICBs in particular. In a string of cases over recent years dealing with end of life decisions for patients with persistent disorders of consciousness, the court has emphasised the role of the commissioner of that care to ensure in their routine reviews not only that the care itself remains clinically appropriate, but that there is appropriate and timely best interests decision making about whether that care should continue, including proactive applications to court as need be. We will come back to this on the issue of delay, below.

For example, in *XR*,[28] Theis J, Vice President, made the following trenchant observations:

> *"92. In my judgment the ICB has an important, critical role to play. As the Clinical Lead for the ICB set out in her statement 'The ICB will undertake as a minimum an annual review of the care commissioned* ***to ensure that the care package remains appropriate to meet the service user's assessed needs****' (emphasis added). For these reviews to be an effective mechanism they should include active consideration by the ICB at each review to be vigilant that the care package includes an effective system being in place for best interest decisions to be made in these difficult cases so that drift and delay is avoided. The ICB should not just be a bystander at these reviews.*
>
> *93. As Hayden J stated in GU*
>
> *[103] '...where the treating hospital is, for whatever reason, unable to bring an application to the court itself, it should recognise a clear and compelling duty to take timely and effective measures to bring the issue*

28 [2024] EWCOP 66 (T3), https://www.bailii.org/ew/cases/EWCOP/2024/66.html

to the attention of the NHS commissioning body with overall responsibility for the patient.'...

> *[105] 'Regular, sensitive consideration of P's ongoing needs, across the spectrum, is required and a recognition that treatment which may have enhanced the patient's quality of life or provided some relief from pain may gradually or indeed suddenly reach a pivoting point where it becomes futile, burdensome and inconsistent with human dignity. The obligation is to be vigilant to such an alteration in the balance'.*

94. The wholly unacceptable delays in GU, AB and now this case send out a blunt but clear message that such delays in effective best interest decision making are unacceptable and wholly contrary to the patient's best interests which there is a clear statutory obligation on the responsible care providers to protect."

Hayden J in turn endorsed and amplified these comments in the important decision of *JP* in February 2025[29], dealing with the issue of delay in making an application.

> *"For the best interests reviews to be effective, the ICB is required to be vigilant and proactive in the process... they should not be "passive bystanders""*

Certainly, it is unlikely to be looked on kindly by a judge if an application is significantly delayed as a result of a disagreement between public bodies about which of them should take the lead in doing so. If need be, it is always open to one organisation to start proceedings, and then to argue at the first hearing that another organisation should be taking the lead instead, and should replace them as the applicant in the proceedings.

---

29 [2025] EWCOP 8 (T3) – https://www.bailii.org/ew/cases/EWCOP/2025/8.html – also mentioned in Chapter 5 re best interests decisions and the role of the family.

The court will certainly expect a collaborative and proactive approach where there is more than one organisation involved in a patient's care, and there is nothing to stop an application being made by more than one organisation on a joint basis (as is commonly seen for example in cases where a patient is under the care of both a mental health and an acute NHS Trust where both are involved in the issues at stake). And where there is no difference of opinion or conflict between the organisations, it is often possible for them to jointly instruct one firm of lawyers and one barrister to represent them, so that the costs can be split.

Delay and timing

As I have heavily trailed, the court is especially concerned by any delay in bringing a case to court, most obviously where that delay is detrimental to the treatment options available to the patient, or their prospects, but also where delay is seen to have impaired the due process of the case, or to have simply lost sight of the need to make best interests decisions actively rather than simply allow the status quo.

Once a patient no longer has capacity to consent to ongoing treatment, then the legal basis for continuing it is that it is in their best interests. As Hayden J said in GU, quoted above, that can change over time, so must be kept under active review. And if it is no longer in the patient's best interests, it is not only lawful to stop that treatment, but *continuing that treatment becomes unlawful*.

The timing of an application is critical and is emphasised in Hayden J's guidance: "*it is important … to recognise that delay will invariably be inimical to P's welfare and where resolution cannot be achieved within P's own timescales proceedings should be issued*".[30]

In the JP case mentioned above, Hayden J was dealing with a man in his 60s who had led an active life until a heart attack had left him in a

30 As above, at paragraph 14(b).

persistent vegetative state, where he had remained for more than 9 years, sustained with artificial feeding and hydration. When the question of whether this should be continued was considered, a clear decision was stymied by disagreement among the family (see chapter 5), but the court was damning about the delay in bringing the case to court, and the impact that this had on JP himself. Having made the decision in January 2025 that the treatment should be withdrawn,[31] the judge gave a further separate judgment in February 2025 to deal with the issue of delay.[32]

There was, the judge said, ample evidence that JP would have hated the situation in which he was left for so long, losing sight of his "inviolable right to be valued, respected, and treated ethically solely because he is a human being", as a result of "*years [of] hand wringing procrastination*" on the part of the organisations involved.

The judge acknowledged that there was a "well-meant attempt to mediate the family dispute about JP's best interests", which resulted in further delay, but made clear that "there is no onus on the ICB or healthcare providers to broker an agreement between the family members", and that any attempt to do so, however well intentioned, risks losing sight of the point of the consultation with the family, which is – he said – to get their evidence on the patient's own wishes, feelings, values and beliefs to inform the proper best interests decision making for that individual.[33]

This can feel like a damned if you do or don't scenario. Sometimes, a delay can be indefensible, born of a misunderstanding of the MCA or an indifference to its obligations. In many more cases, though, aware that court should be a last resort, situations can just drag on for very much longer than they should, with the best of intentions. Over a period which

31 [2025] EWCOP 4 (T3) – https://www.bailii.org/ew/cases/EWCOP/2025/4.html

32 [2025] EWCOP 8 (T3) – https://www.bailii.org/ew/cases/EWCOP/2025/8.html

33 See Chapter 5.

may look far too long, in hindsight, everyone may be hoping, for example, that a reluctant patient will engage with the proposed treatment, and so could be spared the trauma caused by a coercive retrieval into hospital. Or that an apparent dispute about best interests might be resolved with some discussion. The MCA Code of Practice emphasises, after all, that applications to court should be a last resort. It is also natural to be mindful, no doubt, of the legal costs and the stress to the clinicians and family of the court process.

I am sure that there have been cases in which an NHS body has been criticised for an application to court being made too soon, where the dispute and the actual treatment options being proposed had not yet crystallised sufficiently for the judge to make a decision. But cases like that are rare enough that I can't readily think of one in my own experience, and in medical treatment cases it is far more common to be criticised for delay than prematurity.

In *PG*[34], the court approved a proposed care plan in which a 57 year-old woman would <u>not</u> be investigated or treated for cancer where it was thought likely that any such treatment would cause her greater harm in terms of her mental health. However, commenting on the delay in making the application, the judge commented that:

> *"It may be that it flowed from an understandable concern by the Applicants that it would be inappropriate to trouble the court with an inchoate application in the absence of an agreed "fully-worked up" care plan, in respect of the investigations. If so, I would wish to encourage these Applicants and/or any other applicant in such circumstances with such a case, to be less concerned about ensuring that every 'i' is dotted and every 't' crossed before making the application where speed of decision-making may be of the essence:* ***<u>perfect in this instance may well be the enemy of the good</u>****. Once it became apparent that NHS*

34 [2024] EWCOP 49 (T3) – https://www.bailii.org/ew/cases/EWCOP/2024/49.html

> *Guidance regarding the investigation and/or treatment of PG's condition could not be complied with timeously, and/or where it was clear that PG's treating/receiving clinicians could not agree upon a care plan to facilitate the investigations and/or treatment, the application could or should have been issued. The Court could then have ensured with the assistance of counsel and solicitors that evidence was filed from the necessary factual and expert witnesses to enable the detail of the care plan to be completed, and a decision to be reached promptly in respect of PG's best interests." (emphasis added).*

There is naturally a concern that we should be clear about what the available options are, and a reluctance to go to court without a proposed care plan. But sometimes the application to court itself – and the directions timetable this brings – can focus the minds, not least as starting proceedings brings the benefit of the involvement of the Official Solicitor, acting on behalf of the patient, to help to tackle the issues, and refine a plan.

In a number of cases the court has found that a delay in bringing the application has been detrimental to the patient's options, or outcome.

For example, in *H*[35] before Mr Justice Hayden – just days before he issued the January 2020 guidance, perhaps not coincidentally – an application was made for approval of a treatment plan for a 71 year-old lady with a squamous cell carcinoma on her left cheek, which would involve bringing her into hospital against her wishes, because her mental health problems meant that she was in denial about her condition, and she lacked capacity for the relevant decisions. Unfortunately, the application was only made some 7 months after that assessment of her incapacity, and by the time that she was brought into hospital, it was found that the cancer had progressed too far for there to be a surgical

35 [2020] EWCOP 5 – https://www.bailii.org/ew/cases/EWCOP/2020/5.html

option, and the parties were soon back in court to explain the position and seek approval for a proposed palliative care plan instead.

Even if the treatment options are the same, the court will see a delay in issuing proceedings that then brings unnecessary urgency as being detrimental to the patient's right to proper process. In *PW*[36] Mrs Justice Lieven was told that the patient needed an amputation of a leg within 48 hours of the application, given the high risk of sepsis, but "it was entirely apparent from the papers that the application had been in the course of preparation for at least a month, and that the clinical team at the treating hospital had been contemplating the need for the surgery for 9-12 months." As such:

> *"In these circumstances this application could and should have been made some weeks ago, even if at that stage it was on a slightly more precautionary basis. The effect of the delay has been detrimental to PW's interests and to a fair process which could fully take into account his wishes. The timing of the application has meant that the Official Solicitor had no time to visit PW and discuss the operation and his views with him; it has meant that there has been no time for the Independent Mental Capacity Advocate (IMCA) to visit him before the hearing ...; and the OS has had no time to instruct an independent doctor for another opinion if he had felt one was justified."*

The timescale is, perhaps, all the more predictable in cases about pregnancy and childbirth. As long ago as 2014, Mr Justice Keehan gave guidance in a case in which approval was sought for a birth plan to include – if need be – a Caesarean section to be given on a best interests basis against a woman's wishes, saying that any application to court should be made at least 4 weeks before the expected date of delivery,[37]

36 [2019] EWCOP 10 – https://www.bailii.org/ew/cases/EWCOP/2019/10.html

37 Re FG [2014] EWCOP 30 – https://www.bailii.org/ew/cases/EWCOP/2014/30.html

but it is still all too common that applications about this are made on a much more last minute basis, sometimes without obvious justification.

The imperative to get applications into court in good time is unmistakable, and the message is ignored at our peril, with potential sanctions available in adverse comment and publicity as well as legal costs.

More fundamentally than that, of course, I would not wish on anyone the experience of a case in which an initially optimistic diagnosis had become much more grim by the time treatment was eventually attempted, after a delay in being brought to court. And I am well aware that the lawyers are some distance in this from the depth of impact on the clinicians, the family and, most of all, the patient himself.

If the situation feels stuck or impossible, it is unlikely to improve with keeping, and on balance it is much better to be very occasionally berated by a judge for coming to court too soon than to ever find that you have come to court too late.

In the meantime

However quick the court process is, there remains a question of what treatment should be given in the meantime, while a dispute is resolved.

As we saw in Chapter 6, in the Supreme Court in the Charlie Gard case Lady Hale recognised that ongoing delay in the proceedings would mean complicity in continuing a course of treatment that had already been determined to be against Charlie's best interests.

In broad terms, it is usually prudent to maintain the status quo and to take reasonable steps to keep a patient alive for long enough for the court to make the decision / resolve the dispute, even if this means that in the meantime treatment must be given that is no longer felt to be in the patient's best interests for that period. They key is to make that period as short as possible, by making the application to court in good time, having all the right evidence ready, and making the court aware of the reasons for the urgency.

In that situation, there is even more reason to be mindful of the impact on staff, sometimes called "moral distress", from putting them in a position of providing interventions that they do not consider to be in their patient's best interests. In the past I would have had to make this point to courts, and perhaps produce evidence of the harm being done, but I have found that – though the best interests of the patient is, strictly, their sole concern – judges are increasingly aware of and sympathetic to these issues. For the healthcare provider, it is important to recognise that there are duties and responsibilities to their staff, as well as to the patient / family, and appropriate support should be arranged. Certainly, for my part, I see support for the individual clinicians involved in any case as an absolutely central part of my role in advising the organisation.

Though it is usually best not to be seen to pre-empt the decision of the court where there is a dispute, there may be cases in which it is appropriate to see ongoing interventions – or escalations in treatment – as unconscionable, and for the clinicians to say so. The crucial thing is to be clear what can / will be done, at least pending the court's decision. Stopping (or not starting) a particular treatment does not mean stopping all care. It can be helpful to see this in terms of setting out, and hopefully agreeing, a particular plan, perhaps with "ceilings of care" setting out the situations in which care would be escalated, involving other interventions, or would not.

As we saw in the EUP case (above and in Chapter 5 on the role of the family in decision-making), the fact that a family are insistent on a particular treatment does not mean that it is in the patient's best interests, and there can be criticism when a patient comes to harm as a result of such interventions given, if only pending a court decision.

Process and timescale of court applications

Obviously, you'll get more out of some very comprehensive books on the court process,[38] if that's the level of detail you need, and you'll find some of the following terms explained in the Glossary.

In broad terms, though, the Court of Protection[39] process is like any other litigation. The evidence relevant to the application can be documents (including medical records), witness statements and, sometimes, reports by independent experts. These all need to be disclosed (i.e. shared) between the parties in good time before the final hearing, and will then all be worked up by the applicant into a bundle for the court.

The scope and timescale for each procedural step might be set at a directions hearing, at which the court can decide what evidence will be required and when it must be ready. In some urgent cases, the court can go straight to a final hearing, to determine the issues, without a directions hearing.

Overall, in medical treatment cases the process and timescale is driven by the clinical urgency. In appropriate cases it is possible for there to be an urgent application made and decided by phone or online, out of hours, overnight or on Christmas day. There is a judge on call 24/7, and all specialist healthcare law firms will offer a 24/7 service as need be to access this. In most such cases the judge is likely to adopt a holding position if possible, perhaps making only interim declarations about the patient's capacity for the relevant decisions, and that life-sustaining treatment is in his best interests in the meantime, with a direction that detailed evidence

38 For example the "Court of Protection Practice", or "Medical Treatment Decisions and the Law", Serjeant's Inn.

39 Of course in some situations, most obviously if the patient is under 16 years of age, the proceedings would be in the High Court rather than the Court of Protection, but the points made here broadly hold good.

shall be prepared and brought to court very quickly for a more substantive decision.

You will, though, want to have a pretty good reason to give the judge why it is so urgent now as to get him or her up in the wee small hours in the judicial dressing gown and slippers; and expect very short shrift if it is something that could and should have been addressed sooner, or in office hours.

With only one high court judge on call for emergencies out of hours, you will also have to fight for the judicial bandwidth with all kinds of other cases, including for example international abduction child cases where a child may be on a plane about to take off, or where someone seeks an urgent injunction on a Saturday to stop something going into the Sunday newspapers.

Practicalities aside, Mr Justice Hayden's guidance emphasised that out of hours applications should anyway be "exceptional", not least because it compromises the ability of the Official Solicitor (see below) to participate and properly represent the patient.

Where the clinical urgency allows, it is more common for cases to run over several weeks or months (years, in some cases), with the court exercising its powers of case management to try to get the balance right between the need for a decision, and the procedural rights of those involved in the decision making. And of course, usually the longer the case runs, the greater the potential costs involved.

Legal costs

If your mental picture of litigation is of a compensation claim, then you'd expect that the "winner" usually gets their legal costs paid by the "loser". This principle does not apply in the Court of Protection, where the focus is not adversarial but all about establishing the right thing for P. As such, the usual rule in the Court of Protection for applications about personal welfare[40] is that there is "no order for costs"[41] i.e. each party will pay their own lawyers.

Pragmatically, the strictly limited budgets of NHS bodies overall, never mind for paying lawyers, can be a strong disincentive to be anything you might call "trigger happy" in rushing off to court, because even if their application is granted, they will not get back the legal costs incurred.

For contested medical treatment cases, legal costs can be substantial (you're likely to be in the ballpark of the cost of a (modest, second hand) car, rather than the cost of a holiday or a house, but each of these can be fairly elastic!).

Unfortunately, access to legal aid funding to pay lawyers acting on behalf of the patient or family is means tested for medical treatment cases and so all but inaccessible in practice, with the notable exception of cases involving life sustaining treatment for children, in which parents now get non-means tested legal aid, as in Chapter 5.

However, in any case brought as a challenge to a DoLS authorisation,[42] non-means tested legal aid is available, giving a perverse incentive to present a case as a DoLS challenge, if there happens to be a DoLS in place, when the substance is really about the medical treatment itself.[43]

The court has discretion to depart from that general no-costs rule if, for example, it wanted to punish an NHS body for its conduct of the

---

40 As opposed to the property and finances issues that are the bulk of the court's work, where the legal costs are often recovered from the funds being dealt with.

41 Court of Protection Rules 2017 rule 19.3.

42 Under MCA S21A, see Chapter 5.

43 See the Court of Appeal in *Director of Legal Aid Casework et al v Briggs* [2017] EWCA Civ 1169.

proceedings, or for delay, by making it pay some or all of the legal costs of the other parties, e.g. family members.[44]

As an applicant – usually the NHS body in a medical treatment case – you'll also have to pay the application fee when you issue proceedings (currently £408) and the fee for a final hearing (£494, the invoice for which might turn up only many, many months later).

The Official Solicitor and costs and CAFCASS

One well established exception to the general no-costs rule is that by convention (albeit one approved in the case law after it was challenged by an applicant trust) in medical treatment cases the applicant NHS body will agree in any case to pay 50% of the legal costs incurred by the Official Solicitor.

The Official Solicitor (currently Sarah Castle) is a statutory office holder whose responsibilities include acting as a litigation friend of last resort for adults in the Court of Protection. This means acting on the patient's behalf if there is no one else appropriate to conduct the litigation and instruct lawyers for them. A family member or an IMCA can act as the litigation friend, but in medical treatment cases, whether or not there is a family member appropriate or available, it is common for the Official Solicitor to have this role, given the great depth of expertise and experience of her team.

---

44 One example was in P v Manchester City Council and others [2024] EWCOP 43 (T1) in which District Judge Matharu ordered that the local authority, mental health trust and ICB involved should all pay, shared between them, the legal costs of P's mother, after they made an unsuccessful application for material in the proceedings to be withheld from the mother where, the judge held, this was ill-considered and had no reasonable prospect of success. https://www.bailii.org/ew/cases/EWCOP/2024/43.html

In urgent applications made out of hours, it will be up to the judge to decide whether to contact the Official Solicitor in that situation. Otherwise, it is good practice to give the Official Solicitor notice of a potential application about medical treatment as soon as possible, and in my experience the early involvement of the Official Solicitor is invariably a good thing.

I am grateful to Sarah Castle for her kind agreement to the use in this book (at Appendix Two) of a checklist for the preparation of a serious medical treatment application, which I hope is helpful[45].

Of course, if the patient has the capacity to conduct the litigation (as distinct from their capacity to make the decision about the medical treatment in question) then they can instruct their own lawyers without a litigation friend, but this situation is relatively rare.

In proceedings about children in the High Court family division, the child, if joined as a party, will be represented separately, usually by CAFCASS (Children and Family Court Advisory and Support Service). This gives a voice in the proceedings on behalf of the child, which as we have seen can be distinct from the position being advocated by one or both parents. One meaningful distinction for lawyers for NHS providers bringing medical treatment cases to court between CAFCASS and the equivalent role of the Official Solicitor for adults is that there is no conventional provision for the applicant to pay costs to CAFCASS.

Technology at Court

It has become commonplace for witnesses and experts to give evidence by phone or video-link where practicality demands it, and the court is

45 Prepared for the Official Solicitor by a working group including Bridget Dolan KC (Serjeant's Inn), Kate Rashid (University Hospitals of the North Midlands NHS Trust), Gavin Knox (Welsh Health Legal Services), David Edwards (Official Solicitor's office) and myself.

usually content to allow this, especially to minimise the disruption to other clinical commitments, and to allow the family to participate without the cost and time of travel, when the time available with P may be limited.

The impact of the coronavirus drove us a step further, with full hearings all being conducted online, the first of which was *A Clinical Commissioning Group v AF*, on 17-20 March 2020 before Mostyn J.[46] a case about the withdrawal of CANH. The judge said "In the current national crisis, it must be expected that hearings will be conducted remotely in this way as a matter of routine practice".

Having established the feasibility and become more accustomed to the greater use of technology, a great many cases are now simply heard remotely, especially directions hearings or shorter final hearings. Though the feedback on this has been broadly positive, it is important to note the corrective account given on behalf of the patient's daughter of her rather different and less satisfactory experience, where it seemed that some of the formality and gravitas of the proceedings had been lost.[47]

One obvious advantage of online hearings is that they may be more accessible to observers – see for instance the great work of the Open Justice Project.[48]

Anonymity, Media & Social media

The impact of going through medical treatment litigation on the clinicians, and the family, should not be forgotten, and another

46 [2020] EWCOP 16. https://www.bailii.org/ew/cases/EWCOP/2020/16.html

47 http://ukmedicaldecisionlawblog.co.uk/rss-feed/115-skype-in-the-court-of-protection-the-courts-in-the-time-of-coronavirus .

48 https://openjusticecourtofprotection.org/

development of modern technology can be that litigation plays out in real time in the media and in social media, as we saw most powerfully in the cases of *Charlie Gard* and *Alfie Evans* (see Chapter 6).

In each of those cases, the identities of the child and the treating trust were public, though the judgments anonymised the treating clinicians, but nonetheless it became necessary to consider further legal and practical steps to protect them.

Previously, it was typical for cases to be called *A v B NHS Trust and C local authority*, entirely anonymised. The need to dispel the misperception of the court as "secret" has led to ever more transparency and openness. Usually now any case is heard in "open court" i.e. the public and press can attend, but subject to an Order which prevents the patient or family members being identified publicly by the press or anyone else.

The public bodies such as NHS trusts and local authorities will almost always be identified, unless doing so would compromise the protection of the patient's identity.

In a judgment in the family court on 11 May 2020 in *A Local Authority v A & B*,[49] Mr Justice Hayden reflected on the issue of proposed anonymity for the local authority to protect the child's identity in terms which ought to be heard loud and clear by public bodies:

> *"A reading of my substantive judgment reveals my conclusion that this social work team, within this Local Authority, disregarded fundamental principles of safeguarding and child protection. The nature and extent of the failings, as well as their persistence, can only give real cause for public concern. There is an undoubted public interest in the Local Authority being named, in order that they might be subject to the kind of public scrutiny that many would regard as*

49 [2020] EWHC 1162 (Fam), https://www.bailii.org/ew/cases/EWHC/Fam/2020/1162.html

> *necessary. Mr Perkins has told me that, at the highest level within the Social Services Department for this Local Authority, there is real concern as to what has happened and a determination that there should be a full investigation. I am told and accept that there will be. Mr Perkins submits that there are "lessons to be learned". It has to be said that this phrase is deployed so regularly when public bodies fail that it is in danger of becoming platitudinous. It is easy to see how lessons might be learned more thoroughly in the spotlight of media scrutiny".*

An important part of the preparation for court in a medical treatment case is to ensure that the trust comms team is prepared for the likely media coverage.

The position of individual clinicians is more nuanced, and was the subject of a very recent Supreme Court decision – *Abbasi v Newcastle upon Tyne Hospitals NHS Trust*[50], handed down on 16 April 2025. The case involved the families of two children who had already died, Zainab Abbasi and Isaiah Haastrup, but the principles are likely to be applied in the same way to Court of Protection cases involving medical treatment for adults.

In each case, the treating NHS trust had made an application to court for a decision about withdrawal of life sustaining treatment and an order had been made that individual treating clinicians should not be identified. The family of each child felt that this ongoing injunction – which would continue indefinitely unless lifted by the court – hampered their ability to speak out freely about their concerns about the care that was provided in each case, and they applied for the injunctions to be lifted.

---

50 Though the case was conjoined with another – Haastrup v King's College Hospital NHS FT – which raised the same issues, the case is generally known as "Abbasi" – [2025] UKSC 15 – https://www.supremecourt.uk/cases/uksc-2023-0052

The argument went all the way up to the Supreme Court, with the NHS trusts involved, supported by formal interventions in the proceedings by various professional groups arguing for anonymity for clinicians[51], on the basis of concern about the risks of abuse (in person and online) in these fraught and emotional cases, as well as the broader impact on morale and efficiency of working in the clinical teams involved and – ultimately – the ability to recruit and retain staff in the fields most likely to be involved in such cases, such as paediatric critical care.

The Supreme Court recognised these concerns, but the families won their argument, and the injunctions against naming the individual clinicians in those cases are to be lifted.

The BMA's reaction[52] was:

> *"This is a hugely disappointing judgment that will cause a great deal of concern not just to the doctors in this specific case, but doctors across the country, who may find themselves at the centre of similar situations in the future.*
>
> *"Clinical decisions around the withdrawal of life-sustaining treatment are not taken lightly, and applications to court are always a last resort, and made in the patient's best interests. Doctors and other healthcare staff treating these patients need to be able to make these very difficult decisions free from fear of abuse."*

The key, though, as always, is timing, and the Supreme Court thought that not enough consideration had been given to the passage of time:

---

51 The British Medical Association, the Royal College of Nursing, the Faculty of Intensive Care Medicine, the Royal College of Paediatrics and Child Health and the Paediatric Critical Care Society.

52 https://www.bma.org.uk/bma-media-centre/supreme-court-ruling-in-abbasi-and-haastrup-case-will-cause-a-great-deal-of-concern-to-doctors

- The basis for an injunction to protect the anonymity of the clinicians involved when proceedings are started does not apply in the same way when proceedings are concluded, and in particular if the child has already died.

- In proceedings, the key concern is the child's best interests. This can justify an order for anonymity for the clinicians because, for example, the quality of care might be compromised if they are affected by abuse or intimidation etc. As the employer of the clinicians, it is appropriate for the trust to seek the orders that provide for their anonymisation.

- However, if the child has died and proceedings are concluded, things change. There is simply no longer any jurisdiction or rationale for the court to make such injunctions for anonymity for clinicians premised on the benefit to the child.

- The court anticipated that once proceedings were concluded, and especially after the child had died, the prospect of social media or other abuse or harassment would be much reduced. On the other hand, the burden to the parents of being unable to speak freely about their concerns would endure, and may perhaps increase after the child's death.

- It may be possible for the trust to say that anonymity is also needed to allow the hospital to carry out its functions generally, but there will need to be evidence to support this. Otherwise, once a child has died the only basis for any injunction would be to uphold the individual rights of the clinicians.

- The individual clinicians do have rights, of course – and there are legal mechanisms for these to be protected, for instance in common law actions for privacy, as well as protection from harassment etc. But enforcing those rights is best done by the clinicians themselves, rather than by the trusts on their behalf.

- As such, the court talked about the need to join the individual clinicians who seek to be anonymised (or a representative of them) as a party to the proceedings, so that they can make their case about these issues.

I can see why the judgment has been received with alarm, but – read carefully – in some important ways it is actually a win for clinicians.

For instance, the families argued that anonymising the clinicians at all was contrary to the principle of open justice, which the Supreme Court rejected entirely.

The judgment makes clear that the starting point is that – especially in cases of dispute between parents and clinicians, where the temperature might be higher – the court would expect an injunction to be made to anonymise the clinicians (though not forever).

That injunction will need to be specific about who is to be covered, but at the outset of proceedings it is likely to be acceptable to rely on generic evidence about the potential concerns of naming the clinicians, all justified by the potential impact on the child's own care.

Such an injunction should be limited in time, perhaps running only until the child's death, for example, plus a "cooling off period" which is "likely to be measured in weeks rather than months or years".

The purpose of the "cooling off period" is to allow the individual clinicians to consider making their own application to continue any injunctions further into the future. No doubt the Trust involved would support any such application, but it would need to be justified by specific evidence about the potential risks to those particular clinicians in this particular case, and at that particular stage (ie after the child's death). The court recognised the concerns from what happened in the Charlie Gard and Alfie Evans cases (see Chapter 6), but noted that in both those cases the problems were mainly during proceedings, while the child was alive.

The only thing on which the court was really against the clinicians was on whether clinicians should be anonymised indefinitely, after the child's death, in these cases. And it still held open that such an order could be made in an appropriate case, but said that it would need to be justified in terms of the individual clinician's rights, and based on specific rather than generic evidence.

"Lawfare"

Though it is hoped that litigation in the Court of Protection in particular is less adversarial and more collaborative than elsewhere, with the focus squarely on the patient's best interests rather than on "winning" or "losing" the argument, there are still cases in which this has not been the case, raising issues about – for example – use of covert recordings made of the clinicians, injunctions to control the behaviour of the parties, and even in some cases committal to prison for contempt of court.

Relationships with families is a regular theme in the Court of Protection, but few cases are as fraught as An ICB v G,[53] in which the judge described the litigation as being "lawfare" between the family and ICB.

The case ought to have been simply about the welfare of G, a 29 year-old woman with a profound, degenerative neurological condition. Instead, the proceedings became a "theatre of conflict" and involved extreme and florid allegations made by the family about the care being provided (as "abusive", "negligent" and "torture").

The ICB in turn had concerns about the family allegedly tampering with equipment (which were upheld by the judge), as well as being abusive to staff. This meant very lengthy and costly litigation, which had been

53 [2024] EWCOP 13 – https://www.bailii.org/ew/cases/EWCOP/2024/13.html – also mentioned at the end of Chapter 5.

running since 2021, and a fact-finding hearing on this occasion over 21 days of court time, involving 8 barristers including 4 King's Counsel.

This generated a predictably lengthy (80 page) judgment, but it covers some really useful issues, including the role of family, and especially parents of adult children (see Chapter 5 and 6), but also:

- The family's use of covert recording of the clinicians (deplored by the judge as "a violation of the personal and professional privacy that each member of staff is entitled to" as well as a violation of G's privacy);

- The impact on professionals of the family's behaviour (there was "a pattern of sustained, controlling and bullying behaviour" with a "wounding" and "traumatising" impact on professionals; the more than 100 complaints made against the professionals "sap time, energy and are caustic to professional morale");

- And even some guidance on how best to prepare witness statements (it was "poor practice" that statements were taken initially from recollection, without reference to the relevant documentation, meaning that they were less reliable, though the judge had emphasised the "forensic discipline required" given the allegations).

It is an extraordinary case, in every sense. These are very rare, but it shows where the essential loss of trust between families and professionals can ultimately lead. It might help if the legal framework around decision-making in health and care were better understood, and especially the proper role of families in this (see Chapters 5 and 6).

We would hope that relationships and trust can be built on openness and good communication. But there are extreme cases in which it is appropriate to ask the court to make orders to restrict someone's behaviour where it is compromising a patient's best interests, as was done by a District Judge on an ICB's application in one case, imposing a lifelong injunction on AK to limit his rights to visit his adult son.[54]

Finally, there are cases in which things have gone even further and prison sentences have been imposed by the Court of Protection for contempt of court where its orders have been breached, for example an order to stay away from P to allow her care to be given without obstruction.[55]

Some practicalities

Finally, since this is a "practical guide", I'll offer a few practical observations and tips on applying to court, wrangling the medical records, on preparing witness statements, and (if need be) giving evidence in court. This may be very simplistic, but I hope that it might be useful if not to the lawyers then to the clinicians or others who may be less familiar with the process.

Applying to court

1 Discuss between the key clinicians, family and lawyers as soon as possible if a case might need to go to court. Do not leave it too late.

2 A medical treatment case can move very quickly. The first thing I do is get a single document with contact details for all key people, including email and their mobile numbers, and later use it to collate their availability dates for court.

---

54 An ICB v MK [2024] EWCOP 27 – https://www.bailii.org/ew/cases/EWCOP/2024/27.html

55 As for example in Derbyshire County Council v Grundy [2025] EWCOP 2 (T1)

3 The court forms to start Court of Protection proceedings (the COP1 – application form, COP1B – additional information re a personal welfare case and COP3 – evidence of lack of capacity) repeatedly ask for the same information, and only allow boxes the size of a tweet to put it in. My habit now is to attach a simple A4 word document with a bit more detail in it, titled "Application Document", so that I can say "refer to the Application Document" in each box and avoid the constraint and repetition. I use that document to paint a picture for the court what the case is about, the decision that needs to be made and how urgently, to help with deciding the listing and initial directions.

4 Don't lose sight of the timescale. Try all you can to pin down the window in which the proposed treatment can and should be given and when the prognosis is likely to decline or the options narrow. Sometimes, fixing an appropriate date for treatment, subject to prior court approval, can be really helpful to focus minds, and helps the court to ensure timely listing and disposal of the case before then. Equally, sometimes if there is a sense of drift around a case, issuing proceedings can bring it under the court's scrutiny to unblock practical solutions.

5 It is good to have a clear plan before you go to court but it is ok to make an application saying that you really don't know what to do for the best among several possible options, where that is the reality, if the alternative is a long delay due to uncertainty.

6 Work with the Official Solicitor (or any other litigation friend for the patient) as much as possible. It is always appreciated to give them a heads up that a case is coming so appropriate resource can be allocated. The experienced and dedicated team in the Official Solicitor's office have always been tremendously helpful, in my experience.

7 One key role for the Official Solicitor is often to ensure that P's views are presented fully to the court (though increasingly judges

have wanted to meet P themselves as well). In most cases either someone from the Official Solicitor's office or an agent appointed on their behalf will go to visit P and discuss the issues and the proceedings, so that a detailed witness statement can be prepared. In other cases, P's views can be set out in a report from an IMCA.[56] As the trust's lawyer, leaving it too late in the proceedings to secure the appropriate evidence of P's views or the family's views is easily done, in the understandable focus on gathering the evidence from the clinicians, but is a common way in which these cases can go awry.

8 As the trust's lawyer, for example, supporting an unrepresented family through proceedings is a fine line to walk. You will no doubt answer their questions openly and fully and want to help. You will want to explain things and offer reassurance throughout and will often find that you become a conduit for their communication back to the clinicians. It is easy to feel quite close to the family in that role. But you will need to keep saying (and documenting clearly that you have said) that you are not *their* lawyer, that you represent the NHS trust, and that they ought to get their own legal advice if they wish. It can be helpful to signpost them to appropriate specialist advice of their own.

9 Remember that the Court of Protection is not adversarial and not about winning or losing, so don't treat it like a battle. All parties are there to do right by the patient, and the collaborative approach typically seen is, I think, a much more appealing environment than other litigation. (That is, of course, all relative). If things change, it is of course much better to change your position accordingly and explain than to try to defend an outdated position at all costs. Any such focus on "winning" the litigation risks losing sight of the welfare of the patient.

56 Independent Mental Capacity Advocate, see Chapter 5.

10 That said, don't give the judge any good reason to shout at you at the hearing. Trivial as it may seem, a poorly prepared, mis-numbered or late court bundle really does get you off on the back foot. For any extra documents too late for the bundle, I used to say to bring plenty of (hole-punched) copies to court. Nowadays, bundles are typically in PDF, submitted electronically, but you can still annoy a judge if these are not paginated / indexed / hyperlinked, or if we still end up with late documents flying around on email after the bundle has been filed.

11 Instructing the right counsel is key. There are several very well-established chambers in this field which can offer huge strength in depth and expertise.[57] You ought to take technical excellence for granted. Have a look previous reported cases on the issue in question for the counsel involved then. For my part, though, it is just as important for counsel to be responsive and collaborative, as well as being decent company as there is usually an awful lot of hanging about at court.

12 For the hearing itself, remember that attending in person can be a practical as well as an emotional challenge for family members, perhaps in terms of the travel and any accommodation costs. An offer to cover that by the applicant NHS body can be appreciated. And if the whole hearing or just the family's input is to be by phone or online, then it is vital that thought is given to arranging a quiet and private room where they can do this, perhaps on or near the ward if the patient is there and the family wants to remain nearby. NHS bodies have been roundly criticised in cases where this thought was not given, making an already unwelcome experience for the family much harder and more distressing.

---

57 See for instance the reviews in Chambers and Partners directory, for Court of Protection work, both for barristers and solicitors.

13 It can make a positive impression on the court if an appropriately senior manager of the NHS body applicant is at court in person, alongside any witnesses, especially if it is a case in which there may be any criticism of the care or the conduct / timing of the proceedings.

Medical Records

1. There is some truth to the medico-legal cliché that "if it is not written down, it didn't happen". The notes made at the time are likely to be powerful and persuasive evidence of exactly what has happened, whatever is in the witness statements made later.

2. The notes should include careful records of the communication with the patient and with the family, as appropriate. If there have been attempts to communicate that have not been possible for whatever reason, that should also be documented.

3. Remember that the medical records will all be disclosable – ie made available to the judge and to the other parties and their lawyers. Everything that is written in the records can be read out in court, and can therefore find its way into the press coverage of the case and the published judgment. It is important that the content is factual, and the language is kept professional. We have seen that disclosure of an email written in frustration can further damage the relationship between clinicians and family, and can compound the distrust that makes the litigation more likely or more difficult.

4. Legal advice, however, is "privileged", ie protected from disclosure, and should not be filed away in the medical records to reduce the risk that this is handed over inadvertently. Some care might be needed with the documentation where the legal advice is part of an MDT for example, where part of the discussion was about planning the care, and part was about the legal issues.

5. Delay in disclosure of the records, or this being incomplete or illegible in places, is unfortunately common. The records in these cases can be extensive, and complex, often held in several different teams and on separate systems, as well as sometime split between electronic records and hard copies. However, such problems with disclosure of the records can cause delay or increased costs in the litigation, as well as reinforcing any distrust or breakdown in the relationships between the parties. The patient or the family are dependent on the treating clinicians to provide full records.

6. In the very recent judgment in KB[58] Mrs Justice Morgan was critical of problems in the disclosure of records by the trust, and gave this guidance:

    i) An index at an early stage should be compiled by the applicant of the records held by the Trust including, as well as the clinical and medical records any therapeutic records. A senior person at the Trust should be responsible for reviewing whether all categories of material have been included.

    ii) It is likely to be helpful to identify a person with responsibility for ensuring that the index is kept up to date.

    iii) If records are duplicated or held in more than one place, this should be indicated on that index.

    iv) At the first hearing of the application the index should be available to the court.

58 [2025] EWHC 1292 (Fam) – https://www.bailii.org/ew/cases/EWHC/Fam/2025/1292.html

v) Once disclosure into proceedings (or to the parties) is directed from the index the material disclosed should be indexed and paginated. Ideally pagination should be in a form which is then added to rather than changed.

vi) Once disclosure into proceedings (or to the parties) is directed any material which is copied from paper records should be inspected (and a person from the Trust identified to have responsibility for inspection) to ensure that the copies are of sufficient quality, before it is added to the indexed and paginated material.

vii) Recognising that human error may occur in any organisation a senior person should be identified with responsibility to ensure that material readied for disclosure is sent out.

viii) It is likely to be helpful at the first hearing of any application for the parties to have discussions before disclosure of material as to whether it is reasonably possible for that material to be disclosed in a form which makes it text searchable. It will not always be realistic, but it is an issue to be raised early rather than later in the process of disclosure into proceedings.

Good witness statements

1 Any witness statement must comply with the formal rules[59] and be signed with a statement of truth, the form of which is

59 At present see the Court of Protection Rules 2017 Rules 5.2 and Rule 14, and Practice Direction 5B, https://www.judiciary.uk/wp-content/uploads/2014/05/pd-5b-statements-of-truth.pdf

currently: "I believe that the facts stated in this witness statement are true".

2 At the start, set out professional background, expertise and qualifications; essentially, the reasons for your credibility. A couple of paragraphs is usually enough, and if you need more than that consider attaching a CV as an exhibit.

3 Put the statement in your (the witness') own words. As a lawyer, the worst feeling in the world is to be in court and hear a witness respond to any challenge about the statement by saying "I never said that, my lawyer wrote it!" The witness should have the final word on the content and the drafting.

4 Use clear and simple language.

5 Get someone else to read it to spot any ambiguity. It is harder to see this in our own drafting, as we always know what we mean!

6 Get the balance right of detail, background and relevance. In the Court of Protection in particular, background that helps to form a real picture of P as an individual can be important. Sometimes it can be the telling detail – that Doris was once the carnival queen of the village – which captures the essence of someone, to help the court make the right decision about their life and limb.[60] You want the kind of answer you might get from asking someone who knew her well: "tell me about her?"

7 Err on inclusion. You don't want a surprise at court, and the judge may not allow evidence to be given on stuff that is new or

60 Though in some cases the judge may then choose to exclude reference to such details from the final published judgment where they might be so distinctive as to risk compromising P's anonymity.

which can be complained about as an ambush. However unintentional, any appearance of that can increase distrust.

8 On the whole, chronological or another methodical structure is best.

9 Include times where possible as well as dates.

10 Use sections and sub-headings.

11 Separate numbered paragraphs for each issue. And try to keep sentences and paragraphs fairly short.

12 The statement should be just as long or short as it needs to be. Don't pad it and don't curtail it.

13 Attach exhibits as appropriate.

14 Write fact, not speculation. If you give your opinion, make this clear and give your reasons.

15 Avoid loaded words or technical terms (e.g. "neglectful" / "negligence" / "neglect" which have a term of art meaning in law). It is very hard to row back from a witness who has used that language, however inappropriate, and trying to do so smacks of cover up or conspiracy.

16 Set out how you know the facts, e.g. a review of the records, or that you were there when something happened.

17 Especially if it was a long time ago, how do you remember? Was there something distinctive?

18 Make it up to date, but don't worry about the risk that things might change. As they do, you can always submit an additional statement.

19 Avoid (or at least explain) medical jargon or technical terms, and explain any abbreviations the first time they are used.

20 Use balanced and courteous rather than emotive language, but don't pull your punches; say what you mean and don't use euphemisms, which can only make things worse.

21 If the statement needs to directly quote someone swearing (as they often seem to!) that's OK. The judge may well be your granny's age, but you don't need to temper your language.

22 Refer to colleagues by their full name and explain their role.

23 Refer to the patient respectfully (perhaps, for example, explaining at the outset that "Mr Daniel Smith always asked that we refer to him as 'Danny', so I will refer to him by that name in this statement", or otherwise err on the side of formality: "Mr Smith"). Calling them "the patient" (or "the deceased") can seem impersonal and may not go down well with the family or judges / coroners.

24 It is OK to express condolences, if appropriate, at the end. To do so – or to make an apology for a patient who has come to harm in your care – is not an admission of fault or liability (see Chapter 1).

25 If there are lessons to be learned or changes have been made already, consider with your manager / lawyers whether your statement is the place to set this out, or if there will be a separate statement from someone else covering that. It is much better if that material is all clearly in one place, to avoid any inconsistency or confusion.

26 You should prepare the statement expecting to be asked questions about it, but taking the time to do it thoroughly and clearly gives

a better chance of not having to give evidence in person, as the statement can be relied on without calling you as a witness.

Attending and giving evidence at court

1 A hearing will usually be listed taking into account the availability of the key witnesses as much as possible, but in some medical treatment cases the urgency makes this very difficult. Bearing in mind the pressure of clinical commitments already, this is all the more reason to aim for a written statement so good that attendance can be avoided. It is not always possible, but we try to agree with other parties as much as you can to minimise the need for witnesses to attend in person. Sometimes availability by phone or remotely is all that can reasonably be done, but it is inevitably inferior to attendance in person when everyone else is in court. Sometimes the Official Solicitor may agree to ask written questions based on the statement before the hearing to test whether attending to give evidence in person is really necessary.

2 If you receive a witness summons, then it can be a contempt of court to fail to attend.

3 Prepare. Review your statement, the relevant medical records and any other documents as appropriate. Make sure you are clear where you are supposed to be and when. Ask your lawyers anything. However short the listed hearing, expect to be there for far longer and probably all day, and arrange cover accordingly.

4 On the day, bring something to read. There can be an awful lot of hanging around outside court, either because a number of cases are listed before the same judge and waiting their turn or, very commonly in the Court of Protection, because the parties are making some progress on the issues, given the chance to speak face to face. Often you can be there all day long in discussion

between the parties shuttling between various side rooms, and then go into court late in the day to tell the judge what's been discussed and agreed, hopefully having narrowed if not resolved the issues in dispute.

5 Bring a copy of your statement[61]. You can re-familiarise yourself with it beforehand, and you can take a copy with you into the witness box if you're called (there should be a court bundle in the witness box, containing your statement and all other relevant documents, but it can be easier to have your own copy handy). It is not a memory test.

6 It is usually OK to sit in court throughout the case, usually behind the solicitors, who are behind the barristers, so you can hear what's going on, and hear any other witnesses.

7 If you are called to give evidence in person, you'll be guided by the clerk to the witness box, and invited to swear on the bible (or according to another religion) or to make a secular affirmation, as you prefer (if your requirements are unusual, it may be helpful to give your lawyers a heads up).

8 Your lawyer will ask you questions first, usually starting with the easy stuff, to confirm that it is your statement, your signature, and to confirm your name and qualifications. After that, you are likely to be taken only to the key parts of the statement, rather than going through it all line by line.

9 When your lawyer is done, the other parties' lawyers can ask questions, which are likely to be a little more testing, but remain courteous and try to be helpful. You might well be smarter than

61 Subject of course to proper care with such sensitive personal data, and respect for confidentiality and information security. It may be that in many cases the personal identifying information about P is anonymised or removed from such documents as much as possible.

the lawyer asking you questions, but it is asking for trouble to set out to try to prove it.

10 If you feel that you've been misrepresented by the questions asked by the other side's (slippery) lawyer, bide your time as you should get a chance to correct anything in re-examination by your own (savvy) lawyer. If your own lawyer doesn't want to go there, rest assured it's because it wasn't as bad as you may think, or because going back to it again will only make it worse.

11 The judge can ask questions at any time, but whoever asked the question, always address your answers to the judge.

12 My key advice on answering questions is three-fold, and insultingly simple:

a) Listen to *the question that was actually asked* (not the question that you think *should* have been asked, or that you worried *would* be asked), and take a moment to think about your answer

b) After thinking about it, give that answer

c) *Then stop talking*. (This can be the hardest part, and lawyers will often use a prolonged silence to make the witness feel like blurting out something else).

13 Speak slowly and clearly. Follow the "judicial pen", i.e. speak at a pace that allows the judge to write it down comfortably, and slower if you can see that he's trying to keep up.

14 The judge ought to have had your written statement, and read and digested it, but don't assume that he has. There can be huge amounts of documents, sometimes they don't all reach the judge in good time, and sometimes many cases are listed for the same judge on the same day.

15 Don't assume that the judge will understand the background or any jargon without a full explanation. If in doubt, ask the judge if it would help to explain the difference between a thrombectomy and thrombolysis.

16 Before any hearing, the most common questions witnesses ask us are what to wear and what to call the judge. I suggest that you take dressing formally, as if for a job interview, as a benchmark. Don't worry too much about what you call the judge, as you will not be the first person to speak to him (or her) and you can just safely copy the lawyers who go first.[62]

17 If you're asked a question you don't understand, say so, and ask for it to be repeated.

18 If you're asked a question that is outside your expertise, say so.

19 If the answer to the question is that you don't remember, then say so.

20 If you're not sure of the answer, say so and explain why. Authentic doubt is always safer, and will make a better impression on a judge, than undue certainty.

21 Remember (in this context at least) you are there to help the court, not because you've done anything wrong or are in trouble.

---

62 For the record, a Court of Protection hearing might be before a district judge, addressed as "Sir" or "Madam", a circuit judge (e.g. Her Honour Judge Smith), addressed as "your honour" for either gender, or a High Court Judge (e.g. Mr Justice Jones) addressed as "My Lord" or "My Lady". (A coroner is addressed as "Sir" or "Madam"). By and large they are not too precious, especially with non-lawyers, but if in doubt it does no harm to go high. I heard a coroner once addressed as "your majesty" by a witness, and he seemed to quite like it.

22 Remember to turn off your phone!

Key points

- Some things can make conflict less likely (or less acrimonious) but we should not expect it to be avoidable altogether. We are dealing with inherently controversial, emotional and vital issues.
- Informal approaches to resolution can include the complaints process and ADR such as mediation. Going to court should usually be a last resort, but it is appropriate in some cases, and for some decisions it is unavoidable.
- Even in a non-adversarial forum such as the Court of Protection – focussed not on winning / losing, but on establishing the capacity / best interests of the patient – the litigation can be a stressful and difficult experience for everyone involved, including the professionals as well as the family and appropriate support should be made available.
- The timescale for court proceedings can adapt to the clinical urgency of the situation, including dealing with cases out of hours as need be.
- Do not allow good intentions and seeking compromise to delay starting proceedings where appropriate, or to compromise the appropriate care in the meantime.
- Get advice early – delay is unlikely to be in anyone's interests, least of all the patient's.

CHAPTER 8

CONCLUSIONS – AND TAKING CONTROL

My narrow qualification for this is 25 years or so as a lawyer only for clinicians and hospitals, so I know that there are others better qualified to take some other perspectives. But from this overview of some of the issues and the legal framework around medical treatment decisions, there are some themes and thoughts to draw out, respectfully, relating to the different roles that we might each play at different times:

For the adult patient

1 It is all about you ("no decision about me, without me", as the NHS slogan has it). You should be at the centre of decision-making about any treatment, whether or not you are able to make that decision for yourself.

2 But some decisions are not yours to make. Treatment options may be ruled out as clinically ineffective or futile, unaffordable on the NHS, or simply because no clinician is willing to give them. The only route to challenge those decisions is in public law, through judicial review, in which you face the high hurdle of showing, broadly, procedural error, manifest unreasonableness, irrationality, or broken promises.

3 If you are able to make the treatment decision, you can always *refuse* any medical treatment, but you can only *accept or choose* among options which are actually being offered.

4 If a decision needs to be made while you can make it yourself, then make sure that you have all the information you feel you

need. Ask questions. Tell the clinicians what's important to you and why, to make sure that they are telling you everything that will be relevant to inform your decision as an individual (and it will help a lot if and when any best interests decisions need to be made later). Where circumstances permit, take your time; discuss it.

5 Where it is possible to plan ahead a little for a course of treatment, it is possible to give "advance consent" for several foreseeable steps, including some that may need to be taken while you temporarily lack capacity, for example in the immediate post-operative period.

6 To exercise control for a time after some decision-making capacity may be lost, you can make an Advance Decision to Refuse Treatment, now, to set out the things you do not want to happen to you in particular circumstances. It is your body and your life. (Some resources on how to do this are in the Appendix).

7 If you are not able to make a decision about treatment that needs to be made now, despite the best efforts to support and empower you, then the decision must be made for you on a best interests basis.

8 Your views still matter, and you ought to be involved as much as possible in the best interests decision-making process anyway, to establish your past and present wishes and feelings, beliefs and values.

9 Who the best interests decision-maker will be depends on the decision, but typically for medical treatment it will be the clinician responsible for the care, because they will face the consequences if treatment is given without either consent from a patient who can decide, or a proper assessment of capacity and best interests decision-making process for a patient who cannot.

10 No family member becomes the best interests decision-maker simply by virtue of being a family member, and *there is no such thing as "next of kin"*! If someone uses that phrase to you, ask if they mean who you want to be contacted in case of emergency? Or, who do you want to be involved in best interests decisions about you if need be?

11 But the family almost always need to be involved in best interests decisions because of the duty on the decision-maker to consult to the extent practicable and appropriate with "those engaged in caring for the patient or interested in his welfare". And so could friends, neighbours and any others who fall into that category.

12 The main purpose of that consultation is to help the decision-maker make the right decision for you as an individual, taking account of your past and present wishes and feelings, beliefs and values. Help them out! Talk to them now about what is important to you, and what kind of decision you want to be made for you, if it comes to it.

13 You can go a step further and put those wishes in writing, which can help to make sure that full weight can be given to them[1].

14 And if you don't like the idea of clinicians making this decision in your best interests for you, even with the involvement of family, friends and others, you can appoint someone else, through a Lasting Power of Attorney for health & welfare decisions, to be the decision-maker (see the resources in the Appendix).

---

1 This might be called a "living will" or an "advance decision" but those terms are best avoided, I think, as potentially a bit confusing because they only say what you want to happen, which must be taken into account but might not be decisive. The only thing you can do in advance which is binding is *refuse* specific treatment in an ADRT. See Chapter 5.

15 If you do so, the Attorney still has the same obligations under the MCA as any other best interests decision-maker, including the duty to consult with others "engaged in caring for you and interested in your welfare", i.e. the clinicians and others.

16 Any dispute about your welfare or a medical treatment decision should be referred to the Court of Protection for a judge to resolve, if it cannot be sorted out more informally.

17 Doing what you can now – making a clear ADRT, and appointing an LPA if you wish, as well as fully informing them and others about your beliefs and feelings, wishes and values relevant to medical treatment – will make it much less likely that there would be any dispute in future, avoid adding any unnecessary strain on your family, and give the best chance that things will happen as you would want them to.

For the child patient and your parents

1 Lots of the above is relevant for you as well, in terms of making your own decisions if you are over 16 and have capacity to do so, or if you are under 16 you are *Gillick* competent for the relevant decision (see Chapter 6).

2 One exception is that you cannot make an ADRT or appoint an LPA until you are 18.

3 Anyone who has parental responsibility for you has this until you are 18, and this enables them to make decisions about your medical treatment, where you cannot do so.

4 The scope of parental responsibility dwindles as you attain the ability to make particular decisions for yourself.

5 Parental responsibility can only be exercised in your best interests or for your welfare, and from the age of 16 decisions about best interests ought to be taken within the framework of the MCA.

6 Disputes can be taken to the High Court family division for children under the age of 16, or to either the High Court or the Court of Protection for 16–17 year-olds.

7 In High Court proceedings under the Children Act 1989, the simple test is that the welfare of the child is "paramount".

8 It would be wise to get a judge to make a decision where the consent of someone with parental responsibility might be used to force treatment onto an unwilling child, and all the more so as the child approaches or attains Gillick competence or capacity to make that decision for themselves.

For the family of an adult patient

1 If the patient has capacity for the treatment decision, or has made a valid and applicable ADRT, then it is simply their decision.

2 If they have capacity to make decisions about sharing information, and do not want some or all of the family told something, then it is the clinicians' obligation to respect the patient's confidentiality.

3 There is no such thing as "next of kin", and you do not become the decision-maker about an adult patient's medical treatment, when they cannot decide for themselves, by virtue of a family relationship.

4 There is no such thing as "consent on behalf of..." an adult. If an adult patient cannot decide for themselves then, unless there is a

relevant ADRT, it is a best interests decision to be made under the Mental Capacity Act.

5 It is likely that the best interests decision-maker will be the clinician principally responsible for providing the treatment, unless someone else has been appointed as a health & welfare attorney (LPA), relating to this decision, and it has been registered with the Office of the Public Guardian.

6 Much more important than who has the "best interests decision-maker hat", is the need for the decision-making to be open, inclusive and collaborative, and in particular that the decision-maker must take account as far as practicable and appropriate the views of "anyone engaged in caring for or interested in the welfare of the patient".

7 This means that either a clinician is the decision-maker, with an obligation to consult and involve the family, friends and any others; or someone else may be the decision-maker with an obligation to consult and involve others including the clinicians and carers. I am not sure it makes much difference since any dispute that cannot be resolved informally must go to the Court of Protection anyway.

8 Something is going wrong if you feel that clinicians are riding roughshod over the family, but equally neither should clinicians feel the family expect to call all the shots.

9 The process of best interests decision-making is collaborative and inclusive. It is focussed on the patient and their wishes and feelings, beliefs and values. There is no priority status or role for any particular family members over any other, or over friends or neighbours. The question is who can inform the process to help make the right decision for the patient as an individual, in his best interests.

For clinicians

1 Managing expectations and good communication (both ways) are critical.

2 Try to use to the word "decision" much more often than the word "capacity", and be really careful of "capacity" starting to appear right before a full stop.

3 The decision about what treatment options to put "on the table" is for you (or NHS management) in terms of what is clinically indicated or effective (or affordable and actually available). As such, these are not decisions for the patient to make (and so are not a matter of best interests, in the case of a patient who "lacks capacity").

4 There is no power to force clinicians to offer or provide treatment that is not clinically indicated, or against your judgement.

5 Before taking off the table something which could be available, be clear in your mind whether this is because it is futile (i.e. it offers no benefit at all), which is your decision, or because of a value judgement about the balance of benefits and burdens, which ought to be up to the patient if they have capacity to make that decision, and therefore ought to be a best interests decision if the patient cannot.

6 Nowhere is this more important than in the murky ground around DNACPR decisions, where there is anyway a duty of consultation with the patient, or someone on their behalf as appropriate, to explain the decision and the reasons.

7 A way to clarify the thinking is to consider whether particular treatment would be given to a patient with capacity to make the decision, who wanted it, making their own choice as to the balance between the benefits and burdens. If so, then this

shouldn't be unavailable to a patient who lacks capacity to make that decision, and a best interests decision needs to be made about it, in line with the Mental Capacity Act.

8 In making a best interests decision, involve others appropriately (including those "engaged in caring for the patient and interested in his welfare") and do not be misled by the myth of "next of kin". Ask the persons consulted not just what they think should be done, but about the patient, and his past and present wishes and feelings, values and beliefs.

9 Attempts to resolve disputes should be made informally first, including considering mediation, but if need be any dispute can be referred to the Court of Protection (or the High Court). And if something needs to go to court, **do not delay!**

10 Focus on the decision-making process and getting this right, rather than on the decision itself. There is often subjectivity and scope for reasonable disagreement about the decision, but if the process of making the decision is reasonable then you'll be protected by MCA s5.

11 Write down not only your conclusions, but also the thinking, the things you took into account and who you spoke to.

12 But don't write down anything – including in "private" emails – you would not be comfortable hearing read out in court or seeing in a newspaper.

13 With the benefit of hindsight, you don't have to have been right, but you do have to have been reasonable, and the better your documentation, the easier it is to show this.

14 If someone says that they have an LPA, that's not the end of the discussion – is it registered with the OPG? Is it for health & welfare or property & finances? Is this decision within its scope?

And even if the LPA makes someone else the best interests decision-maker, you still have an obligation to see the proper best interests decision-making process is followed, and to contribute fully.

15 Remember that an attorney can only make a decision that is in the patient's best interests.

16 If you have doubts about how an attorney is exercising their powers then you should refer this to the Office of the Public Guardian.

17 The best interests decision-making process should feel collaborative, consultative and inclusive. If it is feeling adversarial, hostile or exclusive, then something is going wrong, and it may be as well to take a step back and seek some support and advice before things go any further awry.

18 The same principles of empowering the individual patient to exercise their autonomy as much as possible apply to dealing with patients *with* capacity and supporting their individual decision-making, taking account of the *Montgomery* approach (i.e. that the test for information to be given to the patient is what is material to the patient, not what a reasonable doctor would tell them). Ask plenty of questions to establish (and document) what is important to them.

19 Don't get too hung up on worrying about deprivation of liberty at the expense of getting capacity / best interests right: most often any problems with DoL are as a result of getting the basics of the MCA wrong, and that is where your focus should be first.

20 Have a low bar for seeking legal advice, following the process within your organisation. It's a good idea to find out how to access this before you need to do it in a hurry.

21 Be sympathetic to the lawyers pressing you to give an opinion *on the balance of probabilities* – that's what we need for the standard of proof, not certainty, though we know that lawyers and clinicians can see and express things differently. The clearer you can be in writing a statement for court, the better the chances that you won't have to turn up in person to explain it. We are trying to help!

22 Remember that the law does not set out to trip you up. For all it is easy to see it as a stick to beat you with, properly understanding and applying the law gives you a shield to protect your decision-making, your practice, and your patients.

For clinicians' lawyers[2]

1 It is relatively rare for cases about medical treatment to really be a dispute about the law itself. The legal framework is mostly fairly clear, though it can be fiendishly difficult to apply in practice in situations which are fraught, emotional and (often) under intense time pressure.

2 Some cases have to go to court because of the nature of the decision itself, but the ones that end up in front of a judge due to a dispute are very often rooted in an initial failure to manage expectations, to communicate effectively, or to establish or maintain trust between clinicians and the patient / family.

3 It can be really difficult to know what the right thing to do is, because we are often dealing with principles pulling in different directions, most often respect for autonomy, and the beneficent (or paternalistic) drive to do good or prevent harm. It can be

2 I won't presume to offer any advice for lawyers acting for patients or families, which is outside my experience, though I would guess that some of this is common ground.

comforting to recognise and articulate this tension as being inherent, and appropriate, in these decisions.

4 Sometimes these issues can raise ethics as much or more than law, and it can be helpful to seek support from an ethical perspective, perhaps from the trust's ethics committee if there is one.

5 It is more reassuring to see clinicians recognise the doubt, ambiguity and complexity of the issues in front of them than to see undue certainty of their own rightness, any intolerance of dissent or someone being dismissive of others' views, including colleagues or family. In my experience that is actually extremely rare. It is equally alarming to see lawyers (equally rarely) litigate with those characteristics.

6 While the court will expect you to take all reasonable steps to come to a view of your own, where there is genuine uncertainty about whether a patient has capacity or, if not, what to do in her best interests, it OK to go to court saying so and seeking the help of a judge, as well as the benefit of the input of the Official Solicitor.

7 Of course, appropriate work needs done on the assessment of a patient's capacity and on the best interests decision-making, but take care not to allow this to drift. An imperfect decision in good time is better than a decision too late.

8 Be mindful of the timescale and urgency. Setting aside the benefits of hindsight, it is important to get to court, if need be, before a window of opportunity is lost.

9 As an area of legal work, I cannot think of anything more interesting, important or rewarding than this. But recognise the strain that comes with dealing with advising about medical treatment decisions. It can feel a heavy, overwhelming responsibility to give advice on an urgent case or about life-

sustaining treatment. Seek support from colleagues. But don't forget that, as lawyers, we are at least at one step removed from the clinicians making their decisions, and our role is merely to support them. They are really doing the heavy lifting.

10 Sometimes, where a situation is especially stuck, the frustration of those involved can easily transfer itself over to you as the advisor they are asking for help. It is easier to deal with this if you can recognise it is happening, and remember the limits of your own role[3].

11 As with the clinicians, focus on the decision-making process itself, rather than the decision. There is scope to be wrong, in hindsight, but reasonable.

12 Though I've said that the legal framework is mostly clear, the case law in the Court of Protection in particular is quite young and still evolving fairly quickly. It is important to stay on top of this, and I'll signpost a few useful resources or this in the Appendix.

Finally, thank you.

I have learnt a lot in the process of thinking about this to write it all down. Please do drop me a line with any feedback to help me keep learning (and to improve any further future editions!).

For now, I hope that at least some of this is helpful.

3 In the training to be a telephone counsellor at Childline they used the model of "the pit". The caller is in a pit, and it is your role is to listen to them unflinchingly, encourage them to describe the pit, and to help them to explore the pit and any way out. But it does them – and you – no good if you jump into the pit with them.

APPENDIX 1

RESOURCES

Many of the following organisations / websites have material about the things we have discussed:

Alzheimer's society – https://www.alzheimers.org.uk/get-support/publications-factsheets-full-list

British Medical Association – https://www.bma.org.uk/advice-and-support/ethics/adults-who-lack-capacity/mental-capacity-act-toolkit

Compassion in dying – https://compassionindying.org.uk/

Dying matters – https://www.dyingmatters.org/page/updated-resources

Essex Autonomy Project – https://autonomy.essex.ac.uk/

Medical Defence Union – https://www.themdu.com/guidance-and-advice/podcasts-and-videos/mental-capacity-act

Medical and Dental Defence Union of Scotland – https://www.mddus.com/resources/publications%20library/fyi/issue%2008/who%20decides

Medical Protection Society – https://www.medicalprotection.org/uk/articles/assessing-capacity

Mencap – https://www.mencap.org.uk/get-involved/campaign-mencap/treat-me-well

My adult still my child – https://myadultstillmychild.co.uk/

My decisions – https://mydecisions.org.uk/

National Centre for Post Graduate Social Work –
https://ncpqsw.com/news/mental-capacity-act-guidance/

To keep up to date, you will find that many specialist law firms will produce regular newsletters, articles or webinars on the case law. Some barristers' chambers and individual barristers also produce updates and commentary, for example:

https://www.serjeantsinn.com/news-and-resources/blogs/

https://www.39essex.com/resources-and-training/mental-capacity-law/

https://www.mentalcapacitylawandpolicy.org.uk/

I also recommend this site, collated with great dedication and expertise by a specialist mental health solicitor, which covers mental health more widely as well as mental capacity issues, and facilitates useful discussion groups: http://www.mentalhealthlaw.co.uk/Main_Page

Advance Decision to Refuse Treatment

Detailed guidance, aimed at health and social care professionals, is available from NHS England.[1]

Remember that an ADRT does not need a particular form, and indeed unless it relates to life sustaining treatment it does not need to be in writing at all (though it is much better if it is, for evidential reasons).

A sample ADRT form is available at
https://www.macmillan.org.uk/documents/cancerinfo/advancedecisiontorefusetreatmentform_2013.pdf

---

1 https://www.england.nhs.uk/improvement-hub/wp-content/uploads/sites/44/2017/11/Advance-Decisions-to-Refuse-Treatment-Guide.pdf

Advance care planning

I prefer this term to "living will" or "advance decision" to avoid any impression that binding decisions can be made in advance, other than the refusal of specified treatment as above.

But don't get hung up on the different language. Whatever the documents are called, making it clear what your wishes and priorities are, when it comes to future medical treatment decisions which you may be unable to make for yourself, is hugely important and valuable for those trying to make best interests decisions for you.

There are some useful documents here:

https://www.dyingmatters.org/sites/default/files/user/Planning_for_your_future_care_FINAL_010212.pdf

https://compassionindying.org.uk/making-decisions-and-planning-your-care/planning-ahead/advance-care-planning/making-acp

Lasting Power of Attorney (LPA)

To appoint an attorney to be the best interests decision-maker for you for heath and welfare decisions you must complete the form on the government website:

https://www.gov.uk/power-of-attorney

You do not need a lawyer.

To be effective it needs to be registered with the Office of the Public Guardian:

https://www.gov.uk/government/organisations/office-of-the-public-guardian/about

There is a fee of £82 to register the LPA.

Making a Will

Finally, if you do not want your worldly possessions to go by default to whoever is considered your (so-called) "next of kin" under the Inheritance of Estates Act 1925, then you need to make a will.

A useful guide is available here:

https://www.ageuk.org.uk/information-advice/money-legal/legal-issues/making-a-will/

It is a legally binding document, and it may be best to get legal advice though this is not strictly necessary.

Many charities will offer a will writing service where they cover the legal cost of the will to encourage a legacy gift (though this is not obligatory). See for example www.willaid.org.uk.

APPENDIX 2

BEST PRACTICE SERIOUS MEDICAL TREATMENT CHECKLIST (PRE ISSUE)

Introduction

- This document is drafted in the hope that it might be helpful for NHS Trusts and clinicians who may be involved in potential applications to court in relation to serious medical treatment issues.
- The same issues, broadly, will arise whether proceedings would be in the Court of Protection, for adults, or the Family Division of the High Court, for cases involving children.
- The focus here is on preparation of the cases for issue of proceedings, rather than on conduct of the litigation.
- This is not intended to be a sequential, step by step, guide but a list of issues to consider, the relevance of which will vary from case to case.
- It applies equally to cases of proposed treatment, non-treatment or withdrawal of treatment.
- The overall timescale can be compressed due to clinical urgency where appropriate.
- This document does not purport to set out the substantive law on mental capacity or decisions for children, nor to depart from

authoritative guidance and case law on the issue of when a case needs to go to Court, including the Guidance of the Vice President of the Court of Protection, in January 2020, available here Serious Medical Treatment, Guidance [2020] EWCOP 2 (17 January 2020) (bailii.org)

Issue	Comments
1. **Recognition by the relevant clinicians of an issue that may need legal advice / an application to court. This can be helped by:** a) MCA awareness and training b) Having a robust Trust policy on 'consent' and clinical bedside guidelines which are accessible in the clinical setting c) Reflection on previous medical treatment cases and sharing widely lessons learned d) Accessibility to the legal team (whether internal or external), and clear structure for escalation e) Clear communication to clinicians (via clinical guidelines and Trust policy) of appropriate triggers to seek legal advice (not necessarily that these are triggers to court applications), such as: I. Where there is doubt or dispute about the patient's capacity to make the decision for themselves; II. Doubt or dispute about the best interests decision to be made, including where it is clearly against the patient's expressed wishes - this may be a dispute between clinicians and/or between the clinical team and those with a legitimate interest in the welfare of the patient;	

III. The best interests decision is finely balanced and / or the consequences are very grave; IV. The proposed treatment is experimental; or V. Carrying out the proposed treatment is likely to need significant coercion, whether by sedation, physical restraint or deception of the patient.	
2. Get specialist legal advice a) Whether in house Trust team or external solicitors as soon as possible, once it becomes clear that there is an issue which you are unable to resolve or which may benefit from a multidisciplinary discussion (including the legal team). b) Do not delay and do not seek to perfect your evidence before seeking advice, your lawyers can help do you this and provide guidance on what is required.	
3. Is it clear exactly what decision needs to be made? a) Are we clear about the patient's condition and prognosis? b) What are the treatment options that are appropriate and available in practice and are they achievable for this particular patient? c) Be clear what the clinicians are not willing to do. But consider whether there are further options that the clinicians would be prepared to offer if the court were to decide, contrary to their opinion, that it was in the patient's best interests d) What are the risks / benefits of each treatment option, and of no treatment?	

e) What will the proposed surgery mean for the patient post-operatively; will they be able to manage their health independently or with available help? f) Are there any conflicting views among the treating team?	
4. What is the timescale? a) What is the clinical urgency? b) How soon might the opportunity to treat be lost / options become more limited / prospects of "success" reduced? c) Is there any further warning sign we can still rely on to show that the urgency has increased, while the opportunity to intervene remains – is there a critical clinical point for treatment d) Is it helpful to identify a proposed treatment date, so all plans can be in place, subject to Court approval? e) DO NOT DELAY – it is better go to court too soon than too late, and awful to find that the opportunity to treat has been lost. f) DO NOT DELAY trying to perfect your evidence – starting proceedings can focus minds and make it possible for the Court to control the evidence and the timescales. g) Do not let sight of this timescale be lost in the fog of complex preparations – the Court can deal with it as quickly as it needs to (including out of hours if need be); keep the focus on the patient and the treatment decision that needs to be made. h) DO NOT DELAY in particular for obstetric cases, where Keehan J has given guidance on	

the process and timing, that cases should be brought at least 4 weeks before the expected delivery, save in exceptional circumstances A NHS Trust v FG [2014] EWCOP 30 – see link in resources section below.	
5. **Capacity (for adults, over 16 years)** a) Is there a clear, well documented current assessment relating to the actual treatment decision? b) Does it reflect the MCA s2/3 – i.e. detail the relevant information for the decision that must be made, and whether the patient can understand / retain / use or weigh that information (or can communicate their decision)? c) Is there an impairment or disturbance of the function of the mind or brain that is the cause of that functional inability to make a decision? d) Is there any disagreement about the patient's capacity to make this decision? e) Do you need a second opinion from another clinician or psychiatrist? f) Do you need to involve your Mental Health Liaison Team in house? g) Has everything been done to enable the patient to regain capacity, or enable them to make a decision? This may include involving wider members of your clinical team such as Learning Disability leads and using individualised patient information tailored to the patient's needs. h) Is it possible to defer the decision until capacity is regained? Consider whether it is	

clinically possible and what the timescales for this may be. i) Does the patient have capacity for decisions about sharing information with others (i.e. their views on who their confidential information can be shared with will effectively limit who can be involved in any discussion about best interests)? j) Does the patient have capacity to conduct litigation about the substantive treatment decision? k) DO NOT DELAY an application if assessment of capacity is difficult – resolving that is part of the function of the Court. l) NB for 16-17 year olds, the possibility remains of the Court using the Inherent Jurisdiction of the High Court (rather than the Mental Capacity Act) to override a refusal of treatment even where the P has capacity to make the decision for themselves.	
6. For children (under 16) a) For children, where appropriate, is there a clear assessment of whether they have the maturity and understanding of the relevant decision? ("Gillick competence" - NB it is still possible for the Court to override a refusal of treatment by a Gillick competent child) b) Are you clear who has parental responsibility? c) Do you need a second opinion? d) Do you need to involve your Mental Health Liaison Team? e) Involve CAFCASS and a guardian for the child	

7. Is there an Advanced Decision to Refuse Treatment? a) Is it relevant to this proposed treatment? b) Does it meet the formal requirements (in writing, signed, witnessed) if it relates to life saving treatment? c) Is there a legitimate reason to think that the patient has changed their mind since making the ADRT?	
8. Is there an LPA / Deputy for health and welfare? a) Is the LPA relevant to this proposed treatment? b) Is it registered with the OPG? c) Is there a copy held in the medical records?	
9. Mental Health a) Is it clear that the Mental Health Act cannot / should not be used in relation to the proposed treatment? b) Do you need to involve your Mental Health Liaison Team? c) If the patient receives, or should be receiving mental health input from another Trust, does that Trust need to be joined to the proceedings? Have you got access to all their records?	
10. What is the plan? a) The plan need not be finalised until the Court approves it, and the input of the Official Solicitor is important to improve a draft plan, but do you know broadly how is it proposed that the treatment be given?	

b) Bear in mind that the plan needs to cover not only the proposed treatment itself, but also any issues of conveyance to or within the hospital, post-operative care and rehabilitation, and going home, as appropriate c) Do you anticipate non-compliance (why?) and how will that be minimised or managed; how will this impact on the ability to treat the patient resulting in positive outcomes? d) If physical restraint is required, do you have sufficient, suitably trained and experienced staff to undertake this? e) If sedation is required, what drugs / doses / routes are proposed, who will administer it, and with what clinical oversight? You may need to involve the pharmacy team if controlled drugs are required. f) In either case, what is the step by step plan for escalation if need be? g) Is there an issue of getting P to hospital, and does the proposed plan cover that conveyance (or return home after treatment)? h) Will your local ambulance service be able to assist with retrieval? i) Do you have an anaesthetist with 'BASICs' training and experience to assist with retrieval and can they follow the patient journey if anaesthetic is required for the proposed treatment? j) How will post treatment recovery / rehab be delivered, and will any non-compliance then reduce the potential benefit of the proposed treatment?	

k) If anaesthetic is (or might be) involved, can you see P's anaesthetic history from the records? l) Do the records / history show experience of recovery from / compliance with similar procedures? m) DO NOT DELAY an application trying to perfect your proposed plan – that is part of the function of proceedings.	
11. Patient's wishes a) What is P saying about the proposed treatment? b) What's the consistency/ strength of feeling? c) Expression of wishes before capacity was lost or during more lucid periods if capacity fluctuating? d) Evidence of similar decisions being made by the patient in the past, when s/he had capacity to make them?	
12. Views of others a) Especially any LPA / Deputy, those with parental responsibility for a child b) And "others engaged in caring for P or interested in their welfare" for the purposes of MCA s4(7) (there is no such thing as "next of kin" although this may be a starting point in identifying those who the patient has named previously as someone to consult) c) Ensure that good and current contact details (mobile phone and email) are held for each person likely to be consulted about best interests decisions	

d) Need to involve an IMCA?	
13. Other organisations to involve? a) GP? b) Social worker / local authority (especially if the post discharge living conditions / housing / access for follow up are important) c) Other NHS bodies – e.g. a community or mental health trust? An ambulance trust / private provider if conveyance to hospital may be required d) Care Home Manager	
14. Making a best interests decision a) Is it clear who is the best interests decision maker? This is usually the Consultant responsible for the patient's care b) Consultation – who with / contact details and discussions recorded c) Is the impact of overriding P's wishes being factored into the best interests thinking, especially as regards their mental health and possible non-compliance with therapy, rehab, post op wound care etc? d) Are you confident that the appropriate wide view of the patient's best interests is being taken, not "just" the best clinical outcome? e) Are you confident that the decision being taken is individualised for this patient, and not just generic to any patient with that condition, considering this treatment? f) Importance of good notes of best interests decisions / best interests meetings – consider having someone nominated as a minute taker,	

and draft minutes being circulated and agreed (by key clinicians and by family) promptly g) You may have a Trust template / document that will assist with documenting the Best Interest decisions and one that will prompt important considerations h) Would it be useful to discuss the case with your Trust Ethics Committee?	
15. Comms with family, in case of a dispute: a) Consider a single point of contact for the family or their representatives. b) Encourage the family to get legal advice, and for the family lawyers to speak directly to the Trust's appointed solicitor. c) In cases of very aggressive or unreasonable behaviour by the family, be clear about what will not be tolerated, and why (perhaps consider a behaviour contract). d) Ensure appropriate support is provided to staff as well. e) Update your Executive team, where necessary. They may wish to approve certain applications.	
16. Other ways to resolve a dispute, depending on the circumstances and timescale, consider offering: a) a second independent opinion from outside the Trust b) a meeting with the family and senior clinicians / management c) mediation	

d) would discussion at an ethics committee be helpful (making it clear that it is not a decision-making body)?	
17. Medical Records a) Plan ahead, as copy records can take some time to gather, though the Court will want up to date notes. Make a copy of the full (relevant) records early in the process, and then arrange for a smaller batch of updating records later? b) Are any records held by other organisations which may need to be requested earlier, or perhaps a third party disclosure order which could be sought on the issue of proceedings, rather than waiting for a directions hearing. c) Can records be made available to other parties electronically? d) Can the scope of records which are relevant for disclosure be agreed with the OS / other parties? e) Can a small number of core essential records be agreed with the OS / other parties for inclusion in the court bundle or a separate bundle? f) Note the guidance in KB [2025] EWHC 1292 (Fam): i. "An index at an early stage should be compiled by the applicant of the records held by the Trust including, as well as the clinical and medical records any therapeutic records. A senior person at the Trust should be responsible for reviewing whether all categories of material have been included.	

ii. It is likely to be helpful to identify a person with responsibility for ensuring that the index is kept up to date. iii. If records are duplicated or held in more than one place, this should be indicated on that index. iv. At the first hearing of the application the index should be available to the court. v. Once disclosure into proceedings (or to the parties) is directed from the index the material disclosed should be indexed and paginated. Ideally pagination should be in a form which is then added to rather than changed. vi. Once disclosure into proceedings (or to the parties) is directed any material which is copied from paper records should be inspected (and a person from the Trust identified to have responsibility for inspection) to ensure that the copies are of sufficient quality, before it is added to the indexed and paginated material. vii. Recognising that human error may occur in any organisation, a senior person should be identified with responsibility to ensure that material readied for disclosure is sent out. viii. It is likely to be helpful at the first hearing of any application for the parties to have discussions before disclosure of material as to whether it is reasonably possible for that material to be disclosed in a form which makes it	

text searchable. It will not always be realistic, but it is an issue to be raised early rather than later in the process of disclosure into proceedings".	
18. Witness Evidence a) Who are the key witnesses? I. on capacity (who will do the COP3 form)? II. on the detail of the proposed treatment / risks / benefits / reasons for urgency – unless there are exceptional reasons why this is not possible, the statements should come from the clinician/s who will carry it out and those who may be involved in aftercare (i.e. oncology) III. anaesthetist's evidence on the anaesthetic risks including retrieval? IV. on the practicalities / care plan overall, including any plans for restraint etc (nurse / ward manager / team involved in proposed restraint?) b) The right witness may not be determined by clinical hierarchy – if the issue is "tell us about Bob" it might be that nursing staff or more junior medical staff have most contact and know him best. c) Make sure there are no surprises about the (non)availability of key witnesses over the relevant period of the potential application; seek confirmation of days that they will not be available as soon as possible. d) Keep on one document contact details (mobile / emails) for all key contacts, including all potential witnesses; include	

details of clinicians' secretary as they will often have knowledge of theatre lists / clinics etc and will know the day-to-day whereabouts of the clinician e) Consider preparing draft statements, to be made available to the OS before they are finalised, alongside issuing proceedings. f) Consider appropriate support for the clinician witnesses – including in rare cases prevention of harassment etc, protection on social media etc?	
19. The Official Solicitor (OS) a) When it is clear that a case is likely to go to Court, involve the Official Solicitor asap b) Make sure that this gives the OS reasonable time to make contact with the patient / their family and arrange their own investigations c) Provide the usual undertaking that the applicant trust/s will pay 50% of the OS costs d) Consider asking the Court to make an initial order with the issue of proceedings to invite the OS to represent P, to enable her participation from the outset [attach a draft?] e) Consider what evidence can be made available to the OS in draft – e.g. witness statements and a draft care plan, inviting the OS's input to help improve the planning? f) Can the OS and counsel be offered an opportunity to discuss the case with the clinicians directly (to narrow the issues, reduce the likelihood of independent expert evidence, and avoid the clinicians giving oral evidence if possible)?	

<table>
<tr><td>20. Drafting the application

a) For adult / COP cases, the appropriate forms are COP1, COP1B and COP3, but the boxes to complete to describe the purpose of the application are small and repetitive so consider provision of a separate Application Document of a few pages setting out the background, proposed approach and the urgency.

b) Seek the input of experienced solicitors / counsel early.</td><td></td></tr>
<tr><td>21. Patient's participation in proceedings

a) Can you arrange access to a video link / private room and appropriate support for the patient to join a hearing / speak to the judge?

b) Does the patient want to attend in person and is this achievable / appropriate? Can you arrange transport and clinical escort?

c) Ensure that the clinical team have discussed the application with the patient, as far as is practicable</td><td></td></tr>
<tr><td>22. Family participation in proceedings

a) Can you refer the family to specialist legal advice, including advice on legal aid funding? It can be helpful to have a relationship with a handful of local firms.

b) Can a private room be made available for the family at the trust to access a remote hearing?

c) Consider offering to pay for family travel expenses to attend a hearing in person?</td><td></td></tr>
</table>

d) Ensure good communication with the family throughout the litigation, especially if they are unrepresented. e) A single point of contact may be useful if this is appropriate and achievable.	
23. Comms and PR a) Hearings are usually now in public, subject to orders which prevent identification of P and the family, though the Trust may well be named, and clinicians may be. Is the Trust prepared for publicity, including in social media, from any coverage of the proceedings? Contact your Trust comms team. b) Consider if a senior manager may be appropriate to attend the hearing, especially if there may be any criticism of the Trust's conduct or any delay in bringing the proceedings. c) Prepare a briefing for the Exec Board. d) Consider an internal briefing to the Trust's clinicians on the case / outcome, to improve practice and support identification of cases which need legal input in future, and avoidance of delay.	

Suggested further reading / resources:

- Guidance of the Vice President of the Court of Protection, in January 2020, available here Serious Medical Treatment, Guidance [2020] EWCOP 2 (17 January 2020) (bailii.org)

- Guidance of Keehan J in relation to obstetric cases – NHS Trust & Ors v FG (Rev 1) [2014] EWCOP 30 (28 August 2014) (bailii.org)

- Guidance of Morgan J on disclosure of medical treatment records – Birmingham Women's and Children's Hospital NHS Foundation Trust v KB & Ors [2025] EWHC 1292 (Fam) (12 May 2025)

LEGAL GLOSSARY

A word on law and lawyers

As I hope to make this as accessible as possible for non-lawyers, it might be helpful to say a little bit to introduce the legal system and those who work in it.

There are two basic kinds of law in the English (and Welsh) system – statute law and common law. Statute means what it says: made by legislation i.e. Acts of Parliament, and is typically set out methodically and relatively comprehensively. Ideally, legislation establishes the law on a particular issue all in one place, perhaps updating or replacing previous bits of legislation over time. The Care Act 2014, for example, covers the basic elements of adult social care law and consolidated and replaced a patchwork of different bits of legislation that had been around for decades. The NHS Act 1946 set up the National Health Service and was then updated and replaced by subsequent Acts of Parliament over the years, most recently the NHS Act 2006, though this in turn was heavily amended, rather than replaced, by the Lansley reforms in the Health and Social Care Act 2012, and then the Health and Care Act 2022.

In dealing with decisions for adults who cannot decide for themselves, the law is statutory: the Mental Capacity Act 2005. But even though you might find the principle in the legislation (e.g. "an act done, or decision made, under this Act for or on behalf of someone who lacks capacity must be done, or made, in their best interests" – MCA section 1(5)) the application in practice will be guided by the way in which this has been interpreted by judges in cases over the years.

Some judges have been more creative and activist than others in stretching legislation to do justice, as they see it, but the starting point is the legislation, and "case law" is the flesh applied to that bone structure.

In contrast, some areas of law are entirely judge made, without a legislative basis. The law of negligence is an example of this. There is no "Negligence Act" which sets out the whole basis of compensation claims. Instead, though aspects have been codified into legislation later,[1] it is essentially built brick by brick by case law (or the "common law"), starting from a woman made sick by a snail in a bottle of ginger beer.[2]

One of the oddities of this is that case law can necessarily only deal with the facts before the court in that particular case. Cases always involve individuals or organisations in a real dispute; it is not the court's role to rule on an academic point of principle (a "moot point"). And yet, when a judgment[3] has been given about an individual dispute, it may (depending on the seniority of the judge) become a point of reference (a

1 For example in the Law Reform (Contributory Negligence) Act 1945.

2 *Donaghue v Stevenson* [1932] UKHL 100. Briefly, a woman was ill after drinking from a bottle of ginger beer which, it turned out, had a decomposing snail in it. She sought compensation, but the legal problem was that her friend had bought it, and so the contract (including the express or implied term that it was fit for consumption) was between the seller or manufacturer and the buyer. The victim had no claim as there was no contract with her, and the buyer who had the contract had no claim as she wasn't ill herself and so suffered no loss. Creatively, the House of Lords said that there is a duty of care in this case, laying down the foundations of the law of negligence: "*The rule that you are to love your neighbour becomes in law, you must not injure your neighbour; and the lawyer's question, Who is my neighbour? receives a restricted reply. You must take reasonable care to avoid acts or omissions which you can reasonably foresee would be likely to injure your neighbour. Who, then, in law, is my neighbour? The answer seems to be – persons who are so closely and directly affected by my act that I ought reasonably to have them in contemplation as being so affected when I am directing my mind to the acts or omissions which are called in question.*"

3 Note that conventionally judgment (as in the formal decision of a judge) is spelt without an e in the middle, in contrast to judgement (as in the general ability to make a considered or sensible decision).

"precedent") for the way in which the lawyers advise and, in turn, the courts decide cases which raise similar points.

Effectively, we take a still photo of a very particular set of circumstances, project it across a cinema sized screen and then try to infer the whole movie, looking for the reasoning behind the decision so that we can apply it to other people in similar situations. All the while, of course, arguing that our client's case is just the same as the precedents we like, and totally different from the ones we don't.

In case law terms, there is a hierarchy; some cases are worth more than others. "First instance" judgments are given by courts of the lowest appropriate level to determine the issue in dispute. For instance, for issues under the MCA that is typically the Court of Protection before a District Judge (Tier 1), a Circuit Judge (Tier 2 eg His Honour Judge Smith) or, for serious medical treatment decisions, a High Court Judge sitting in the Court of Protection (Tier 3, eg Mr Justice Smith); for issues about medical treatment of a child it may be the family division of the High Court. From there an appeal can be made, if the necessary permission is given, usually firstly up to the Court of Appeal (typically made up of three more senior judges, e.g. "Lord/Lady Justice Jones", or "Jones LJ") and then up to the House of Lords / Supreme Court (typically made up of five or more of the most senior judges – "Lord/ Lady Smith". The House of Lords was the highest court in England and Wales until October 2009 when it was reformed into the Supreme Court). If the issues raised involve the European Convention of Human Rights then a further appeal to the European Court of Human Rights in Strasbourg may also be possible.

Where there is a clear prior judgment on a particular issue only a higher court can depart from it. So a judge has to follow an earlier Court of Appeal judgment on an issue, even if she (respectfully) thinks it is wholly wrong.[4] So would the Court of Appeal itself in a later case, even if constituted of three different judges. Only the Supreme Court can overrule a Court of Appeal judgment. And as the Supreme Court is the top trump, it can also choose to overrule an earlier Supreme Court judgment, though it is often very reluctant to do so.

Of course, the larger the body of case law, the clearer and more well-established the central principles may be, but equally the greater the volume of material there may be to sift through to find a case that suits the position you want to take.

The Mental Capacity Act 2005 is now coming of age at 18 years old (coming into force in 2007) so there is a relatively young but growing body of case law to work with. In a sense we are all still finding our way together how best to implement what parliament intended. Equally, not a week goes by without a handful of interesting new cases, constantly challenging and refining our understanding. For a lawyer with an interest in the law (which isn't all of us!) it is a wonderful area to work in, for this as well as many other reasons, which I hope shine through in the previous chapters.

So who are the lawyers?

"Lawyer" is a general term, a bit like calling someone a "doctor" can mask whether they are a GP or a hospital cardiologist. Most but not all lawyers will have a law degree (or equivalent), as well as some further professional qualifications. "Lawyer" could cover an array of people including qualified legal executives, paralegals and trainees, but conventionally the two main branches of the profession are solicitors and barristers.

Historically, solicitors were the accessible, high street generalists (the GP parallel is fairly apt). You would see a solicitor if you needed legal advice,

---

4 Though in that scenario she may try to reach a plausible view that the present case is very different from the precedent she is seeking to avoid, which she will try to "*distinguish*".

and he[5] would often be able to deal with the issue. In some cases the solicitor would instruct a barrister (sometimes known as "counsel"), either for a more specialist opinion on a particular issue or because there would be proceedings in court which required a barrister's "rights of audience" (on qualification as a barrister, you are entitled to appear before any court). The traditional model is the client alongside the instructing solicitor sitting in court behind the barrister who is doing the advocacy (i.e making submissions to the judge and asking the witnesses questions). Solicitors only had rights of audience to do the advocacy themselves in the "lower courts" (e.g. the magistrates and county court, as well as the Court of Protection, but not the High Court or any appeal courts).

In fact, the distinction between solicitors and barristers has been breaking down for a while. Some solicitors have become just as specialised as any barrister, with whole departments and whole firms dedicated to medical law, for example. I have always done my own advocacy in the Court of Protection, often appearing alongside barristers acting for the other parties.[6] On the occasions, often at short notice, I have had to appear and do the advocacy in the High Court when strictly I had no rights of audience, it is always within the discretion of the judge to grant temporary rights of audience to do the hearing[7]. Solicitors can now take

---

5 At that time, usually, "he". We have recently celebrated the centenary of women in law, after the Sex Disqualification (Removal) Act 1919 allowed women to be awarded a degree, and so to enter the profession. The first woman solicitor qualified in 1922. By 1990 60% of newly qualified solicitors were female, but women remain underrepresented at more senior levels even today.

6 Though I must say that it sticks in the craw that the convention is that we respectfully refer to a barrister in court as "my learned friend", but for referring to a solicitor it is just "my friend", no matter how experienced the solicitor or how junior the barrister. It takes a year longer to qualify as a solicitor than it does to qualify as a barrister, by the way.

7 I've always loved the story of a solicitor who misunderstood the point about rights of audience that was being made when the judge repeatedly

a course to get full rights of audience in the higher courts too, the same as a barrister (known as "solicitor-advocates").

Equally, the traditional rule that a client could not go directly to a barrister but had to first get a solicitor has now been relaxed (look for barristers advertised as available for "direct access") though you'll find that many barristers still prefer to be instructed by an experienced solicitor on the client's behalf.

As to seniority, in a firm of solicitors the conventionally ambitious will aim for partnership. Beneath that, firms can be structured very differently, with layers variously called solicitor, associate, senior associate, principal associate, legal director and so on.

Barristers typically cluster in something called a "set" or "chambers" where they can share premises and expenses, though they are usually all self-employed. Confusingly, a barrister is known as "junior" counsel even if they have donkey's years' experience, unless or until they are elevated to King's Counsel (KC or leading counsel, sometimes called "taking silk" from the conventional court dress). This leads to the absurdity that if a case does not justify a KC, but you want a barrister with plenty of experience, you need to ask the clerks (who manage the barristers' diaries) for a "senior junior".

The leading independent directory of solicitor and barristers in any particular field is called Chambers and Partners, updated annually, freely available online, and is a good place to start if you are looking for advice.

---

said "I can't hear you" to the solicitor, who responded by gradually raising his voice until he was shouting!

Some medico-legal terms explained

ADR – Alternative Dispute Resolution. To lawyers this means anything apart from litigation (the process of going to court), so could be mediation (described in Chapter 7) or negotiation, for example.

ADRT / ADVANCE DECISIONS TO REFUSE TREATMENT – an advance refusal of a specified treatment made by a person at a time when they have capacity to make that decision, to be brought into play when that person is no longer able to make that decision for themselves. If it meets certain formal requirements, an 'ADRT' is legally binding (see Chapter 5).

ADVANCE STATEMENTS – (sometimes called a "living will" or "advance decision") a statement about the sort of care that someone would wish to receive in any aspect of their future health or social care. An advance statement is not legally binding, but must be taken into account by anyone who is making decisions about your care in your best interests, as evidence of your wishes, feelings, values and beliefs (see Chapter 5).

APPLICANT – the party starting the court proceedings. In medical treatment cases, this is usually the organisation responsible for the proposed treatment.

ASSESSMENT OF CAPACITY – the Mental Capacity Act 2005 sets out how you can assess capacity to make a particular decision (see also "LACKING CAPACITY" and "MENTAL CAPACITY"). Anyone carrying out an assessment must apply the following principles:

i. Every adult has the right to make their own decisions. You must assume that someone is capable of making a decision unless it is established otherwise, applying the tests set out in the Mental Capacity Act. You should not assume that someone can't make a decision just because they have a particular disability or condition, or if they have been unable to make that decision at some point in the past, that they are necessarily unable to make that decision now.

ii. Before applying the test, all practicable steps should be taken to provide help and support to the person concerned to enable them to make and communicate the decision. The person should be given all the information they need to make the decision presented in a way that is as easy to understand as possible e.g braille, pictorial, sign language. Blinking or squeezing a hand may be enough to communicate a decision. If any doubt remains, you may wish to consider obtaining a second opinion from a healthcare professional.

iii. You should not treat someone as lacking capacity just because they choose to make an unwise decision. The test concerns the ability to make a decision, not how sensible others think that decision is.

ATTORNEY – A person given power to act as best interests decision-maker on someone's behalf through a Lasting Power of Attorney (LPA) or an Enduring Power of Attorney (EPA). EPAs are only legal if made prior to 2007; after 2007 a person must have made a LPA at a time when they had capacity to do so. An attorney under an EPA only has power in relation to a person's property & financial affairs, while an LPA can cover decisions relating to a person's property & finances, or health & welfare, or both.

BEST INTERESTS – If anything is done or any decision is made for a person who lacks capacity to make a decision for themselves, it must be in their best interests. This means what is best for the person, rather than just what anyone else wants, although the best interests decision-maker must take into account the views, if practicable and appropriate, of various persons; specifically anyone named by the person, anyone engaged in caring for them or interested in their welfare or a legally appointed attorney or deputy. The person's own wishes and feelings, values and beliefs, both now and before losing capacity, are likely to weigh heavily. Best interests must be interpreted very widely, to include social, and emotional factors, and not just medical welfare or safety. See Chapter 5.

CAPACITY – (see "MENTAL CAPACITY")

CORONER – The official appointed by the crown to hear inquests, at which it is determined who the deceased was, and how, when and where he or she came by his or her death. The finding of an inquest is not supposed to lay any blame.

COUNSEL – a barrister.

COURT OF PROTECTION – The specialist court that deals with cases relating to capacity and best interest issues.

DECISION-MAKER (BEST INTERESTS) – Typically the person responsible for delivering the treatment or care about which a best interests decision is required will be the best interests decision-maker. For example, for day to day decisions that may be the person's primary carer, and for medical treatment it would usually be decided by the person delivering it e.g. the doctor or nurse (see Chapter 5). A relevant lasting power of attorney or deputyship may mean that the attorney or deputy is appointed the best interests decision-maker instead.

DEPRIVATION OF LIBERTY (DoL) – A person lacking capacity to consent to it is deprived of their liberty if they are 'under continuous supervision and control' and are 'not free to leave' and it is in some way the responsibility of the state (see Chapter 5). A person's compliance with their care, or the quality or appropriateness of the care they receive is not relevant to the question of whether or not that person is deprived of their liberty. See also "DEPRIVATION OF LIBERTY SAFEGUARDS (DOLS)" – and, of course, "A Practical Guide to the Law of Deprivation of Liberty", Law Brief Publishing (2024).

DEPRIVATION OF LIBERTY SAFEGUARDS (DoLS) – Article 5 of the European Convention on Human Rights states that 'everyone has the right to liberty and security of person. No one shall be deprived of his or her liberty [unless] in accordance with a procedure prescribed in law'. The Deprivation of Liberty Safeguards are the legal procedure by which the deprivation of liberty of a resident or patient in a registered care home or hospital can be legally authorised, under certain circumstances. See Chapter 5. DoLS will be replaced entirely by the Liberty Protection Safeguards (LPS) if the Mental Capacity (Amendment) Act 2019 is ever brought into force, but at the moment that is looking doubtful, with dates of implementation having drifted from October 2020 to April 2022, and then an announcement in April 2023 that it would not happen prior to the general election that took place in 2024. We now await confirmation of the current government's intentions, but even if there is an appetite to bring in the LPS, the implementation itself is likely to need 2-3 years to complete.

DEPUTY – A person appointed by the Court of Protection to deal with a specific issue or a range of issues to help a person who lacks capacity for those decisions and who hasn't got an attorney to do so.

DIRECTIONS – the timetable and procedural steps in litigation to get to a final hearing. This can be set out by the court in an Order with or without an initial "directions hearing", or more than one, and will reflect the scope of the evidence required and the urgency. The steps may typically be the exchange of documents ("disclosure"), then exchange of witness evidence ("statements"), and then exchange of expert evidence, if any has been allowed. To avoid delay and costs, the court has a duty to restrict expert evidence to what is necessary to assist the court to resolve the case, and so there will not be expert reports in every case.

DISCLOSURE – The stage in court proceedings at which each party must tell the other parties about all the information and documents in its possession that are relevant to the proceedings, and (if requested) must provide copies. Such documents are "disclosable", while other documents (such as the advice from your lawyers, for example) are "privileged" i.e. protected from disclosure.

ECHR – European Convention of Human Rights 1950. The most significant bits for the purposes of medical treatment are Article 2 (the right to life), Article 3 (the right not to suffer torture or inhuman or degrading treatment), Article 5 (the right to liberty) and Article 8 (the right to private and family life).

FIRST INSTANCE HEARING / JUDGMENT – The first judge to make a final decision about the case i.e. before any appeal.

FLUCTUATING CAPACITY – When a person has capacity to make a particular decision at times, but not at other times (for example, during an acute phase of illness). This should be treated with some care because, of course, capacity is time and decision specific i.e. the question is whether the person has capacity for the specific decision, at the particular time it needs to be made. Decisions should be deferred until the person has capacity to make them, if possible. See Chapter 4.

FUTILE – Treatment that would be ineffective or offers no benefit.

GILLICK COMPETENCE – the ability of a child (under 16) to make a decision for themselves, having gained sufficient understanding, intelligence and maturity. See Chapter 6.

Human Rights Act 1998 – (HRA) – the legislation that incorporated key parts of the ECHR into English and Welsh law.

IMCA (INDEPENDENT MENTAL CAPACITY ADVOCATE) – a person who provides support and representation for a person who lacks capacity to make decisions in certain defined circumstances (usually in relation to major decisions where that person does not have any family, friends, an attorney or a deputy to provide that support).

INQUEST – see Coroner.

JUDICIAL REVIEW – a procedure by which a court can review an administrative action or decision by a public body. In broad terms, the principle of judicial review is to test that the public body has acted properly within its powers, and not to substitute the court's own decision for the public body's.

LACKING CAPACITY – See Chapter 4. When someone is unable to make a particular decision at a particular time due to a temporary or permanent impairment in the function of their mind or brain, because of which they cannot do one or more of the following four things:

i. Understand the information relevant to that decision.

ii. Retain that information long enough to be able to make that decision.

iii. Use or weigh the information necessary to make that decision.

iv. Communicate their decision by any possible means, such as talking, using sign language or even simple muscle movement such as eye blinking or squeezing a hand.

LASTING POWER OF ATTORNEY (LPA) – A legal document that lets a 'donor' appoint one or more people (known as 'attorneys') to make decisions on their behalf. There are formal requirements, and an LPA must be registered with the Office of the Public Guardian before it can be used. There are two types:

i. Property & financial affairs, e.g. paying bills, organising a pension, which can be used at any time.

ii. Health & welfare, e.g. making decisions about medical treatment and how someone is looked after. This can only be used when the donor lacks capacity for the decisions in question.

LITIGATION – Court proceedings.

LITIGATION FRIEND – The person who conducts the litigation on behalf of a patient, if they lack the capacity to do so for themselves (see Chapter 7). This is distinct from any lawyers who may be instructed by the litigation friend. In most medical treatment cases, the Official Solicitor will act as litigation friend for the patient, and will typically deal with the case through one of the solicitors in her team and instructing counsel.

MEDIATION – one kind of ADR in which a mediator who is impartial tries to help the parties in dispute towards finding a resolution for themselves (see Chapter 7).

MENTAL CAPACITY ACT 2005 – See Chapters 4 and 5. The Mental Capacity Act (or MCA) aims to empower and enable people to make their own decisions, and to make sure that people who lack capacity to make decisions are protected by structured decision-making, involving them and focussed on their best interests. The five key principles are:

i. A person must be assumed to have capacity unless it is established that he lacks capacity.

ii. A person is not to be treated as unable to make a decision unless all practicable steps to help him to do so have been taken without success.

iii. A person should not be treated as unable to make a decision merely because he makes an unwise decision.

iv. An act done, or decision made, under this Act for or on behalf of a person who lacks capacity must be done, or made, in his best interests.

v. Before the act is done, or the decision is made, regard must be had to whether the purpose for which it is needed can be as effectively achieved in a way that is less restrictive of the person's rights and freedom of action.

MENTAL CAPACITY – Refers to the ability of a person to make a particular decision at a particular time, whether minor, like what to eat, or major like medical treatment decisions. If you have mental capacity for a particular decision, you are able to make that decision for yourself. See also "LACKING CAPACITY".

MENTAL HEALTH ACT (or MHA) 1983 – legislation dealing with the treatment of mental illness or disorders. It does not, on the whole, allow for provision of treatment for physical health needs, which is the province of the MCA, though this can be more complex if the physical health need is a symptom or manifestation of a mental disorder.

OFFICE OF THE PUBLIC GUARDIAN – The "OPG" monitors court-appointed deputies, and keeps a public register of attorneys and deputies. It also investigates concerns about attorneys and deputies, and provides general information / advice on becoming a deputy, and registering Lasting Powers of Attorney.

OFFICIAL SOLICITOR – A government office whose responsibilities include acting as a litigation friend of last resort (i.e. if there is no other suitable litigation friend available) for patients who lack capacity to litigate, though the "OS" will typically act as litigation friend for P in any medical treatment case in any event.

P / PATIENT – P is the shorthand used in the MCA to refer to the person who may lack capacity, i.e. the patient or service user. (But equally it is important to remember that this reductive term easily glosses over the fact that "P" is not just a vignette of characteristics and circumstances relevant to a case about medical treatment, but is also likely to be a brother/sister, father/mother, husband/wife, son/daughter, colleague, employer, friend and so on with rather more breadth and depth to their life and their story.[8])

8 As observed by Nathan Filer in "This Book Will Change Your Mind About Mental Health", p1.

PARENTAL RESPONSIBILITY – A set of duties, responsibilities and powers enabling specific adults (or a local authority with a care order) to make significant decisions about a child up until the age of 18. See Chapter 6.

POSITION STATEMENT – before any hearing in the Court of Protection each party will usually file (i.e send into Court) and serve (i.e. send to each of the other parties) a short written summary of the issues in dispute, as it sees them, its position on them, and what orders it will be asking the Court to make.

POWER OF ATTORNEY – see "LASTING POWER OF ATTORNEY"

PROOF, BURDEN OF – This is *who* has to prove their case to "win". Usually it is up to the claimant or prosecution to prove their case, and failure to do so means the defendant wins. In the Court of Protection of course you have no such adversarial process, but the assumption of capacity in the MCA means that the burden of proof is on whoever is trying to displace that assumption, to prove that P lacks capacity for the relevant decision, i.e. usually the applicant seeking to persuade a judge to make decisions about P's best interests.

PROOF, STANDARD OF – This is *how high* is the hurdle to get over to "win". In the criminal courts it is "beyond reasonable doubt", but in the civil (i.e non-criminal) courts including the Court of Protection, it is simply the balance of probabilities i.e. more likely than not.

PUBLIC LAW – The body of law, including judicial review, which applies to the way that public bodies (in this context notably central and local government and NHS organisations) make decisions and exercise their powers.

RESPONDENT – Each of the parties to court proceedings which are not the applicant. In a Court of Protection medical treatment case, for example, you might expect the treating NHS trust to be the applicant, P to be a respondent acting by the Official Solicitor as litigation friend, and any other parties such as other organisations involved in the care or family members who want to influence the litigation to be second, third or fourth respondents etc.

S49 REPORT – MCA s49 gives the Court of Protection the power to order that any NHS body or local authority must provide a report to the court to assist it in dealing with any issue relating to a case. This might often be to try to minimise or avoid the need for independent expert evidence.

WITNESS STATEMENT – The evidence of an individual witness in written form. See Chapter 7 for some guidance on preparing this.

MORE BOOKS BY LAW BRIEF PUBLISHING

A selection of our other titles available now:-

'A Practical Guide to Probation Breaches and Other Applications' by Mark Thomas
'A Practical Guide to Remarriage and Divorce' by Cordelia Williams & Claire Howard
'A Practical Guide to Privacy, Transparency, Reporting Restrictions and Closed Proceedings in the Court of Protection' by Laura Mannering
'Beaumont on Barristers – A Guide to Defending Disciplinary Proceedings (Second Edition)' by Marc Beaumont
'A Practical Guide to Payments for Environmental Services' by Ben Sharples
'A Practical Guide to the Law of Pregnancy and Maternity at Work' by Rebecca Thomas
'A Practical Guide to Redundancy – Second Edition' by Philip Hyland & Collette Moore
'A Practical Guide to International Issues for Scottish Family Lawyers' by Susie Mountain, Donna McKay, Ken MacDonald
'A Practical Guide to the Law on Deprivation of Liberty' by Ben Troke
'A Practical Guide to Rights over Airspace and Subsoil – Second Edition' by Daniel Gatty
'A Practical Guide to the Law in Relation to Inquests' by Ramya Nagesh
'A Practical Guide to the Construction and Rectification of Wills and Trust Instruments (Second Edition)' by Edward Hewitt
'A Practical Guide to Data Protection in Social Housing' by Clare Paterson
'A Practical Guide to Spousal Maintenance – Second Edition' by Liz Cowell
'A Practical Guide to International Parental Child Abduction Law (England and Wales)' by Dr Onyója Momoh
'A Practical Guide to Deprivation of British Citizenship' by Sean Ell
'A Practical Guide to Commercial Property Service Charges' by Rachel Garton
'A Practical Guide to Clinical Negligence – Third Edition' by Geoffrey Simpson-Scott (Geoff)
'A Practical Guide to the Rights of Grandparents in Children Proceedings – Second Edition' by Stuart Barlow

'The Electronic Communications Code: A Practical Guide – Second Edition' by Kerry Bretherton KC, James Castle, Mark Loveday
'A Practical Guide to the Independent School Standards – September 2023 Edition' by Sarah McKimm
'A Practical Guide to Estate Administration and Crypto Assets' by Richard Marshall
'A Practical Guide to Parental Alienation in Private and Public Law Children Cases' by Sam King QC & Frankie Shama
'Contested Heritage – Removing Art from Land and Historic Buildings' by Richard Harwood QC, Catherine Dobson, David Sawtell
'The Limits of Separate Legal Personality: When Those Running a Company Can Be Held Personally Liable for Losses Caused to Third Parties Outside of the Company' by Dr Mike Wilkinson
'A Practical Guide to Transgender Law' by Robin Moira White & Nicola Newbegin
'A Practical Guide to 'Stranded Spouses' in Family Law' by Mani Singh Basi
'A Practical Guide to Residential Freehold Conveyancing' by Lorraine Richardson
'A Practical Guide to Pensions on Divorce for Lawyers' by Bryan Scant
'A Practical Guide to Challenging Sham Marriage Allegations in Immigration Law' by Priya Solanki
'A Practical Guide to Digital Communications Evidence in Criminal Law' by Sam Willis
'A Practical Guide to Legal Rights in Scotland' by Sarah-Jane Macdonald
'A Practical Guide to New Build Conveyancing' by Paul Sams & Rebecca East
'A Practical Guide to Inherited Wealth on Divorce' by Hayley Trim
'A Practical Guide to Practice Direction 12J and Domestic Abuse in Private Law Children Proceedings' by Rebecca Cross & Malvika Jaganmohan
'A Practical Guide to Confiscation and Restraint' by Narita Bahra QC, John Carl Townsend, David Winch
'A Practical Guide to the Law of Forests in Scotland' by Philip Buchan
'A Practical Guide to Health and Medical Cases in Immigration Law' by Rebecca Chapman & Miranda Butler
'A Practical Guide to Bad Character Evidence for Criminal Practitioners by Aparna Rao
'A Practical Guide to Extradition Law post-Brexit' by Myles Grandison et al
'A Practical Guide to Hoarding and Mental Health for Housing Lawyers' by Rachel Coyle

'Stephens on Contractual Indemnities' by Richard Stephens
'A Practical Guide to the EU Succession Regulation' by Richard Frimston
'A Practical Guide to Solicitor and Client Costs – Second Edition' by Robin Dunne
'Constructive Dismissal – Practice Pointers and Principles' by Benjimin Burgher
'A Practical Guide to Religion and Belief Discrimination Claims in the Workplace' by Kashif Ali
'A Practical Guide to the Law of Medical Treatment Decisions' by Ben Troke
'Fundamental Dishonesty and QOCS in Personal Injury Proceedings: Law and Practice' by Jake Rowley
'A Practical Guide to the Law in Relation to School Exclusions' by Charlotte Hadfield & Alice de Coverley
'A Practical Guide to Divorce for the Silver Separators' by Karin Walker
'The Right to be Forgotten – The Law and Practical Issues' by Melissa Stock
'A Practical Guide to Planning Law and Rights of Way in National Parks, the Broads and AONBs' by James Maurici QC, James Neill et al
'A Practical Guide to Election Law' by Tom Tabori
'A Practical Guide to the Law in Relation to Surrogacy' by Andrew Powell
'A Practical Guide to Claims Arising from Fatal Accidents – Second Edition' by James Patience
'A Practical Guide to Asbestos Claims' by Jonathan Owen & Gareth McAloon
'A Practical Guide to Stamp Duty Land Tax in England and Northern Ireland' by Suzanne O'Hara
'A Practical Guide to the Law of Farming Partnerships' by Philip Whitcomb
'A Practical Guide to the Law of Unlawful Eviction and Harassment – Second Edition' by Stephanie Lovegrove
'A Practical Guide to Costs in Personal Injury Claims – Second Edition' by Matthew Hoe
'A Practical Guide to the General Data Protection Regulation (GDPR) – Second Edition' by Keith Markham
'A Practical Guide to Working with Litigants in Person and McKenzie Friends in Family Cases' by Stuart Barlow
'Protecting Unregistered Brands: A Practical Guide to the Law of Passing Off' by Lorna Brazell
'A Practical Guide to Secondary Liability and Joint Enterprise Post-Jogee' by Joanne Cecil & James Mehigan

'A Practical Guide to the Pre-Action RTA Claims Protocol for Personal Injury Lawyers' by Antonia Ford

'A Practical Guide to Neighbour Disputes and the Law' by Alexander Walsh

'A Practical Guide to Coercive Control for Legal Practitioners and Victims' by Rachel Horman

'A Practical Guide to the Law of Driverless Cars – Second Edition'

by Alex Glassbrook, Emma Northey & Scarlett Milligan

'A Practical Guide to TOLATA Claims' by Greg Williams

'A Practical Guide to Elderly Law – Second Edition' by Justin Patten

'A Practical Guide to Responding to Housing Disrepair and Unfitness Claims' by Iain Wightwick

'A Practical Guide to the Law of Bullying and Harassment in the Workplace' by Philip Hyland

'How to Be a Freelance Solicitor: A Practical Guide to the SRA-Regulated Freelance Solicitor Model' by Paul Bennett

'A Practical Guide to Prison Injury Claims' by Malcolm Johnson

'A Practical Guide to Advising Clients at the Police Station' by Colin Stephen McKeown-Beaumont

'A Practical Guide to Antisocial Behaviour Injunctions – Second Edition' by Iain Wightwick

'Practical Mediation: A Guide for Mediators, Advocates, Advisers, Lawyers, and Students in Civil, Commercial, Business, Property, Workplace, and Employment Cases' by Jonathan Dingle with John Sephton

'The Mini-Pupillage Workbook' by David Boyle

'A Practical Guide to Crofting Law' by Brian Inkster

'A Practical Guide to the Law of Domain Names and Cybersquatting' by Andrew Clemson

'A Practical Guide to the Law of Gender Pay Gap Reporting' by Harini Iyengar

'NHS Whistleblowing and the Law' by Joseph England

'Employment Law and the Gig Economy' by Nigel Mackay & Annie Powell

'A Practical Guide to Noise Induced Hearing Loss (NIHL) Claims' by Andrew Mckie, Ian Skeate, Gareth McAloon

'An Introduction to Beauty Negligence Claims – A Practical Guide for the Personal Injury Practitioner' by Greg Almond

'Intercompany Agreements for Transfer Pricing Compliance' by Paul Sutton

'Zen and the Art of Mediation' by Martin Plowman

'A Practical Guide to Adoption for Family Lawyers' by Graham Pegg

'A Practical Guide to Industrial Disease Claims' by Andrew Mckie & Ian Skeate
'A Practical Guide to Conducting a Sheriff Court Proof' by Andrew Stevenson
'A Practical Guide to Vicarious Liability' by Mariel Irvine
'A Practical Guide to Applications for Landlord's Consent and Variation of Leases' by Mark Shelton
'A Practical Guide to Relief from Sanctions Post-Mitchell and Denton' by Peter Causton
'A Practical Guide to Equity Release for Advisors' by Paul Sams
'A Practical Guide to Financial Services Claims' by Chris Hegarty
'A Practical Guide to Financial Ombudsman Service Claims' by Adam Temple & Robert Scrivenor
'A Practical Guide to Running Housing Disrepair and Cavity Wall Claims – Second Edition' by Andrew Mckie & Ian Skeate
'A Practical Guide to Holiday Sickness Claims – Second Edition' by Andrew Mckie & Ian Skeate
'Arguments and Tactics for Personal Injury and Clinical Negligence Claims' by Dorian Williams
'A Practical Guide to Drone Law' by Rufus Ballaster, Andrew Firman, Eleanor Clot
'On Experts: CPR35 for Lawyers and Experts' by David Boyle
'An Introduction to Personal Injury Law' by David Boyle

These books and more are available to order online direct from the publisher at www.lawbriefpublishing.com, where you can also read free sample chapters. For any queries, call us on 0844 587 2383 or email us at mail@lawbriefpublishing.com.

Our books are all generally in stock at www.amazon.co.uk with free next day delivery for Prime members, and at good legal bookshops such as Wildy & Sons.

We are regularly launching new books in our series of practical day-to-day practitioners' guides. Visit our website and join our free newsletter to be kept informed and to receive special offers, free chapters, etc.

You can also follow us on Twitter at www.twitter.com/lawbriefpub.

www.ingramcontent.com/pod-product-compliance
Lightning Source LLC
LaVergne TN
LVHW052223200926
848481LV00001B/194